ASPIRATION

ASPIRATION

The Agency of Becoming

Agnes Callard

OXFORD
UNIVERSITY PRESS

OXFORD
UNIVERSITY PRESS

Oxford University Press is a department of the University of Oxford. It furthers
the University's objective of excellence in research, scholarship, and education
by publishing worldwide. Oxford is a registered trade mark of Oxford University
Press in the UK and certain other countries.

Published in the United States of America by Oxford University Press
198 Madison Avenue, New York, NY 10016, United States of America.

© Oxford University Press 2018

First issued as an Oxford University Press paperback, 2019

Library of Congress Cataloging-in-Publication Data
Names: Callard, Agnes, author.
Title: Aspiration : the agency of becoming / Agnes Callard.
Description: New York : Oxford University Press, 2018. |
Includes bibliographical references.
Identifiers: LCCN 2017033630| ISBN 9780190639488 (hardback) |
ISBN 9780190085148 (paperback) | ISBN 9780190639501 (epub)
Subjects: LCSH: Change. | Becoming (Philosophy) | Practical reason. | Ethics.
Classification: LCC BD373 .C35 2018 | DDC 116—dc23
LC record available at https://lccn.loc.gov/2017033630

*This book is dedicated to my teacher Amy Kass,
who made her classroom a theater of aspiration.*

CONTENTS

PART I

PRACTICAL RATIONALITY

CONTENTS

PART II

MORAL PSYCHOLOGY

PART III

MORAL RESPONSIBILITY

ACKNOWLEDGMENTS

The University of Chicago provided the context in which this book could be written. Especially helpful at the final stage were a fellowship I received from the Franke Institute for the Humanities at the University of Chicago for the 2015–2016 academic year and a workshop attended by my colleagues Jason Bridges, David Finkelstein, Anton Ford, Gabriel Lear, Jonathan Lear, and Martha Nussbaum.

For encouragement and feedback at vulnerable moments in my trajectory, I thank Sarah Buss, Rachana Kamtekar, Kate Manne, Berislav Marušić, Julie Tannenbaum, and Steve White. For patient support over the many years that this project has taken to congeal, I thank my editor, Peter Ohlin. For generously providing the beautiful cover art to a perfect stranger (though longtime admirer), I thank the artist Istvan Banyai. Arnold Brooks and Ben Callard read every draft, debated every argument, and helped me think every thought in this book. What clarity it has is due to the fact that Ben fought as hard as he did to remain a skeptic of aspiration. Its optimistic spirit comes from Arnold, who would always help me find my way back to the central idea.

Writing this book, I have relied on extensive firsthand observation of the aspirants who have presented themselves to me both at home and at work. I owe thanks to both constituencies. First, my three children. Abe is such a bundle of outsized aspirations that those who know him have asked me whether this book is based on him. Macabee, who has the gift of feeling deeply and of understanding the feelings of others, is the glue that holds our family together. Izzy, the youngest, is just beginning to come into being, and that is wonderful in itself.

My students have, for the past decade, been leading me to the topic of this book. Perhaps they did not always know they were doing it, and I certainly did not recognize it at first, but it is nonetheless true that they are responsible for not only my faith in the possibility of rational self-transformation but also my conviction in the urgency of demonstrating that possibility to others. In this regard, I owe a special debt to Amichai Amit, Stina Bäckström, Jason Bern, Gabrielle Bowyer, Noah Chafets, Maximilian Chaoulideer, Stephen Creighton, Danie Dorr, Romelia Drager, Daniel Drucker, Kenneth (Paul) Dueck, Cait Duggan, Alex Elnabli, Josh Epstein, Garrett Fox, Josh Fox, Peter Goldberg, Henry Gruber, Helen Hailes, Alex Hale, Dzan Herba, Kayla Higgins, Mark Hopwood, Julie Huh, Dan Ioppolo, Todd Isenstadt, Ethan Jerzak, Dake Kang, Claire Kirwin, Josh Kramer, Louis Levin, David Lind, Jennifer Lockhart, Michael Malpass, Matt Mandelkern, Anya Marchenko, Olivia Markbreiter, Max (Haney) Maxwell, Jeremey McKey, Maria Mejia, Santiago Mejia, Bodhi (Shane) Melnitzer, Gillian Moore, Parysa Mostajir, Maya Nguen, Rory O'Connell, Claire O'Grady, Anne (Anastasia) Quaranto, Ajay Ravichandran, Emmett Rensin, Erika Rist, CJ Schei, Gabe Shapiro, Dan Telech, Eric Thurm, Josh Trubowitz, Doug Vaaler, Gareth Walsh, Sam Wigutow, and Sophia Wyatt.

The book also draws on my own experiences as an aspirant, and so it seems appropriate to thank a few of the key players along that route. Among the many things for which I have my parents to thank, I would single out the difficult decision they made to leave their homeland and raise me in the United States. I thank my sister, Kata Gellen, for enduring my earliest and most irritating aspirational efforts, many of which were, for one reason or another, enacted on her. Even as adults, we are still growing up together. Likewise I thank my best friend, Yelena Baraz, for holding tight to me over the years, even as we each twisted, Proteus-like, through a variety of shapes. Finally, I thank my teachers Leon and Amy Kass, who fueled my own aspirations in the same classrooms in which I now do my best to emulate their example.

ASPIRATION

Introduction

I. OVERVIEW: REASONING TOWARD VALUE

(a) How We Got Here

We can all think back to a time when we were substantially different people, value-wise, from the people we are now. There was a time when we were not even aware of the existence of some of the people, activities, institutions, and ideologies that now figure centrally in our lives. Maybe we had different political views or no political views at all; maybe we used to be religious, or used not to be; maybe we now feel deep ties to a place that is spatially, culturally, and linguistically far from where we grew up; maybe we find our interests and concerns resembling those of our parents more than we ever thought they would. We care about many things that we once did not care about. How did that change come about?

In accounting for the genesis of our new values, we often have occasion to mention the effects on us of forces outside our control, such as a fortuitous coincidence, an influential mentor, an inspiring locale, a tragic loss, a bitter betrayal, a domineering parent, the emergence of an innate facility, the process of getting older. Nonetheless, none of these sorts of factors can amount to the whole story. A mentor cannot implant a love of music; the betrayal cannot, of itself, create a devotion to independence; coincidence cannot produce love; being in a culinary mecca cannot make one into a chef; talents do not develop themselves. There is no doubt that our parents, friends, and romantic partners influence us deeply, but they do not fashion us. We have a hand in answering the question as to what things in the world are important to us, and our answers need not be, and typically are not, arbitrary or random. Agency, as distinct from mere behavior, is marked by practical rationality. Insofar as becoming someone is something someone *does*, and not merely something that happens to her, she must have access to *reasons* to become the person she will be. Giving a philosophical account of how it is possible for value-acquisition to be a form of practically rational agency is the project of this book.

This project faces a difficulty: people do not seem to be able to *choose* or *decide* to have different values. A decision or choice is an act of the will that prefigures, accompanies, or is a constitutive part of some single action. The transition from indifference to love cannot typically be effected by way of deciding: no matter the strength of my will, it does not seem that I can muscle myself into suddenly caring. To be sure, the path to valuing sometimes includes momentary expressions of commitment: the moment when you say "I do," or sign the adoption papers, or buy the one-way plane ticket to a foreign country. But these moments are themselves only part of the story, punctuating a longer process. Coming to value something tends to represent a deep change in how one sees and feels and thinks. Acquiring a new value often alters the structure of one's priorities by demoting or even displacing something one valued before. Such changes take time, over the course of which one has done many different things in the service of value-appreciation. The later actions are shaped by the small changes that the earlier ones have engendered in such a way as to allow someone to slowly develop new priorities, concerns, and attachments. The process as a whole exemplifies a distinctive form of practical rationality, one not structured by a single moment of intention or decision at its inception; the rationality of the agent I seek to describe changes and indeed solidifies over time, as the agent becomes increasingly able to respond to the reasons for action associated with her new values.

we become more rational and more able to respond to things as we become able to acknow. why we do things

(b) Valuing and Aspiring

We have a rich vocabulary for the many forms that positive practical orientations can take: in addition to valuing, we speak of desiring, wanting, loving, approving of, being attracted to, caring about or for, endorsing, preferring, being identified with, seeing as valuable, feeling impelled to, etc. Setting aside other differences between such terms, we can group them roughly into two psychological strata. There is a shallower stratum to which "desire," "urge," and "attraction" often belong, and a deeper stratum—one that runs closer to the heart of who the person in question is—to which "value," "endorsement," and "identification" usually belong. These terms are quite flexible, and context can suffice to make clear that, in a given case, the urge in question is a deep one, or the endorsement a superficial one. One marker of whether a given term, in a given context, runs shallow or deep is whether we're inclined to preface it with "mere"—*mere* desire, *mere* attraction, etc.

I will have occasion to refer to both kinds of practical attitudes over the course of the book. When I speak of "values" the reader can be sure I am picking out a deep practical orientation. Beyond this, I am disinclined to invoke a technical vocabulary that would reliably mark the difference between, e.g., loving chocolate and loving one's child. For I would have to either artificially relegate such a term to a specific stratum or introduce a term of art to cover the lower stratum; and the risk of messing with natural language is that of becoming alienated from intuitions about the phenomena one is trying to describe. I prefer to speak loosely and colloquially of agents wanting, desiring, etc., and allowing context to clarify whether the practical orientation I am describing represents what really matters to the agent or is a case of *mere* wanting.

Our interest is, for reasons I will elaborate later in the chapter, specifically an interest in the rational process by which we arrive at new elements in the deeper stratum. Grasping new values is hard for us because, to paraphrase Augustine,[1] our hands are already full. Without denying that parents and teachers may play an important role in such a process, we might nonetheless characterize it as one in which one habituates or educates oneself. It is a mark of being old enough to engage in such an activity that one already has interests, concerns, and projects that can serve as obstacles to acquiring new ones. Gaining a value often means devoting to it some of the time and effort one was previously devoting elsewhere. Sometimes one's new value requires complete divestment from an old value, for instance when a former pleasure-seeker turns herself toward asceticism. Even in cases where our old value-outlook does not specifically contradict our new one, we often experience the effort of coming to apprehend value as a struggle with ourselves. Leisurely self-contentment is ruled out for someone who sees herself as being in a defective valuational condition. Grasping new values is work.

The name I will give to the rational process by which we work to care about (or love, or value, or desire . . .) something new is "aspiration." Aspiration, as I understand it, is the distinctive form of agency

1. "God wishes to give us something, but cannot, because he sees that our hands are already full." Cited in Schillebeeckx (1969: 242).

directed at the acquisition of values. Though we do not typically come to value simply by deciding to, it is nonetheless true that coming to value can be something the agent does. The explanation of how we come to value, or to see-as-valuable, so many of the things that we once did not is that we work to achieve this result. The aspirant sees that she does not have the values that she would like to have, and therefore seeks to move herself toward a better valuational condition. She senses that there is more out there to value than she currently values, and she strives to come to see what she cannot yet get fully into view.

The work of aspiration includes, but is by no means limited to, the mental work of thinking, imagining, and reasoning. If a callow youth gets an inkling of the value of classical music or painting or wine, and wants to come to appreciate these values more fully, it will not suffice for him to think carefully about these things. He must listen to music or visit museums or drink wine. Let me offer a few more examples, some of which may strike the reader as more familiar than others. If one aspires to be a doctor, one goes to medical school. If one aspires to be more attuned to values of healthy living, one might become a member of a gym and transition one's eating habits toward vegetables and whole grains. If one seeks to appreciate some person, one might invite him for coffee. If one aspires to be religious, one might spend more time at one's church or synagogue or mosque—or, in another kind of case, one might deliberately stay away from those places in an effort to (re)connect with God on one's own terms. If one's goal is to value civic engagement, one might explore community activism. We aspire by doing things, and the things we do change us so that we are able to do the same things, or things of that kind, better and better. In the beginning, we sometimes feel as though we are pretending, play-acting, or otherwise alienated from our own activity. We

may see the new value as something we are trying out or trying on rather than something we are fully engaged with and committed to. We may rely heavily on mentors whom we are trying to imitate or competitors whom we are trying to best. As time goes on, however, the fact (if it is a fact) that we are still at it is usually a sign that we find ourselves progressively more able to see, on our own, the value that we could barely apprehend at first. This is how we work our way into caring about the many things that we, having done that work, care about.

The English word "aspiration" is a good, if not a perfect, label for the concept I aim to explicate. Since I use the word to describe the process of rational value-acquisition, I end up emphasizing certain of the ordinary language features of the word and de-emphasizing others. For instance, we often speak of someone's aspiring to some career, as I did a moment ago when describing an aspiring doctor. In this kind of context, we may think that such a person's primary hope is to acquire the skills and qualifications that further enable her to secure an extrinsic reward such as status, money, or parental love. The aspirant, as I use the word, doesn't aim exclusively at any of these things. To be sure, she wants to go to medical school, to pass her exams, to succeed in her residency, to gain a position at an excellent hospital. Perhaps she even wants to please her parents. But her desire for all these things is a secondary manifestation of what she really wants, which is to provide the kind of medical assistance whose particular nature it is the job of her medical education to convey to her. Though she takes herself, before attending medical school, to have some understanding of medicine, she (knows that) she will only really grasp the specific good she is seeking to bring about by way of engaging in the work in question. (Consider the variety of medical professions: anaesthesiologists, obstetricians and psychologists provide very different kinds of help to people. The full

[margin note: only grasp the good when you engage w/ the work]

understanding of the kind of medical assistance each provides is the province of the experienced practitioner, not the first-year medical student.)

A medical student whose final target was money, the approval of her parents, or social status would not count as an aspirant in my sense; I discuss this distinct phenomenon, which I call "ambition," in chapter 6. The ambitious medical student is not seeking to acquire a value: she takes herself to have full access, even before entering medical school, to the value of having money, the approval of her parents, or social status. She does not hope that medical school and residency will teach her the value of these things. She hopes only that they will help her satisfy the values she already has. She has too much access to the value in question to count as aspiring toward it. More generally, the word "aspiration" is sometimes used to describe any kind of hope or wish or long-term goal to bring some result about. These agents will not count as aspirants in my sense, unless the sought-after end is one whose value those agents are also seeking to learn.

I will also restrict the term "aspirant" at the other end of the spectrum, by withholding it from people who have *too little* antecedent access to any value that they might acquire. It is not a stretch of the English word "aspirant" to describe a young adult who sets out for Europe to "find herself" as an aspirant. She won't count as an aspirant in my sense, however, unless there is something more specific she is trying to find.[2] Adventures are not typically aspirational, and a sign of this is that they rarely feel like work.[3]

---

2. In my paper "Liberal Education and the Possibility of Valuational Progress" (Callard, forthcoming), I identify a form of aspiration that may be an exception to this rule. Colleges and universities provide aspirants with the kind of support that makes it possible for a person to aspire even if she possesses only an aspirational goal as vague and schematic as that of "becoming someone" or "learning how to think" or "self-discovery."

3. I develop this idea by contrasting aspiration with Talbot Brewer's "dialectical activities" in chapter 6, section II.

to be an "aspirant" requires specificity and seeking to learn

The aspirant is trying to change herself in some particular dimension; she is not merely open to changes that might come. She grasps, however dimly, a target with reference to which she guides herself.

It is not always easy to determine how much of an antecedent grasp of value someone has or to ascertain how much of a grasp someone would have to have in order to count as an aspirant. I won't offer any guidance for assessing borderline cases, though I will discuss why this is a difficult problem and why such assessments may presuppose specialized knowledge of the value in question (see chapter 2 part IV). My point here is only that my use of the word "aspirant" is philosophically charged in such a way as to pick out all and only the cases in which the project of becoming someone is also the process of appreciating the values distinctive of becoming that kind of person.

Aspiration is rational, purposive value-acquisition. In the second part of this introduction, I offer a case study of an aspirant taken from Plato's *Symposium*. Alcibiades' closing speech gives us access to what it feels like to struggle to be better than one is, and Plato's presentation of that speech makes it possible for us to assess the rationality of Alcibiades' attempts at value-acquisition. My discussion of Alcibiades presupposes that there is such a thing as a rational pursuit of one's own fundamental values; the book goes on to defend this claim. Before turning to Alcibiades, I now briefly outline the structure of that argument.

II. OUTLINE OF CHAPTERS

Throughout this book, I describe myself as "giving an account" or "presenting a theory" of aspiration. As this outline will make clear, the work of the book is somewhat more rudimentary than those descriptions might suggest. The topic of aspiration lies at the crossroads of three sub-areas of ethics: the theory of practical rationality, the theory of moral psychology, and the theory of moral responsibility. In each of the three areas, the concept of aspiration emerges as a problematic one—it is difficult to see how aspiration can be rational, how it can be psychologically real, and how it is possible for someone, via aspiration, to "create himself." I aim to identify those elements of the received framework in each field that foreclose the possibility of aspiration and to propose emendations that would accommodate it. This book describes what an aspiration-friendly theory of rationality, moral psychology, and moral responsibility would look like. In addition, by way of motivating my emendations, I explain the payoffs available, in each area, for making the required changes. The theory of aspiration must begin somewhat earlier than the theory of a phenomenon that does not require such emendations. It must begin with an explanation of how it is so much as conceivable that human beings aspire.

(a) Rationality

If aspiration is to be an exercise of human agency, aspirants must be responding to practical reasons of some kind. Behavior qualifies as agency insofar as it exhibits the distinctive intelligibility of being a response to reasons. "I do what happens," as Anscombe said (1963: 52), but only when what happens happens for some reason. There are, however, problems in identifying the reason on which the aspirant acts. In chapter 1, I explore two recent attempts to account for aspirational activity within the framework of decision theory. If that project fails, then it might seem—as one of the authors in fact concludes—that the process of substantive value-change simply cannot be rational. I argue instead that it has a distinctive rational form that is not the rationality of deliberation, calculation, preference, or decision.

In chapter 2, I discuss the special practical reasons peculiar to aspirants, which I call "proleptic reasons." If someone takes a music class in order to come to appreciate music, her behavior does not serve a current end of hers in the same way it would if she got a cheeseburger because she was hungry. In the second case, she already has a desire for food; in the first, she is trying to have a desire for music. The reasons of aspirants are not, to use Bernard Williams's ([1980] 1981) term, "internal reasons" to which an agent can expect complete access if she deliberates correctly from her current motivational condition. Internal reasons are reasons that answer to one's current set of motives. When we reason from them, we reason about how to get what we already want. If we want to understand how substantive value-change is possible, we will have to introduce a new kind of reason, one directed not at satisfying wants but rather at generating them.

(b) Moral Psychology

There is a characteristically aspirational form of angst. In order to bring out what is distinctive about the aspirant's inner strife, it will be helpful to contrast it with two well-recognized sources of psychological conflict: that of a hard or tragic choice and that of a recalcitrant or rejected motive. In the case of a hard choice, an agent may find it difficult to select among her options. Perhaps the values are incommensurable, or perhaps she simply does not want to give up any of the relevant goods: even getting what is better overall involves a substantial loss. Such an agent feels pained at the loss of whichever options she lets go of.

This kind of pain is quite different from that of a recalcitrant or rejected motive. Consider the unwilling addict. She is moved by forces that she views as in some way external to her will. Her motivation to take drugs is not accompanied by the corresponding evaluative judgment to the effect that she ought to take the drugs. The case of the addict is typically taken to be an instance of the more general phenomenon of alienation from affective conditions such as pathological fears or bouts of uncontrollable rage. Such a person might feel that there is nothing to be said for feeding her addiction (or fueling her rage or accommodating her phobias), but she is moved to do so by inner drives she cannot control.

The phenomenon of aspiration opens up a third way of being torn. Though she looks forward to a time when she will no longer find operas boring, the aspiring opera-lover does not currently find her boredom external or alien. It is all too clear that the indifference she feels really is *hers*, which is to say, it represents a point of view that she identifies as authentically her own. This is exactly why she (sees that she) needs to work to see things differently.

Nor does the aspiring music-lover find the choice between love of and indifference to music to be a "hard choice." She is oriented toward the one condition, and away from the other, in such a way as to make the decision an easy one. She does not feel uncertain, nor does she feel that by coming to love music she is choosing between two things, her love and her indifference, both of which are really important to her. Nonetheless, coming to love music can be difficult. Someone who is working at it will often feel torn. I describe this form of conflict, which I call "intrinsic," in chapter 3.

In the fourth chapter, I address the well-known puzzle of akrasia (weakness of will), as to how it is possible for a person to act against her better judgment. I begin by articulating a standing problem with analyses of akrasia since Davidson: they force us to choose between saying that the akratic agent did not (really) know that she should have done otherwise or saying that she did not act willingly. Effectively, the agent is depicted either as not having fully decided the issue between her two options—it was a hard choice—or as having been overwhelmed by a form of motivation that is alien or external to her. I argue that a better account of akrasia is available to those who understand it as an instance of intrinsic conflict.

An aspirant reasons toward value, aiming to resolve her intrinsic conflict by grasping some value more fully. But she must also, sometimes, reason *from* the defective grasp she currently has—we cannot wait to make use of our values until such time as they are firmly in our possession. Agents who attempt to deliberate from a shakily grasped value while in the throes of intrinsic conflict are susceptible to akrasia. Akrasia, on my account, is a result of the fact that we sometimes need to make do with the value-grasp we currently have, however imperfect it may be.

While aspiration may be philosophically neglected, akrasia cannot claim to be. Those who puzzle over how it is possible to act against one's better judgment, are, I argue, grasping a tip of the aspirational iceberg. It is worth noting, however, that my analysis of akrasia is, in an important sense, freestanding from the rest of the book. One needn't accept that akratics are intrinsically conflicted in order to embrace my account of the role of intrinsic conflict in aspiration; rather, the direction of support goes the other way. In applying the framework of intrinsic conflict to the paradoxical phenomenon of akrasia, I aim to illustrate the explanatory power of the theory of aspiration.

(c) Responsibility

In part III of the book, I argue that the theorist of aspiration offers us an important piece of a solution to a long-standing puzzle as to how we can be responsible for being the kinds of people we are. Much of who we are either is or flows from our values—but we cannot, according to this puzzle, choose our values. For if we are inclined to choose to value something, that must (so goes the dilemma) be because the valuing of that thing already accords with the values we have—which is, of course, why we are so inclined. Otherwise, coming to value it entails breaking radically with our old values, in which case the transition is neither rational nor agential. The new valuation, on this horn of the dilemma, is something that happens to us rather than something we do.

In chapter 5, I show that we can escape the dilemma by inverting the traditional relation of authority between the creator and the created self. On an aspirational account of self-creation, the creator does not determine, choose, or shape the created self; rather, she looks up to, imitates, and seeks to become the created self. The source of normativity lies at the end of the process rather than at the beginning.

In chapter 6, I develop an asymmetrical aspirational theory of moral responsibility for one's valuational condition. We are positively responsible—praiseworthy—for the good valuational condition we attain via aspiration. We are negatively responsible—blameworthy— for the culpable failure to aspire to a better condition. The account is asymmetrical because aspiration is a learning process: since one can't learn what is not the case, there is no such thing as "aspiring to be evil."

The expression *finis origine pendet* means "the end hangs from [i.e., depends on] the beginning." It is attributed to the Roman poet

Manlius and was adopted as a motto by Phillips Exeter Academy. On one interpretation, the phrase asserts that what happens in the early years has a substantial impact, positive or negative, on the later unfolding of that life. Perhaps this is all Manlius meant to say; perhaps he was simply pointing out that beginnings are important. But once we are operating in the educational context into which the founders of Exeter Academy imported the phrase, it seems fair to append to the motto the clarification that the most important beginnings are those that, in an aspirational sense, hang from the end.

III. A CASE STUDY: ALCIBIADES

As the chapter overview suggests, the very possibility of aspiration has been neglected in the philosophical literature on rationality, moral psychology, and responsibility. The effects of this neglect are visible not in any overt claim that such a thing is *impossible*, but in certain subtle ways in which the space of possibility has been narrowed in each of the three subfields discussed in the preceding section. The theorist of aspiration finds herself pointing to something in the middle of what we might have taken to be an exclusive dichotomy between making a decision to change and being changed by one's environment; between the unwilling addict's alien motivation to take the drug and a form of motivation that one wholeheartedly embraces. In the face of the standing assumption that there is a principled distinction between a process of discovery and one of creation, she points out that the aspirant's value-discovery is at the same time her self-creation. She is forced to stretch the existing concepts into a new dimension by pointing to *degrees* to which one sees a reason, or has a value, or inhabits some point of view.

We cannot prove the need for these innovations simply by offering an example of aspiration, since a skeptic can always read any example in a non-aspirational way. Examples have a limited power to defuse a skeptic bent on reductive elimination of the phenomenon (purportedly) exemplified in them; this problem is particularly acute in the case of aspiration, which can be hard to distinguish from related phenomena such as ambition, adventurousness, indoctrination, and pretense. Nonetheless, an example will help us lay out what an aspirational account of some phenomenon would look like. And a well-written example can do a bit more. For an author who has taken some care to present the details of an aspirant's psychology in a realistic way affords the theorist of aspiration an opportunity to showcase the interpretative power of her innovations in the theory of rationality, psychology, and ethics. I find such an opportunity in the speech of Alcibiades at the end of Plato's *Symposium*. As a first step in arguing for the possibility of aspiration, I propose to argue that an aspirational account of Alcibiades' rationality, psychology, and ethical status offers us the least contrived reading of Plato's text.

In Plato's *Symposium*, Socrates attends a drinking party, the participants of which take turns offering speeches of praise to the god Eros. As the last speaker is finishing up, a drunken Alcibiades crashes the party. Alcibiades was, at the time, a newly minted general whose good looks, charisma, and aristocratic lineage engendered a large base of popular support. Alcibiades' throng of suitors as a teenager is described in Plato's *Alcibiades I*. In the *Symposium* he is a bit older, and what he has lost in boyish appeal—upon entering, he removes a laurel crown from his own head and places it on that of a beautiful, young up-and-coming poet, Agathon—he has gained in political influence. Indeed, given his victories in the 416 Olympic Games[4]

---

4. Mentioned by Alcibiades himself in Thucydides' *History of the Peloponnesian War* VI.16.2, where one can also find a sketch of Alcibiades' arrogance and influence that corroborates Plato's.

and his recent appointment as a general, it is fair to say that in the *Symposium* Plato catches Alcibiades on the cusp of greatness—a greatness that, as I will discuss later, he was never to attain.

Alcibiades opts not to offer a tribute to Eros, as the other symposiasts have done, but to praise Socrates instead. Because his encomium issues from Alcibiades' vantage point as Socrates' would-be lover, it is as much a lamentation of Alcibiades' sufferings as it is a catalogue of Socrates' virtues. Alcibiades recounts the practical consequences of the famed "knowledge of one's own ignorance" with which Socrates infects those around him. He describes his newly discovered need to live a wholly different life, to become a much better person than he is. Unthinkable that *Alcibiades* could feel inadequate!—at least Alcibiades finds it so. What one hears throughout his speech is the shock of finding *himself, of all people* in this position.

Alcibiades discusses his own aspirational condition at length, because he is so struck by the unlikeliness of it. But even as he describes it, he is *in* it—so his speech offers us access to the phenomenon of aspiration, described from the point of view of the aspirant. His speech shows us what aspiration looks like from the outside and what it feels like from the inside:

> You know, people hardly ever take a speaker seriously, even if he's the greatest orator; but let anyone—man, woman or child— listen to you or even to a poor account of what you say—and we are all transported, completely possessed. If I were to describe for you all what an extraordinary effect his words have always had on me (I can feel it this moment even as I'm speaking), you might actually suspect that I'm drunk! Still, I swear to you, the moment he starts to speak, I am beside myself: my heart starts leaping in my chest, the tears come streaming down my face,

even the frenzied Corybantes seem sane compared to me—
and, let me tell you, I am not alone. I have heard Pericles and
many other great orators, and I have admired their speeches.
But nothing like this ever happened to me: they never upset
me so deeply that my very own soul started protesting that my
life—my life!—was no better than the most miserable slave's.
And yet that is exactly how this Marsyas here at my side makes
me feel all the time: he makes it seem that my life isn't worth
living! You can't say that isn't true, Socrates. I know very well
that you could make me feel that way this very moment if I gave
you half a chance. He always traps me, you see, and he makes
me admit that my political career is a waste of time, while all
that matters is just what I most neglect: my personal shortcomings, which cry out for the closest attention. So I refuse
to listen to him; I stop my ears and tear myself away from him,
for, like the Sirens, he could make me stay by his side till I die.
Socrates is the only man in the world who has made me feel
shame—ah, you didn't think I had it in me, did you? Yes, he
makes me feel ashamed: I know perfectly well that I can't prove
he's wrong when he tells me what I should do; yet, the moment
I leave his side, I go back to my old ways: I cave in to my desire
to please the crowd. My whole life has become one constant
effort to escape from him and keep away, but when I see him,
I feel deeply ashamed, because I'm doing nothing about my
way of life, though I have already agreed with him that I should.
Sometimes, believe me, I think I would be happier if he were
dead. And yet I know that if he dies I'll be even more miserable.
I can't live with him, and I can't live without him! What can I do
about him? (215d1–216c3)[5]

---

5. Translations of Plato throughout are from Cooper (1997).

Alcibiades is torn between being inclined, with Socrates, to "admit that my political career is a waste of time" and the powerful inclination to pursue that same career. He is sincere[6] when he acknowledges the importance of attending to the personal shortcomings he goes on to neglect. For even when he is not talking to Socrates, Alcibiades experiences the Socratic point of view as an oppressive presence pouring forth censure onto his way of life. Alcibiades channels Socrates when he castigates his own life as "not worth living" or as no better than that of a slave; and when he says that his "political career is a waste of time" because of his "personal shortcomings, which cry out for the closest attention," his language has an authentically Socratic ring. He claims to know that Socrates is right while nonetheless being overcome by the value—honor—that Socrates has taught him to discount.[7]

Alcibiades insists on a vivid and intense access to the experience of being refuted by Socrates, even now (215de, 216a), that is, when he is not being refuted by Socrates. He dismisses his pursuit of honor as something that "overcomes" him or as a vestige of his "old ways." He describes the effects of Socrates' speech as something he can "still feel even at this moment"—but this cannot quite be right. For when Socrates refutes him, Alcibiades, by his own reckoning, behaves like a Corybant: "I find my heart leaping and my tears gushing forth at the sound of his speech" (215e). But his heart is not, as he speaks, leaping, nor are tears gushing forth. If Socrates *could*

---

6. The following consideration suggests that we can trust Alcibiades' report of their interactions: he opens with the following invitation to Socrates: "If I say anything that's not true, you can just interrupt, if you want, and correct me; at worst, there'll be mistakes in my speech, not lies" (214e). Socrates never interrupts him.

7. In the first few paragraphs of this analysis I draw on the corresponding discussion in Callard (2014). In that paper, I analyze the aspirations of Alcibiades in terms of the understanding of akrasia Socrates develops in the *Protagoras*, but a discussion of Socrates' account of akrasia would take us too far afield.

make him feel that his life is not worth living, that could only be because he doesn't currently feel that way. Alcibiades is clearly referring to an experience that both he and others have had at another time, namely, when they were being refuted by Socrates.

Alcibiades feels that he has a grip on what "Socratism" is and what it does to him: "I know very well that you could make me feel that way this very moment if I gave you half a chance" (216a). This sentence expresses in a wonderfully vivid way Alcibiades' sense that he both can and cannot make contact with the Socratic experience from a distance. Alcibiades is presently aware of his own weakness, of just what he *would be* experiencing at the hands of Socrates. But if Socrates were presently refuting him, that weakness would feel different—worse.

Alcibiades has some grip on the kinds of things Socrates will say to him and the ways that his own actions, choices, and desires will look and feel to him when he is talking to Socrates. But they don't quite look or feel in those ways at the moment. He doesn't, as he speaks to the assembled company, hear Socrates' actual voice, but a simulacrum of Socrates' voice, one that uses Socratic phrasing but lacks the full Socratic bite. When Socrates actually begins to speak, those accusations will ring much louder. Alcibiades experiences a characteristically aspirational form of torture: he can almost see what it would be like to see things differently, but he doesn't get all the way to seeing them differently.

What Plato brings out so nicely in the speech of Alcibiades is the way in which one's old way of seeing things makes trouble for the new way. Alcibiades' conventional honor-loving values move him to flee from and hate Socrates, even as he struggles to recognize that the honor-loving life is not worth living. He can almost see his values as bankrupt—but he can't quite, because they won't go away.

But is Alcibiades really striving to be different? In this opening speech, it is perhaps not completely clear what aspirational work Alcibiades is doing. For what comes to the forefront of Alcibiades' self-description are his attempts to *avoid* the wisdom-loving life by hiding from Socrates. I want to turn to another passage in which Alcibiades' attempts at forward progress toward his aspirational target are more evident.

Alcibiades tells how he hungered for Socrates' wisdom and hatched the following plan: "What I thought at the time was that what he really wanted was me, and that seemed to me the luckiest coincidence: all I had to do was to let him have his way with me, and he would teach me everything he knew—believe me, I had a lot of confidence in my looks." Alcibiades goes on to couch his offer of sex-for-knowledge to Socrates in the language of his newfound Socratism: "Nothing is more important to me than becoming the best man I can be, and no one can help me more than you to reach that aim. With a man like you, in fact, I'd be much more ashamed of what wise people would say if I did not take you as my lover, than I would of what all the others, in their foolishness, would say if I did" (218d). Socrates responds, to Alcibiades' astonishment, by complaining that if what Alcibiades is saying is true, he (Socrates) would be getting the short end of the stick:

> Dear Alcibiades, if you are right in what you say about me, you are already more accomplished than you think. If I really have in me the power to make you a better man, then you can see in me a beauty that is really beyond description and makes your own remarkable good looks pale in comparison. But, then, is this a fair exchange that you propose? You seem to me to want more than your proper share: you offer me the merest appearance of beauty, and in return you want the thing itself, "gold in exchange for bronze." (218e–219a)

Socrates doubts that Alcibiades really can see what he takes himself to be able to see. If Alcibiades were in a position to fully appreciate the wisdom he claims to have recognized in Socrates, Alcibiades would see that no one who had it would trade it for sex. Someone who sees the beauty of the body as being on par with the beauty of wisdom hasn't apprehended how beautiful wisdom is. When Socrates tells Alcibiades that if he, Alcibiades, were even able to see the beauty of wisdom, he would be "more accomplished than you think," Socrates' point is to show Alcibiades that he is in fact less accomplished than he takes himself to be. Alcibiades' Alcibiadeanism—with its concomitant arrogance ("I had a lot of confidence in my looks")—stands in the way of his being able to get his new values into view.

Alcibiades may experience moment-to-moment variations in the strength of his two points of view, but they are both with him throughout his time as an aspirant, each precluding a full experience of the other. He seems to inhabit both the Socratic value perspective he aspires to acquire and the honor-loving values represented by the old ways he aspires to escape. He is not merely pretending to care about wisdom for Socrates' benefit and then cheerfully pursuing honor on his own time. Nor does he flip-flop between two perspectives, comfortably inhabiting each for however short a duration; he's not like someone who is drunk and then sobers up, then gets drunk again. Someone who repudiated his past Socratism would not be so haunted by Socratic thoughts. And someone who was fully under Socrates' spell would not have so much trouble shedding his honor-loving skin.

Alcibiades is, for reasons I will explore later, an especially conflicted aspirant. Aspiration will be smoother sailing for someone who does not make such a sustained effort to escape his own aspiration. Nonetheless, the quality, if not the quantity, of Alcibiades' conflict is typically aspirational. The work of the aspirant is often marked by some resistance to doing that work. We are much less likely to find such resistance among those engaged in work not geared toward value-change. Someone who is, for instance, building a birdhouse, is unlikely to take apart what he has built, throw away his tools, run away from his project, and then return to working. That's because his values are fixed throughout the process. If we are to get aspirational work into view, we must be prepared to encounter its characteristically tortured and disoriented presentation. At the same time, what it is a tortured presentation of is something that bears a crucial resemblance to building a birdhouse. Both aspiring and building are forms of work, activities to be engaged in and not (merely) experiences to be undergone.

It is not difficult to allow that someone may move from being one kind of person to another. We all drift and change in response to our environment, cultural pressures, etc. Sometimes, we change without even noticing it. The aspirant's movement is not of this kind, since she actively moves herself. And that means, as I have noted, that she has some *reason* for doing so: aspiration is a *rational* process. Can what Alcibiades is going through in this period of his life be described as a rational process?

Much of this book is dedicated to articulating both why it is so difficult and why it is so important to get the rationality of aspiration into view. Roughly speaking, the problem is that being practically rational involves acting for the sake of some envisioned end—and, as Socrates points out to him, an aspirant like Alcibiades doesn't fully have in view the end for the sake of which he is acting. Alcibiades cannot fully grasp the value of wisdom, and he therefore cannot fully grasp why it is to be pursued. He offers up his body in exchange for he knows not what, since he doesn't really see the beauty he thinks he sees. Having an end in view is, of course, merely a prerequisite for the characteristic activities that we usually think of as the mark of the practically rational agent: she reflects on whether this end is, in fact, likely to be achieved by her; she compares it with other ends and decides that it is to be pursued over them; she figures out the best means to achieve it.

The aspirant has trouble engaging fully in any of these activities, and that is because she fails the basic prerequisite of acting for the sake of some envisioned end. Her thought about what she is doing cannot be completely clear, both for the negative reason that she has insufficient contact with the value to understand how or why it is to be achieved and because her mind is positively clouded by the presence of distorting values, such as Alcibiades' love of honor. Alcibiades is not in a position to make value-comparisons, such as the comparison between honor and wisdom. He cannot seem to get them both into view at once, as someone might who can "step back" from two things that he values and decide between them from a position of impartial arbitration. His manner of desiring both honor and wisdom at once is to have one of those points of view dominate, at any given time, and have the other present itself in the form of a recalcitrant impulse or sense of shame or incomplete grasp of the dominant value.

His experience of concomitantly loving honor and wisdom does not come in a form where he might occupy the reflective position of impartial judge between the two values. He does not seem to be trying to "decide" whether it is better to be honor-loving or wisdom-loving. Rather, he seems convinced that it is better to be wisdom-loving but is unable to feel the force of this conviction in the absence of Socrates. We can see that Alcibiades doesn't resemble someone trying to make a decision. Though he clearly struggles, his struggle is not that of someone who has difficulty choosing which of two valuable things he should pursue. The love of honor and love of wisdom that threaten to pull him apart do not present themselves to him in the form of a difficult practical problem. He is not trying to figure anything out. He is just trying to become a wisdom-lover, and his love of honor is holding him back. Or, at other times, it seems to be that he is trying *not* to become a wisdom-lover but finds that honor has lost some of its initial appeal ("my heart, or my soul, or whatever you want to call it . . . has been struck and bitten by philosophy, whose grip on young and eager souls is much more vicious than a viper's and makes them do the most amazing things" [218a]). Alcibiades' project is not one of making a decision from the values he already has; it is the project of acquiring more fully the values he currently grasps in an attenuated way.

I am not going to argue that someone in Alcibiades' position is, despite appearances, in a good position to exhibit the rationality of reflective, reasoned, well-informed decision-making. Instead, I am going to argue that that is only one way in which practical rationality manifests itself.

In order to make a good decision, one must already have the desires (values, preferences, etc.) that supply one with (or just *are*) a conception of the end(s) in the light of which one decides. But how does one come by these very desires, values, preferences, etc.? Here are two familiar kinds of answer to that question: (i) non-agential transformation: I acquire it through external influence/accident/ genetic predisposition; (ii) self-cultivation: I acquire it by reasoning that I would better satisfy the desires I have now if I acquired such a desire. Alcibiades' attempt to acquire a desire for wisdom has elements of (i) and (ii), but neither schema fits him perfectly.

One kind of skeptic of aspiration might want to read Alcibiades' story as passive, non-agential transformation along the lines of (i). She would be right to cite the effect of Socrates on Alcibiades' desires and values. Things feel different when Socrates is refuting you; he has a real influence on the people around him. Such a skeptic might also note Alcibiades' innate talents. Socrates has focused his own efforts on Alcibiades because Socrates, like all of Athens, sees great potential the young man.[8] We should acknowledge that Socrates' influence and Alcibiades' innate talent are relevant to Alcibiades' status as an aspirant—but only as backdrop. They might explain why it is easier for Alcibiades than others to get the value of wisdom into view, but this skeptic leaves out of the account Alcibiades' activity of (trying to) bring it into view.

Another kind of skeptic reads Alcibiades' pursuit of philosophy as satisfying a set of desires he already has about the kind of person he wants to be. She will point to Alcibiades' belief that he would be better off desiring wisdom, and try to explain his behavior as rational in the light of his antecedent motivational condition. But Alcibiades' belief does not stem from a judgment that such a desire coheres better with, or helps him satisfy, desires he has anyway. His whole problem is that he thinks his deepest, most fundamental desires, values, and concerns are misdirected. Alcibiades' project of wisdom-acquisition is both less self-directed and more self-transformative than the process of self-cultivation described by the skeptic.[9] Someone who tries to make her desires more coherent derives guidance from the self she already has; the aspirant must take her bearings from the self she doesn't have yet. More specifically, she must take her bearings from some value grasped by that self. Alcibiades' goals of self-improvement require that he fix his attention on the value of wisdom, on seeing *its* beauty. He is surprised to find that his attention is on Socrates, when *Alcibiades* should be the beloved. The aspiring parent is thinking about her

---

8. See *Alcibiades I*, esp. 104e–106a.
9. For further discussion of self-cultivation, see chapter 1, section III and chapter 5, section II.

(potential) children, the aspiring music-lover is thinking about the value of music, the aspiring doctor is thinking about the practice of medicine and her future patients, etc. These people are trying to acquire a desire not because something about them demands that they acquire it, but because they see (that they don't fully see) that there is something of value out there. Let me step back from the details of Alcibiades' story and place it within the broader philosophical framework of the book.

There is a distinctive form of rationality that pertains to the genesis of desire, a way of reasoning toward desire rather than from it. When we reason from desire, our rationality consists for the most part in making and sticking to good choices, knowing what is worth sacrificing, taking prudent risks. The excellent decision-maker knows when to jump on an opportunity and when to bide her time. Such rational activity doesn't, of course, entail the presence of a process of *reasoning*. We often make good decisions without doing much thinking; indeed, we sometimes make better decisions by doing less thinking.[10] The rational decider is good at making the choices that maximize the satisfaction of her desires (the realization of her values, etc.). In hard cases, she deliberates well; in easy cases, she does not deliberate at all, but immediately decides rationally. Decision theory is that branch of philosophy that offers a formal account of the optimal decision procedure that would be employed by such an agent, be it in the form of consciously articulated reasoning, reflexive rational response, or something that partakes of both. The decision theorist tells us what a rational choice consists in.

Edna Ullmann-Margalit and Laurie Paul have discussed the topic of large, life-altering choices from the point of view of decision theory. Since decision theory presupposes a subject who enters the

---

10. See Holton (2004); and for further discussion of the general point that reflective deliberation is not a cure-all see chapter 3, section V.

decision scenario with (some) fixed core preferences, they argue[11] that decision theory cannot tell us how to be rational when the decision's primary import is a fundamental change in those (core) preferences. I find their arguments to be, by and large, sound. I will go through them in the next chapter, though I will draw a very different lesson from their conclusions than they do. Instead of concluding that, because the decision theorist cannot tell us what it would be for an agent like Alcibiades to be rational, there is no fact of the matter about whether he acts rationally, I will argue that agents like Alcibiades—aspirants—exhibit a distinctive form of rationality that is not a matter of decision at all.

Theorists of practical rationality have tended to focus on the question of how we rationally manage the values and desires agents already have. They attend to the case of value-acquisition, to the extent that they do, as a special case of desire-management. There is, of course, a form of desire-acquisition—a secondary form—that is simply a special case of desire-management. My topic, however, is *primary* desire-acquisition. In such a case, the desires one already has are themselves fully intelligible only in the light of the desires one will have. One's present condition is, as it were, a simulacrum of the condition one hopes someday to be in. If there is such a thing as rational change in one's core preferences, one does not make such a change by trying to best satisfy the preferences that one already has.

Aspirants often depend on a teacher or mentor figure, but it is a peculiarity of Alcibiades' case how dependent he is on Socrates. In the absence of Socrates, Alcibiades actively opposes the aspirations

---

11. Here I am glossing over a distinction between the two views. It is Ullmann-Margalit who has the view described here, while Paul hopes to rescue a decision theoretic approach by appealing to second-order preferences. I argue that her rescue does not work, and so her critique leaves us in the same position as Ullmann-Margalit's.

he feels in Socrates' presence, trying to free himself from the demand to be better. Alcibiades is, on all accounts, a failure at the project of aspiration. This is not the same thing as saying that he does not aspire at all, but it does entail that Alcibiades' behavior, considered as a whole, is irrational. This is, I believe, the point of Socrates' cryptic reply to Alcibiades' speech:

> Alcibiades' frankness provoked a lot of laughter, especially since it was obvious that he was still in love with Socrates, who immediately said to him: "You're perfectly sober after all, Alcibiades. Otherwise you could never have concealed your motive so gracefully: how casually you let it drop, almost like an afterthought, at the very end of your speech! As if the real point of all this has not been simply to make trouble between Agathon and me! You think that I should be in love with you and no one else, while you, and no one else, should be in love with Agathon— well, we were *not* deceived; we've seen through your little satyr play. (222cd)

What might strike the reader as an unfeeling or even clueless response to Alcibiades' impassioned confession is, I believe, meant to function as a rebuke. Socrates charges Alcibiades with the ulterior motive of "getting between" himself and Agathon. It is striking, however, that Socrates does not suspect Alcibiades of seeking to court Agathon's affections. Socrates thinks that Alcibiades is trying to be the *lover* of Agathon and the *beloved* of Socrates. The narrator remarks of Alcibiades that "it was obvious that he was still in love with Socrates," but Socrates notes that Alcibiades is fighting this condition. Alcibiades wants *to be in love* with someone else, to pursue the up-and-comer Agathon, whom he came to the party to crown with laurel wreaths ("I want this crown to come directly from my head to the head that belongs, I don't mind saying, to the cleverest and best looking man in town" [212e]). Alcibiades also wants to be loved by Socrates, for that would mean that Socrates would take his "proper" place: older, uglier lover (*erastēs*) of a young, beautiful boy (*erōmenos*).[12] He wants Socrates to want him for his young, beautiful body, so that he can stop loving Socrates and himself pursue the even younger and better-looking Agathon for *his* beautiful body.

Socrates accuses Alcibiades of trying not to love Socrates. "Loving Socrates" has already emerged, through Alcibiades' speech, as a matter of striving for virtue and wisdom. Socrates' response to Alcibiades' sexual overtures was to invite him to be a partner in the shared project of acquiring the wisdom he thinks they both lack: "In the future, let's consider things together. We'll always do what seems the best to the two of us" (219b). Likewise, Socrates' conviction that Alcibiades is evading or resisting the work of love amounts to an accusation that he is unwilling to seek the value he aspires to have. Alcibiades is aspiring irrationally, because he is trying to be better, and trying not to be better, at the same time. He interrupts his own pursuit in such a way as to make it discontinuous, incoherent, and ultimately fruitless.

The reader might be wondering why I would choose, as a model of aspiration, someone who is not a model aspirant. The answer is that by modeling *irrational* aspiration Alcibiades reveals to us that the distinction between rationality and irrationality does indeed have application, even in such murky waters. In hiding from Socrates ("My whole life has become one constant effort to escape from him and keep away" [216b]), Alcibiades is also hiding from the part of

12. Socrates' rebuke thus picks up on one of Alcibiades' remarks toward the end of his speech: "He has deceived us all: he presents himself as your lover, and, before you know it, you're in love with him yourself!" (222b).

himself that hungers for something more than honor and power. And this is surely part of what Plato is trying to expose by having him tell his story.

During the drinking party, Alcibiades is still Athens's golden boy, but by the time the dialogue was written, Athens had witnessed Alcibiades' spectacular downfall as well as the trial and death of Socrates. The disastrous Sicilian expedition urged by Alcibiades in the year after the events described in the *Symposium* was the beginning of the end, leading to Alcibiades' betrayal of Athens to the Spartans, whom he in turn betrayed to the Persians, before briefly returning to Athens until, having been exiled once more, he was executed by a party sent by the Athenian leadership. The nineteenth-century historian and lexicographer William Smith describes his end aptly: "Thus perished miserably, in the vigour of his age, one of the most remarkable, but not one of the greatest, characters in Grecian history. With qualities which, properly applied, might have rendered him the greatest benefactor of Athens, he contrived to attain the inhumane distinction of being that citizen who had inflicted upon her the most signal amount of damage" (1872: 376).

Given its dramatic date and the date when it was written, Plato's depiction of Alcibiades' speech must be read in the light of his trajectory.[13] Arguably, the core of the animus fueling Socrates' accusers is the negative influence they judged him to have on the noble youths who flocked to his company.[14] We do not know what was said in the

13. A reading encouraged by the fact that Plato inserts the tale of the dinner party into a much later narrative frame. He has Apollodorus recount the events of the party to an unnamed friend some years after the deaths of both Socrates and Alcibiades.

14. This charge appears both on the lists of official charges brought by Anytus, Meletus, and Lycon against Socrates (*Apology* 24bc) and on the list of charges Socrates attributes to his "old accusers" (*Apology* 19c). Additionally, the question of the education or corruption of the youth is the bone of contention between Socrates and Anytus in the *Meno* (89e and following) and between Socrates and Meletus in the *Apology* (24d and following).

speech that preceded the one Plato presents in the *Apology*, but the case against Socrates certainly could have referenced Alcibiades as exhibit A. In the *Symposium*, Plato may be offering us an alternative moral to the story of the fate of Alcibiades. Plato seems to be tracing the disastrous outcome of Alcibiades' life to the fact that he didn't try hard enough. Although he had access to the raw materials (talent, influence, the help of Socrates) for a meaningful life, he nonetheless let himself get sucked back into a life he could see was empty. Alcibiades' practical irrationality consists in his culpable failure to aspire sufficiently.

In part III of this book, I will argue that the theorist of aspiration is well placed to vindicate our moral responsibility for ourselves, because she is in a position to solve a puzzle about how we can be "causes of ourselves." The aspirant herself, and not (only) her parents, teachers, mentors, culture, etc., is morally responsible for developing into the kind of person she ends up becoming. The reason Socrates didn't "make" Alcibiades virtuous is that this is not something one person can do to another. The work of appreciating the value of, say, wisdom is not work that someone can do for or to you. As Socrates was constantly telling people, virtue is not teachable.

IV. SELF AND VALUE

There is a conceptual connection I have been taking for granted throughout this introduction. I have described aspiration as, on the one hand, the process by which we acquire values and, on the other hand, the process by which we become a certain kind of person. As I will continue to identify these processes throughout the book, a word of explanation is in order. First, I should note that I use words such as "self," "identity," and "character" and phrases such as "who a person is," "becoming someone," and "the kind of person one is" in a strictly ethical as opposed to metaphysical way. I am, thus, setting aside metaphysical questions as to what, if anything, allows a person to remain one single object over the course of the many changes she undergoes from birth to death. I am not discussing a metaphysical question about personal identity over time, but rather an ethical question about a person's true or real or deep self. This self is composed of those features of a person that have ethical significance—they are the features in virtue of which you are praise- or blameworthy, beloved or hated. When you are proud or ashamed of some feature of yourself, you see that feature as having ethical significance. Which features of a person have ethical significance? They will differ from person to person, and they depend at least in part on what the person *takes* to have ethical significance.

Consider the following list of facts about a person: health, heritage, race, religion, gender, hobbies, profession, fashion sense, physical appearance, citizenship, how her home is decorated, sexual orientation. Most of us will take only some items on this list to reflect "who I really am." One atheist may be passionately committed to her atheism, devoting herself to the cause of undermining religious authority; another rarely gives the matter a second thought. One person treasures her knowledge of multiple languages, taking care to, e.g., pass them down to her children, whereas another is indifferent to the fact that he possesses this capacity. The fact that so-and-so is your next-door neighbor might be a really important fact about your life—you'd be devastated if she moved—or you might barely know her.

Of course, an agent's indifference to a fact is compatible with its having profound ethical significance for her identity. Someone who is indifferent to the needs of her immediate family members or friends, or to the dignity and equal worth of other human beings, manifests an ethically significant form of indifference. Nonetheless, even in these cases the ethical significance is a fact about what she takes to be important: a fact about, as it were, the negative space around her caring. Likewise, if you judge that someone cares too much about, e.g., what others think of her or how she looks, you might fault her for the shape of her concerns. All of these facts— both the facts that have ethical significance (in part) because the person endows them with such and the facts that have ethical significance because they reflect failures in her endowment system—are facts about a person's *values*.

When I speak of a person's ethical self, I am really talking about her values. When I speak of a person making profound changes to herself, I am talking about her changing her values. And when I speak of the aspirant's awareness of a deficiency in herself, I am describing a deficiency in respect of value. But is it really true that a person's values are the ethically deepest and most important facts about her? Giving a complete defense of these theses about ethical identity is beyond the scope of this book, but I do want to call to the reader's mind the intuitive plausibility of the ethical association between a person and her values.

This association is reflected in our ordinary, everyday speech and thought about ourselves. When we say, in the context of apologizing or renewing personal relations, "I'm not that person anymore," we usually mean that the values we have now differ from those we had then. When we promise a loved one to whom we have caused profound hurt that we will change, we mean that we will change not only our behavior but the values from which that behavior springs. We feel shame at being discovered to be in some condition when being in that condition amounts to a failure to live up to our values; and, correspondingly, when we feel pride, it is because we recognize the fact that we have lived up to our values. When we contrast superficial features of a person, such as his appearance or social status, with "what really matters about a person," we are referring to a set of features of the person that either are, or at least include, the person's values. So, for instance, when Martin Luther King, Jr., enjoined us to judge people "not by the color of their skin, but by the content of their character," he was contrasting a superficial feature of a person with a deep one. It is a mistake to judge a person by his skin color, but it might not be a mistake to judge him by the fact that he, for instance, unduly esteems his own skin color and takes it as grounds for treating those with skin of a different color as his moral inferiors. The latter is a fact about a person's (defective) values, and those are the things that constitute a person's character.

But *why* is it the case that a person's values are so central to who she is? To answer this question, we must first explain what values are. Is valuing a form of desiring, as David Lewis (1989) and Gilbert Harman (2000) have argued? Or is it, as Michael Smith (1992) maintains, a kind of belief? Samuel Scheffler has argued against such reductive accounts of value and in favor of an account of value on which it involves "a complex syndrome of interrelated dispositions and attitudes, including (at least) certain characteristic types of belief, dispositions to treat certain kinds of considerations as reasons for action, and susceptibility to a wide range of emotions" (2010: 4). Jay Wallace (2013) and Niko Kolodny (2003) have also espoused a theory of valuing on which it constitutes a response to a variety of reasons: the valuer sees reasons to believe that what she values is good (or valuable or worthy), as well as reasons to do things in relation to it, and to have certain feelings at the prospect of engaging with the value, losing the value, etc. I follow Scheffler, Wallace, and Kolodny in accepting such a hybrid account of value, which I discuss in chapter 3. On such an account, when we identify someone's values, we identify objects around which her ethical self is organized: the valued object elicits from the agent a response that is the product of the cooperation of the various cognitive, motivational, and affective elements of her agency. Values are, therefore, a nexus of the person's various agential functions; when we know a person's values, we know what objects out in the world she is, as we say, "all about."

Finally, I want to address a worry about associating aspiration with the self. Someone who accepts the association I have just described, between aspiration and value-acquisition, might nonetheless object to the idea that what aspirants are engaged in is a kind of self-making, self-shaping, or self-creation.[15] For she might think that aspiration ought to be directed, first and foremost, not at the fact that I will have a certain value but rather at the valuable object itself. Let me return to the case of the aspiring doctor. The objector I am imagining would insist that the aspiring doctor is directed at helping people with their medical problems rather than at discovering the value of helping people with their medical problems. Even granting that the medical student is open to such a learning experience, the objector I am imagining maintains that what she is really "all about" is helping people, not changing herself. The new set of preferences she acquires at the end of her training would then not be her aim, but a consequence of what she aspires to.

Consider, however, the importance of hands-on experience in coming to comprehend the many spheres in which the agency of doctors is operative: there is preventative care, bedside manner, surgical precision, enabling people to make informed choices, consulting with colleagues over a diagnosis, making lifelong connections with patients and their families, etc. The aspiring doctor, like those of us who are not doctors, has only a schematic understanding of the helping activities she will perform in each of these spheres. For

---

15. For further discussion of this objection, see Ch. 5, section IV(e).

instance, she may not have thought much about how she will navigate the dilemma of supporting a patient's autonomy while at the same time advising him on making a medically sound decision. For the main way in which one would come to understand that dilemma, and the distinctive kind of medical help one provides in offering advice, would be by working with actual patients to guide them through the decisions they must make.

The medical student cannot simply aim to realize the value of helping people, or some more specific value such as that of helping people make good medical decisions, because she does not have a firm grip on what she would be realizing. The experienced doctor, by contrast, aware that she is entering a consulting room with a patient who has a difficult choice before him, can straightforwardly possess the relevant aim. She thinks to herself, "I want to help this patient make a good decision without telling him what to do." I do not want to deny that the aspiring doctor aims at the goal of helping people. Rather, I am claiming that aiming at this goal when one's knowledge of it is limited just is a matter of trying to learn what that goal amounts to. This is not because the agent in question is self- as opposed to world-directed, but because the only shape that her contact with the value can take is an educational one. She comes into contact with, or aims at, the value not by realizing it but by learning it. In such a case, one's value-directed activity is simply identical with a self-directed activity. This learning constitutes a change in who she is, which is to say, a change in what she values.

PART I

PRACTICAL RATIONALITY

Chapter 1

Decision Theory
and Transformative Choice

Decision theory lies at the intersection of philosophy and economics, and is concerned with rational preference-structures and rational choice. It is the job of decision theorists[1] to articulate a procedure for deliberating well between any set of options. They explain how one makes the right decision. But are there choice situations for which no such procedure can, in principle, be supplied?

Edna Ullmann-Margalit's 2006 paper, "Big Decisions: Opting, Converting, Drifting," and Laurie Paul's 2014 book, *Transformative Experience*, take up the question of whether decision theory can offer us an account of the rational navigation of life's major crossroads. In addition to familiar examples such as attending college, having children, getting married, and choosing a career, both authors offer us a rich medley of more idiosyncratic examples of life-altering decisions. Ullmann-Margalit considers the early Zionists who had to

---

1. Though it is not necessarily the job of *every* decision theorist. This is because some decision theorists set out to describe how agents actually decide rather than how they ought to decide; in addition, as Pettigrew (2015) points out in his comments on Paul's book, some of those in the latter group are concerned only with what it takes for a set of preferences to be well ordered, and not with articulating a decision procedure that agents might incorporate into their deliberations.

leave their Eastern European heritage behind in order to "become the new Jews of their ideals" (160). Paul discusses the difficult choice a member of the Deaf[2] community faces when offered the opportunity for her infant son to undergo a surgical procedure that would (partially) cure his deafness but would thereby alienate him from the Deaf community. Their question, about all such choices, is what it would be to count any of them as having been made rationally.

Ullmann-Margalit distinguishes such "big decisions" (as she calls them) from both the medium-sized decisions that she takes decision theory to be well placed to handle and "small decisions," such as choosing one token (e.g., a box of cereal) over another nearby token of the same type. In a small decision, an agent finds himself choosing—or as Ullmann-Margalit (1977) calls it in an earlier paper, "picking"[3]—one of several nearly identical items. Why should I choose this cereal box instead of the one next to it? Perhaps there is simply no answer to this question: Ullmann-Margalit argues that the distinction between rational and irrational choice does not get a grip in small decisions, because they are "selection situations without preference."[4] We will, perhaps, not be too troubled to hear that decision theorists offer us no guidance in making small decisions, given that people making those decisions typically are not looking for guidance. We don't, in ordinary circumstances, agonize over the question of which cereal box to select. The silence of decision theory in respect of big decisions would, however, be

---

2. Like Paul, I follow the convention of reserving "deaf" with lowercase "d" for the biological property of being unable to hear and write "Deaf" with an uppercase letter to describe the culture and community that exist among many deaf people.

3. "When preferences are completely symmetrical, where one is indifferent with regard to the alternatives, we shall refer to the act of taking (doing) one of them as an act of *picking*" (1977: 757).

4. Ullmann-Margalit and Morgenbesser (1977: 758); in her later paper, she calls them "decisions without preferences" (Ullmann-Margalit 2006: 171).

much more troubling. We *do* agonize over the choice to have children, relocate, change careers, or take other such forks in the road of life. Ullmann-Margalit argues that it is nonetheless no more possible to draw the distinction between deciding rationally and deciding irrationally when one is deciding between careers than when one is deciding between cereal boxes. Decision theory can help us answer only the "medium-sized" questions such as whether or not we should buy a car.[5]

The problem discussed by Paul and Ullmann-Margalit can be stated at a very high level of generality, one not tied to any particular conception of decision theory. The decision theorist asks an agent placed before any choice to consider each outcome's likelihood of occurring, and her preferences with respect to those outcomes. In order to make a rational decision to φ (for the sake of A) instead of ψ-ing (for the sake of B), one needs to know whether (and by how much) one prefers A to B and whether (and by how much) it is more likely that φ-ing produces A than that ψ-ing produces B. The problem is that because one (or both) of the options promises a substantial change in preferences, the agent doesn't have a single, stable set of preferences that could provide the input for the

---

5. In her earlier paper, she rightly points out that the distinction between small and medium-sized decisions is a matter of attitude (Ullmann-Margalit 1977: 780): a child might take choosing between (what look to the adults to be) two identical pieces of candy to be a medium-sized decision, whereas an unusually indifferent adult—perhaps she is very wealthy, perhaps she is depressed—might see the purchase of a car or house as a small decision. We can elide this point by simply assuming that we are describing ordinary adults having the reaction we might expect to some choice situation. Thus when I describe cereal box choices as small, car purchases as medium-sized, and choices concerning marriage, pregnancy, and career as large, I presuppose that those choices are viewed from the perspective of an ordinary adult. I acknowledge that the situations from which I, like Paul and Ullmann-Margalit, draw my examples of "big decisions"—marriage, emigration, pregnancy, career—can present as small or medium-sized choices for extraordinary people or for ordinary people in extraordinary circumstances.

decision procedure.[6] Over a period of time during which my desires are unstable, there may be no fact of the matter about which option would better fulfill them. Decision theory assumes relatively[7] static preferences, and an agent making a big choice confronts a radical shift in her preferences.

Paul and Ullmann-Margalit make this point in slightly different ways. Ullmann-Margalit examines the rationality of a big decision from the outside, posing the question as to what standard we should use in evaluating the rationality of someone else's big decision. Paul is interested in inspecting a big decision from the point of view of the agent making it. She asks us to consider what it would take to count ourselves justified in our own choice. I think we can gain insight both from Ullmann-Margalit's third-personal perspective on the problem and from Paul's first-personal one. I begin with Ullmann-Margalit.

I. ULLMANN-MARGALIT ON OLD PERSON VERSUS NEW PERSON

Ullmann-Margalit calls making a big decision "opting" and describes the problem thus:

> New Person is now, by hypothesis, a transformed person. Opting transforms the sets of one's core beliefs and desires. A significant

6. Here I subsume questions of the agent's tolerance of risk under the aegis of preference; I also set aside the question of whether there are decisions that agents cannot navigate because they are ignorant as to the relevant probabilities. Paul argues that the value-ignorance of agents making large choices cannot be handled by existent methods of accommodating ignorance about probabilities (2014: 29ff.). It is worth noting, however, that her argument rests on the assumption, challenged later in this chapter, that such agents have not already begun the transformative pursuit in question.

7. The decision theorist can accommodate small shifts in preference that occur against a stable background of core preferences (see Elster 1982); hence Ullmann-Margalit's emphasis on the fact that a decision is "big" in the relevant sense only if it is "core-affecting."

personality shift takes place in our opter, a shift that alters his cognitive as well as evaluative systems. New Person's new sets of beliefs and desires may well be internally consistent but the point about the transformation is that inconsistency now exists between New Person's system of beliefs and desires, taken as a whole, and Old Person's system taken as a whole. I am not questioning his ability to actually make a choice, or his ability subsequently to assess himself as happy (or unhappy) with his choice. The question I am raising is whether it is possible to assess the rationality of his choice, given that this choice straddles two discontinuous personalities with two different rationality bases." (2006: 167)

Here is one of the examples with which she fills out the schema of opting:

> I was told of a person who hesitated to have children because he did not want to become the "boring type" that all his friends became after they had children. Finally, he did decide to have a child and, with time, he did adopt the boring characteristics of his parent friends—but he was happy! I suppose second order preferences are crucial to the way we are to make sense of this story. As Old Person, he did not approve of the person he knew he would become if he has children: his preferences were to not have New Person's preferences. As New Person, however, not only did he acquire the predicted new set of preferences, he also seems to have approved of himself having them. How are we to assess the question whether he opted 'right'? (167, n. 10)

Ullmann-Margalit thinks that we cannot assess the rationality of this choice, because in order to do so we would have to make an arbitrary selection from the two points of view from which we might assess it. If we adopt the value-perspective of Old Person, the choice to have children was the wrong one: it frustrates Old Person's desire to avoid being boring. On the other hand, if we adopt New Person's point of view, the choice was rational: it satisfies New Person's core preference for conventional family life. There is no neutral perspective from which we can answer the question as to whether his choice left him "better off" than he was. Ullmann-Margalit takes the question with which this example ends to be rhetorical: decision theory offers us no way to answer such questions, and they are therefore unanswerable. She concludes that the "opting" we do in big decisions suffers from the same rational unassessability as the "picking" we do in small ones. We are no more able to evaluate the rationality of Old Person's choice to have children than his choice of this box of cereal over that one. Both big decisions and small decisions are cases where "reasons cannot prevail" (171).

She does not charge someone who makes a big decision with irrationality, but rather arationality: "In order to be irrational about something there must also be a rational way of going about it, and the rational way of going about opting is what I am here questioning" (168).

II. PAUL ON DECIDING TO BECOME A VAMPIRE

Paul's book explores the same themes as Ullmann-Margalit's essay, but from a first-personal perspective. Most of her book is dedicated to articulating the difficulty of taking account of the value of the prospective experiences that would arise from what she calls our "epistemic and personal transformations" (2014: 17). Her guiding example is one in which the reader is offered the chance to become a vampire: "As a member of the undead, your life will be completely different. You'll experience a range of intense, revelatory new sense experiences, you'll gain immortal strength, speed and power, and you'll look fantastic in everything you wear. You'll also need to drink blood and avoid sunlight" (1). Paul's claim is that because you cannot know what it is like to be a vampire until after you are bitten, you cannot make an informed choice in the traditional way. In particular, nothing you (think you) know about vampiric life is relevant to your choice.

Your ignorance is unchanged by the fact that, as Paul imagines the scenario, others have walked the road before you: "All of your friends, people whose interests, views and lives were similar to yours, have already decided to become vampires. And all of them tell you that they love it" (1). You might reasonably expect that you'll feel happy with the choice if you make it; nonetheless, you shouldn't think you have any idea of what you're getting yourself into. She considers whether someone could approach such a choice by conducting a scientific study of happiness among those who have, and those who have not, made the choice in question. Such studies have in fact been done on the childbearing decision, and Paul cautiously concludes that the research points in the direction of the conclusion that childlessness is the rational choice:

[I]f you are prepared to ignore all of your subjective assessments about what it would be like for you to have a child, and choose solely on the basis of the empirical research, if you want to maximize your expected subjective value, the research (to the extent that there are clear results) suggests you should not have a child. If we simply follow the dominant empirical conclusions of the experts, it seems that anyone who wants to make a rational decision about parenthood that is based on maximizing expected subjective value must either suspend judgment (given the lack of a clear consensus on the results), or should actively choose to remain childless. (87)

Paul objects, however, to basing one's decision on such studies. She thinks that someone who conforms her choices to what she calls "impersonal, "big data" reasoning" (88) sacrifices her own autonomy:

> Unless robots have taken over the world when humans weren't looking, for many of us, this is an untenable way to approach choices involving our personal goals, hopes, projects, and dreams. In other words, in today's society, when making important personal choices, we want to consult our own, personal preferences and to reflect on what we want our future lives to be like as part of assigning values to outcomes. It is simply unacceptable to be expected to give up this sort of personal autonomy in order to make decisions about how one wants to live one's life. (87)

Her contention is that we feel we don't make our choices rightly unless we make them from a personal point of view, by asking what this experience will mean *for me*. But in cases of big decisions, we cannot answer this question. All we know is that the decision will produce a new and revelatory experience.

III. SELF-CULTIVATION VERSUS SELF-TRANSFORMATION

It is important to note that only some examples of emigrating, motherhood, or becoming a vampire will serve Paul's and Ullmann-Margalit's purposes. We could imagine a dutiful daughter who moves to Israel in order to fulfill a promise to her dying mother; a younger sister who, having observed an older sister's pregnancy and child raising firsthand, feels she has an excellent grip on what those changes will mean for her; a fan of vampire movies who (believes she) wants nothing more than to live an emotionally vacuous, immortal, and fashionable life. The dutiful daughter recognizes that her life may become more difficult as a result of her choice, but counts this as a side effect of a decision grounded, fundamentally, in duty. The younger sister and the lover of vampire movies may be deluded as to the experience of motherhood or vampiricity; nonetheless, the important point is that they take themselves to know what they will be getting themselves into. None of these people makes a transformative choice in Paul's sense or a big decision in Ullmann-Margalit's sense. Likewise, the fact that motherhood or emigration ends up making no mark on someone's preferences doesn't prevent her choice from qualifying as big/transformative, so long as she did not know this would be the case. And, of course, many decisions we make to change the shape of our lives will *not* be large or transformative in Paul's and Ullmann-Margalit's sense. For we may feel, rightly or not, that we know well in advance what we are getting out of, e.g., a new job.

Among these various kinds of cases that will not serve Paul and Ullmann-Margalit's purposes, it will be useful to have a label for those aimed specifically at self-change. I will call a case of self-change "self-cultivation" if someone decides to, e.g., join a gym in the expectation (and hope) that she will thereby, over time, engender in herself an inclination to exercise. Or rather, I will consider her a self-cultivator so long as that inclination serves her current stable interest in living a more healthy life. Likewise, someone might take a speed-reading class, change her sleep habits, or enter psychotherapy, all the while foreseeing, and approving of, the change in preferences that these decisions will occasion. For suppose that I can now see (or think I can see) that I want to be the kind of person who takes pleasure in exercise, who is motivated to do more reading, who is inclined to wake up early, or who has a less anxiety-grounded preference-structure. In these cases, when I change myself, I am driven by my current preferences. For I see the having of those new preferences as a way of satisfying current and more basic preferences, to live a long life, get more work done, etc. Likewise, there are cases in which we cultivate a taste for, e.g., opera or cigarettes or gourmet food in order to reap the social rewards of such an interest. These cases do not raise the puzzles described by Paul and Ullmann-Margalit, because the agent enters the choice fully equipped with the resources to appreciate and value the person she is making herself into. So what could possibly ground a preference-changing decision if those preferences do not support, but rather threaten, one's basic antecedent preference-structure?

IV. PRIVILEGING SECOND-ORDER PREFERENCES?

At the end of her book, Paul proposes that the very fact that our knowledge that the value-experience in question will be *new* might itself form the basis for a rational transformative choice. She suggests that we can ground these decisions on whether we want things to change or stay the same:

> We must embrace the epistemic fact that, in real-life cases of making major life decisions in transformative contexts, we have very little to go on. To the extent that our choice depends on our subjective preferences, we choose between the alternatives of discovering what it is like to have the new preferences and experiences involved, or keeping the status quo. If we decide to choose this way, when facing big life choices, the main thing we are choosing is whether to discover a new way of living: life as a parent, or life as a hearing person, or life as a neurosurgeon, and so forth; that is, we choose to become the kind of person— without knowing what that will be like— that these experiences will make us into. Or, because we value our current preferences more highly than we value the (mere) discovery of new ones, we reject revelation. (2014: 122–123)

[handwritten margin note: but this doesn't necessarily mean we abandon old ways; could just be building upon them]

Paul recognizes that the second-order preference for preference-change (or preference-stasis) is one that itself may change as a result of the choice. She contends that it is nonetheless rational for the agent to privilege her current second-order preference and use it to decide what she wants to do.[8] This procedure, she claims, at least avoids the *irrationality* of "trying to decide based on the character of the particular subjective values of the lived experiences involved," for it allows us to avoid "let[ting] illicit, unjustified assumptions about what it will actually be like to be a vampire . . . infect our decision

---

8. Then why isn't it rational for her to similarly privilege her current first-order preferences? There is a worry here akin to that raised by Watson (1975: 217–219) against Frankfurt's higher-order desire theory. From the fact that one mental state is of a conceptually higher order than another, nothing follows about the relative authority between the two.

procedure" (121). Paul's account of rational transformative choice is sketched in only a few pages of her final chapter; it is, presumably, an account whose details she plans to elaborate in future work. I want to offer an objection to the approach she proposes, at least in its current form.

First, let us note that it applies to only a subset of big decisions. Ullmann-Margalit (2006: 161) draws a distinction between opting (yes, no) and opting (A, B) that I find quite helpful for analyzing Paul's solution. In a case of opting (yes, no), the agent must choose between, for instance, becoming a vampire or not, becoming a parent or not. In a case of opting (A, B), both options are transformative: she is choosing between two careers, or between having a child and traveling the world, or between marrying suitor A and marrying suitor B. Paul's suggestion that the agent choose on the basis of whether or not she wants a change does not offer any guidance to the agent in the opting (A, B) situation. For in those cases, both choices will satisfy (or frustrate) whatever second-order preference one has. In a footnote, Paul effectively acknowledges that in such cases we may be unable to choose on a rational basis: "Perhaps we can only pick a career, not choose a career, in the sense of 'picking' developed by Ullmann-Margalit and Morgenbesser (1977)."

Is the difference between the two kinds of case strong enough to support separate treatment? One might doubt whether even the opting (yes, no) cases offer us the prospect of stasis. As Ullmann-Margalit emphasizes, it seems to be a feature of big choices that "the choice not made casts a lingering shadow." (158) If we choose not to have children, we do not go on exactly as before. For now we are living the life in which we have chosen to live without children. In choosing not to become vampires, we are bringing our own humanity to the forefront of the rest of our lives. To choose but one of the myriad potential practical repercussions of such "stasis": if one's friends have all become vampires or engrossed in their new children, the choice to "remain as is" may entail getting new friends.

Even when the "no" option lacks external practical consequences, it typically has internal ones. As Ullmann-Margalit points out: "The rejected option enters in an essential way into the person's description of his or her life. The shadow presence maintained by the rejected option may constitute a yardstick by which this person evaluates the worth, success or meaning of his or her life" (160). Opting against transformation can turn a previously unnoticed property of oneself into a focus of one's identity: one might proudly wear the banner of "child-free by choice," "mortal by intention". Our subsequent experience of value may well be colored— transformed—by the fact that the other option was available, and rejected. The stasis that Paul's no-opter seeks may not be available to any subject of a big decision, since it seems that even deciding against changing can be transformative.[9]

But this is to cast doubt on whether Paul's procedure is applicable to many actual big choices. We can certainly concoct agents for whom it will be applicable. Suppose that someone who knows she will have the option, after she opts "no," to take an amnesia pill. Such a person really can bring it about that life goes on much as it did before. I want to set aside worries about whether we can apply the second-order-preference solution and ask whether we ought to apply it. I think that even if we could make (yes, no) decisions by looking to second-order preference, we should not do so.

---

9. It isn't even obvious that not having children is *less* transformative than having them. There are people for whom having children would be the conventional and expected choice, and the decision to remain child-free would, in ways they cannot fully anticipate, set them on a radical new path in which they will have broken from their communities. More generally, if I cannot know in advance what a transformative experience will be like, I also cannot know how transformative it will be.

The fact that Paul's solution cannot help us opt (A, B) is connected to the fact that it is troublingly one size fits all. If she is right, someone ought to think about adopting a child in just the way that she would think about embarking on a career as an ultramarathon runner, getting a cochlear implant (for one's child), or emigrating from one's Soviet homeland to help build the state of Israel. If one knows that one wants to do one of these things, one knows one wants to do any of them! This follows from the fact that one's desire to have a revelatory experience cannot (rationally) be conditioned on the way one expects that particular experience to be. In any of these cases, one is setting off on a new adventure that will change one's preferences in ways one, if one is rational, will recognize that one cannot predict. On Paul's account, one should make any of these decisions if one wants to know what it is like to have a new experience.

Couldn't Paul claim that one wants to discover *what it is like to be a mother* without wanting to discover *what it is like to be an Israeli pioneer*? The problem is that, on Paul's view, the relevant difference between these options is subjective and experiential, and it is precisely these features that Paul cautions us against importing into our decision. Recall the fact that the second-order method cannot help us opt (A, B): it must abstract from the details of any particular experience and consider only the question of whether it is new or old. Notice that this problem does not occur in cases of self-cultivation. I can use the fact that I prefer to live longer to ground a second-order preference for preferring to exercise and, on the basis of this second-order preference, decide to join a gym. But in this sort of case is a case of self-cultivation precisely because the second-order preference is grounded in a first-order preference. I prefer to prefer to exercise because I prefer to be healthy. A free-floating second-order preference, such as the preference for preference-change, does not provide a similarly stable anchor for choice.

I would be surprised to hear someone articulate the rationality behind, e.g., her decision to have a child primarily in terms of the fact that she wants to change. I think that we usually do not seek to transform preferences for the sake of doing so, but because we want to have the new set of preferences. We certainly know that by choosing to become parents or pioneers we will see the world in a new way; nonetheless, our reason for opting "yes" is not the newness but the particular value of that perspective.[10] It does not seem true that a reason to have children is also a reason to become a vampire or to move to Israel. Ullmann-Margalit and Paul are right that a person cannot get a full grip on the kind of goodness the new experience offers her from her current point of view—but that, I will argue, is exactly why she needs to aspire.

V. THE DECISION MODEL VERSUS
THE ASPIRATION MODEL

Ullmann-Margalit notes that if we look at how people actually make big decisions, we will be disappointed:

> One would expect the opters to take extra time and care in amassing relevant information as their evidence base, to exercise extra caution in assessing the alternatives open to them . . . In short, one would expect an act of opting to be an exemplary

10. Here I am staying in Paul's metaethical framework, in which all value is translated into the subjective value of experiences. I do not think that this is the right way to think about value, but that issue is immaterial here.

candidate for the ideal rational-choice explanations just delineated . . . There is some evidence that the attitude of people toward their big decisions is quite the opposite of the one that we might expect. That is to say, evidence[11] seems to suggest that people are in fact more casual and cavalier in the way they handle their big decisions than in the way they handle their ordinary decisions. (2006: 165)

Because Ullmann-Margalit's attention is on the normative question of how someone might handle a big decision rationally, she quickly sets aside her own surprise at the social psychological evidence for the conclusion that human beings do not tend to make such decisions rationally. But I think this answer to the descriptive question should give us pause. When we encounter evidence that a domain of rational agency is characteristically (or even just often) peopled by agents who fail with respect to the relevant norms, we need to consider the possibility that we haven't quite grasped the phenomenon, or its norms. I propose that the large transformations in people's lives are rational, though their rationality is not best captured through the framework of decision-making.

The problems with this framework, which I call, "the decision model," do not hinge on any particular conception of what it takes for a decision to be made rationally. Indeed, it is striking how noncommittal both Paul and Ullmann-Margalit can be with reference to any of the technical details of decision theory. Ullmann-Margalit needs only the "core insight" that an action is rational if it is "the best way of satisfying the full set of the person's desires, given his or her set of beliefs formed on the basis of the (optimal amount of)

---

11. Ullmann-Margalit supports this claim with a series of references to social psychology literature I will not reproduce here (see her notes 7 and 8: 165–166).

evidence at their disposal" (164). Paul works from the fact that "the normative decision maker should choose the act that has the highest expected value" (21). Nonetheless, they are both assuming that the transformation into motherhood, for instance, is something whose rationality will be exposed by its being considered a decision by a non-mother to become a mother. They assume that the process of becoming a mother is rational only insofar as it is possible for a non-mother to make a rational decision to become a mother. It is this assumption I wish to question.

Notice, first, that even when people are fortunate enough to have a say in the matter, it may happen that they become mothers or wives or immigrants without deliberating, weighing reasons, and deciding. For it often happens that our point of view on the matter changes little by little, and we transition slowly from someone who is relatively indifferent to the preferences, values, and interests of the new way of being to someone for whom they figure as the centerpiece of her life. Is this a less rational way of going about the transformational process, by comparison with that of making an explicit decision? Ullmann-Margalit suggests that it is when she contrasts opting with what she calls "drifting." She observes that sometimes one's character and values change ("drift") in incremental steps, so that one can see only in retrospect the magnitude of the change that those steps have added up to. She cites cases of people who slip, through a series of small and innocuous-seeming decisions, into criminal activity or marital infidelity. Ullmann-Margalit observes that we are apt to deceive ourselves into drifting through an opting situation by hiding from ourselves the magnitude of the change we are undergoing:

> It is possible for a person to proceed as a drifter while an informed spectator would judge that the person's situation is

one of opting. When this happens, I think that we can view the actor as engaged in self-deception. The actor may be ignoring aspects of his or her decision situation, which reveal it for what it is: a first commitment leading down a core-transforming, irreversible road. (170)

Ullmann-Margalit's discussion of drifting suggests a suspicion that what she calls drifting is the product of having avoided opting. She cites sociological research to the effect that "[i]mportant life decisions are sometimes incremental in nature, the end product of a series of small decisions that progressively commit the person to one particular course of action. A stepwise increase in commitment can end up locking the person into a career or marriage without his ever having made a definite decision about it."[12] The fact that Ullmann-Margalit's final discussion of "the place where opting and picking meet" takes an explicitly existentialist turn moves me to hear a Sartrean subtext in her discussion of drifting: (most?) human beings cannot handle the magnitude of the decisions that sometimes face them; they drift instead of opting, having abdicated their freedom by deceiving themselves into thinking they have no choice. These claims are at most implied by Ullmann-Margalit's suggestive final comments,[13] but I wanted to make them explicit in order to address them here. For I think they are the closest that Paul

12. Janis and Mann, cited in Ullmann-Margalit (2006: 170).
13. In support of ascribing these views to Ullmann-Margalit, I observe that her other paper on this topic, written with Sidney Morgenbesser thirty years earlier, ends with similarly approving reference to existentialism as "a philosophical literature . . . suggesting that at the very deepest level of selection, involving the ultimate and most significant alternatives confronted by man, there can only be picking, there being no possibility of a reasoned choice." That paper ends by gesturing at the position Ullmann-Margalit was to articulate later: "Given our beliefs and utilities, we pick or we choose as the case may be but as to our utilities or values themselves, to the extent that they can be thought to be selected at all, they can only be picked" (Ullmann-Margalit and Morgenbesser 1977: 783).

or Ullmann-Margalit comes to a defense of the decision model for understanding transformations.

I do not think that the months or years someone spends gradually working her way into the value-perspective of, say, a full-fledged mother, wife, or doctor is (necessarily) time spent drifting. That is, I think that gradual transformation of preference can be one way in which a person's agency is manifest; not only is becoming something little by little something that happens to us, it is also, sometimes, something we do. Nor do I think there need be any moment, even one that is ignored, in which a person makes a "a first commitment leading down a core-transforming, irreversible road." Before defending this claim, let me try to describe the difference between the decision model and the non-drifting transformative process I call "aspiration." On the decision model, agency is split into three stages. There is an initial, deliberative stage in which one considers the transformation from a detached, investigative point of view. One is, having not yet begun to be transformed, asking oneself whether or not being in the transformed condition is worthwhile. This process of investigation and reflection culminates in a decision (stage 2), to become a mother or leave one's homeland or take on a career. In stage 3, one does whatever it takes to enact the relevant transformation. Paul and Ullmann-Margalit focus on stage 2 of this process— what Ullmann-Margalit calls the "first commitment." Stage 1 may be barely present, as in cases where one commits without reflecting; moreover, if the act of commitment suffices to hurl one down, as Ullmann-Margalit puts it, an "irreversible road," the agent's role in stage 3 may also be minimal. Nonetheless, it is of great significance for the decision model that it effects a structural separation between the rational activity of coming to value being in the transformed condition (stage 1) and the rational activity of coming to be in it (stage 3). The resulting exaggeration of the ignorance of the agent in

[handwritten margin note: things aren't just changed in us; we might also actively work to change them]

stage 1 and her passivity in stage 3 is, I claim, what makes the transformation as a whole difficult to understand.

Consider stage 1. On the decision model, the person evaluating motherhood or the life of a pioneer can do so only from a detached, reflective distance. She is not a pioneer or mother; she is, rather, looking into becoming one. If that way of life is sufficiently different from her own, it is hard to see how she can come to value it. Paul laments the fact that a wall of ignorance deprives such agents of the knowledge they most desperately need: "So, in many ways, large and small, as we live our lives, we find ourselves confronted with a brute fact about how little we can know about our futures, just when it is most important to us that we do know" (4). Presumably, the guiding example of a choice to become a vampire is supposed to emphasize the alienness of the new experience into which she takes the subject of transformative choices to leap.

When Paul advises the prospective mother, pioneer, or vampire against the inclination to "infect" her decision procedure with "illicit, unjustified assumptions about what it will actually be like to be" the person she's considering becoming (121), her point is not that one should incorporate licit, justified beliefs about what it will be like into one's deliberations. Her point is that, since we cannot know what it will be like, *all* of our antecedent thought about what it will actually be like must take the form of illicit, unjustified assumptions. Her argument for this conclusion is that (really) knowing what it is like to be a mother requires becoming a mother, and the latter process has not yet begun.

One way of responding to this argument might be to insist that one can know what it is like to be a mother without being one; that someone who has taken care of her sister's children, or spent time thinking and reading about motherhood, has come to know something of what it will be like for her to be a mother.[14] I think there is something in this response, but notice that it is possible for someone who, let us suppose, doesn't and never will have any interest in motherhood to take care of her sister's children or read and think about motherhood (say, for her social psychological research) without thereby acquiring a sense of what it is like to be a mother. The person who is likely to emerge from these experiences with an enriched grasp of motherhood is the one who went into them[15] with a view to acquiring such a grasp—when she is taking care of her sister's children or reading about motherhood, she is thinking all the while about what motherhood would be like for her. She sees babysitting as a tentative, experimental foray into motherhood.

Someone who is considering whether or not to throw out the birth control pills began the process of coming to acquire the values, perspective, interests, and concerns of a mother long before that. We will distort her deliberations about motherhood if we sever them entirely from the process that has been long under way. This distortion is also apparent when Ullmann-Margalit asks us to "think of a young talented person who faces a choice between a career as a concert pianist and as a nuclear physicist" (160). There is reason to doubt that anyone has ever found himself poised before these two options, since someone who is in a position to choose a career as a nuclear physicist has directed enough time and energy toward the end of becoming one that he would not have had the time to pursue the similarly demanding trajectory of concert pianist. The general point is this: in order for the transformative options to get a grip on

14. See Harman (2015) for such a response.
15. Or who later reflected on them.

us, the transformative process must *already be under way*. Thus we needn't imagine that the agent evaluating them stands fully outside of what she evaluates.

Now consider stage 3. On the decision model, there is no reason why the transformation that takes place after the moment of decision needs to be understood as a form of agency at all. On Paul's picture, having the values, interests, and point of view of a mother is something that happens to me as a result of a transformative experience I decide to undergo. She models the mother case on the vampire case. When I become a vampire, I first decide to be bitten, and then the bite transforms me. After I am bitten, I will find myself with typically vampiric thoughts, habits, and values: a love of spiders, excellent fashion sense, and cold indifference toward humans.

Notice, however, that while the vampire's bite (*ex hypothesi*) transforms you into a vampire, neither the throwing out of the pills nor the fertilization of egg by sperm transforms someone into a mother. Some pregnant women have no intention of becoming parents, and even those who do might struggle to view themselves that way. Seeing a positive pregnancy test can certainly be an emotional and shocking experience, but it does not magically endow one with the values, habits, and feelings of parenthood.[16] A parent is someone who raises a child, where child raising is an ethical process that includes nourishment, protection, education, and love. It is parenthood, not pregnancy, that represents the endpoint of the relevant transformation. Unlike becoming a vampire, becoming a parent is neither something that just happens to you nor something you decide to have happen to you. It is something you do. And it is not

---

16. The same goes for any of the stages on the way to parenthood: hearing the heartbeat, feeling the baby kick, holding the newborn, giving him his first bath, etc.

something you can do in a moment: we spend a long time becoming mothers and fathers.

When one makes a radical life change, one does not submit oneself to be changed by some transformative event or object; one's agency runs all the way through to the endpoint. The nature of that agency, as I shall argue, is one of learning: coming to acquire the value means learning to see the world in a new way. But this, in turn, means that the process of valuing motherhood and the process of becoming a mother are not two separate events flanking a moment of decision, but rather one and the same process. The job of this book is to describe that process, which I call aspiration. The book as a whole aims to make the case for treating the phenomenon in the unified way I have described here. Part II (chapters 3 and 4) corrects the distortions introduced by the decision model with reference to stage 1: I argue that the aspirant's assessment of her goal is not achieved by way of detached, deliberative distance but rather by way of immersing herself in the point of view she seeks to acquire. Part III (chapters 5 and 6) does the corresponding work with reference to stage 3, highlighting the aspirant's role in making herself into—rather than being made into—the person she is becoming. In this way, the book shows that aspirational assessment and aspirational change are both best understood in the light of one another. It challenges the prevailing assumption that basic or fundamental preferences (desires, values, etc.) are the kinds of things you can only reason *from*, by exposing a way we have of reasoning *toward* them.

Once we remove the barrier of decision standing between assessment and transformation, we expose the possibility of reasoning that engages in the first instance not with what we already succeed in desiring and valuing at the time of the reasoning, but with what we *will* desire and value once the rational process is complete.

Instead of seeing the endpoint of the transformation as "fundamentally inaccessible" (Paul), we see the agent as located on a path of rational access, working her way into a new point of view. An agent can exhibit rationality in coming to apprehend the value of the life she seeks to have. Let me illustrate the point with Ullmann-Margalit's Old Person.

Recall that he is initially committed to the exciting single life, but ends up as a boring parent, New Person. Imagine a movie presenting Old Person's transformation, via experiences with his friends' children, private moments of reflection, developments in his relationship with his partner or his own parents, etc., into the person who says, "Let's go for it!" Suppose that the movie continues to present his slow and sometimes painful growth into his role as a parent until the point where he says he is happier than he has ever been. That is likely to be a bad movie, because the change described is *so* intelligible as to be clichéd. We would not find ourselves forced to classify his decision to "go for it" among acts of the will that are "nihilist, absurd, or leaps (of faith)" (Ullmann-Margalit 2006: 172). It is not like Meursault's or Raskolnikov's decision to become a criminal by killing some random person. And yet it might look that way if we abstract it from the change that Old Person is undergoing. Ullmann-Margalit considers it difficult to judge the rationality of his transition because we cannot choose between adopting his old and his new perspective on the value of parenting. But this leaves out the fact that at some point after the beginning of the movie, Old Person himself starts to try to adopt the new perspective. By the time he says, "Let's go for it," he is actively trying to appreciate the values distinctive of parenthood. His transition from Old Person to New Person will look absurd only so long as we leave out the fact that during it, Old Person aspires to become New Person.

VI. TRANSFORMATIVE CHOICE?

I have claimed that the "decision model" is not the best way to understand rational transformation into, say, a mother, wife, or pilgrim and that these transformations needn't be prefaced by, or even contain, decisions to become the person in question.[17] We do not find human beings engaging in acts of choosing that take as their input a non-parent (or non-pioneer, non-philosopher, non-music-lover, etc.) and output a parent (or pioneer, philosopher, music-lover, etc.). We are not, in that sense, transformed by our choices. But that is no reason to deny that there is a phenomenon to which the label "transformative choice" might be applied. Agents do, of course, agonize over whether or not to board the boat, throw away the birth control pills, accept an admissions offer to grad school, or propose marriage. Once we release these decisions from their status as the lynchpin of the decision model, we are in a better position to understand both how they are made and how they fit into the transformative processes in terms of which, I argue, they must be understood.

On an aspirational model, these decisions are best understood as climactic moments embedded in a longer transformative journey, marking neither its beginning nor its end. The decisions do not come at the beginning of the transformation process, for at that point the answer would be clear: someone who has *none* of the interests, values, attitudes, or preferences of a parent or pilgrim or wife or philosopher would not even entertain the option of discarding the pills, boarding the boat, applying to grad school, or proposing marriage. The one making the decision is, therefore, not entirely an outsider to the life she may opt into.

17. I thank David Finkelstein for helpful discussions of the material in this section.

If aspiration is not begun by way of decision, one might wonder how it gets started. Before we ever have to make a choice such as whether to get married, attend college or graduate school, emigrate from our country, or have children, we undergo extensive education on the value of these activities at the hands of our family, friends, teachers, books, and acquaintances. As I will argue in chapter 6, aspirational agency is distinctively dependent on such environmental support. One important element of such dependence is the orchestration of original contact with the values that will eventually become objects of aspirational pursuit. Aspiration begins before the aspirant is in a position to exercise agential control over her relation to the value: it gets started, but the aspirant herself isn't the one who starts it. This is not only because she may be too young to do so, but also because, for reasons well brought out by Paul, a person would not have any reason to bring herself into contact with something for which she had *no* preference, appreciation, value, etc. Someone could behave in a way that resulted in such contact, but she would not be acting in order to come into contact with it.

There are also important implications to the fact that the climactic choice does not of itself complete the transformation. Vampires aside, no decision magically transforms a person into someone with different values, preferences, etc. As a result, the transformative question can almost always resurface after it has been answered in the affirmative. While some people never ask themselves, "Should I become a . . .?", others find themselves asking and re-asking the question. Indeed, I suspect that people who are, as a matter of contingent psychological fact, inclined to frame the situation in terms of a decision are inclined to do so at repeated points rather than settling the matter once and for all.

Thus, I do not agree with Ullmann-Margalit's characterization of these climactic choices as "irreversible." As she acknowledges (159), in one sense no decisions are reversible—one cannot go backwards in time. All that can be said of transformative decisions in comparison with other decisions is that the costs of reversing them tend to go up as one proceeds down the transformative path. Deciding not to be a wife is one thing before one has proposed, another thing before one has planned the wedding, and yet another thing altogether after one has been married or had children. Nonetheless, if one is prepared to shoulder the relevant costs, which may include one's happiness or even one's life, one can opt out of any incomplete transformative process one previously opted into.[18] More generally, it is important to distinguish between committing oneself to doing a certain kind of work—the work of becoming a mother, wife, philosopher, or pilgrim—and having done it. It does not follow, from the fact that avoiding becoming X-ish after having committed to doing so will be very costly to me, that I am already X-ish.

None of this answers the question as to *how* one decides whether to throw away the pills, board the boat, apply to grad school, or propose marriage, but it does help us understand what such a person is asking herself. The preferences that such a person is poised to acquire are not yet fully her own; nor are they totally alien to her. At the moment, she may be in a better position to grasp the costs of her new life than its benefits. The pilgrim is struck by the fact that she may never see her family again and that she currently prefers caring for her siblings to satisfying her Zionist ideals; the mother-to-be worries about exposing her relationship with her spouse to serious stresses, for she currently cares more about her relationship

---

18. In Amos Oz's memoir, *A Tale of Love and Darkness*, he recounts his grandparents' journey from Odessa to New York . . . and then back to Odessa: "It was utterly unheard of: some two million Jews migrated from east to west and settled in America in fewer than two score years between 1880 and 1917, and for all of them it was a one way trip, except for my grandparents, who made the return journey" (2005: 92).

with her husband than motherhood; the college graduate frets over her job prospects as a professional philosopher: financial stability is, at the moment, more important to her than philosophy. But such a person can also see that her own grasp of the values of Zionism, motherhood, and philosophy is imperfect and attenuated—that if she continues down the relevant path, she will come to care much more than she currently does. Perhaps in some cases it is possible to postpone the decision until one is better acquainted with the values and desires in question—but often it is not, because every step toward acquaintance also raises the costs of departure. Hence, the predicament of climactic choice is one of needing to decide whether the sacrifice is worthwhile before being able to accurately assess the value for the sake of which it would be made.

Nonetheless, she may choose to board the ship, throw away the pills, or go to graduate school. In order for this decision to be rational, it must take in not only the preferences she currently has, but those she seeks to acquire. One lesson of this book is that these are genuinely different categories: facts about where you are headed are not expressible as facts about where you currently are. The fact that she is reaching for a new preference cannot be recast as a current preference—not even the preference to have a new preference. Given that she is embarking on each domain for its intrinsic rewards, she is in no better position to assess the value of having the preference for X than the value of X itself.

In the next chapter, I will describe the special kinds of practical reason that figure in the thinking of such an aspirant. She sees that she does not, at the moment, fully grasp all there is to be said in favor of continuing on her aspirational course. She does her best to make the decision in the way that she would make it if it were feasible to postpone it until she were fully acquainted with the value in question. She may do so by, e.g., imitating fellow aspirants, by seeking advice from mentors, by imagining what things will be like for her in one or two years' time. This kind of reasoning will be imperfect, since the person engaging in it is doing her best to adopt a point of view that is not (yet) her own. What I will argue in the next chapter is that the imperfection characterizing the rationality of the aspirant is not a matter of irrationality, but rather of a distinctive kind of rationality that I call "proleptic."

This book does not attempt to navigate the varied and difficult terrain of climactic aspirational decisions, though I will say something at the end of the next chapter as to why assessing such decisions may presuppose firsthand expertise of more than one kind. The question "How much should one be willing to sacrifice for one's aspirational project?" does not lend itself to abstraction from the particular values and particular people involved. But I do aim to address the skeptic who denies the very possibility that one can navigate either these decisions or the aspirational process as a whole in a rational way. And I also aim to acknowledge Paul's and Ullmann-Margalit's insight that the standard, i.e. decisionmodel-based, understanding of practical rationality, populated as it is by standard, i.e. non-proleptic, practical reasons makes it difficult to see how one can rationally work one's way into a new set of preferences.

Does it *matter* whether we acknowledge the existence of distinctively aspirational reasons for action? What are the stakes of denying the possibility of rational self-transformation? In the conclusion of this book, I will address this question with reference to the case of motherhood in particular. If someone denies the existence of reasons to become a mother, he will be unable to appreciate the fact that, for instance, someone who learns she cannot become one may have *reason to grieve* that fact. And this will, in turn, prevent him from treating her with the respect she deserves.

Chapter 2

Proleptic Reasons

she assumes they can't come to appreciate it

The teacher of a music appreciation class is frustrated with those students who are taking her class for, as she puts it, "the wrong reasons." In her view, the class offers students access to the intrinsic value of music. Students who are taking it for "the right reason" will be taking it for this reason. But only those who already appreciate music appreciate musical appreciation. Or, at any rate, only they appreciate it correctly, for the reason for which (she believes) one should appreciate it, namely, intrinsic musical value. The problem is that if the intrinsic value of music is a reason you respond to, you don't need to take her class. You already appreciate music.

She wants students in the class who care about music. But she's supposed to be teaching them to care about music. Is she being unreasonable? The problem does not go away once we admit of degrees or kinds of caring—it does not help to characterize her job as that of getting people who care a little (or who care in this way) to care more (or in that way). So long as someone enters the class satisfied with his level or type of music appreciation, whatever that may be, the teacher will impugn his motives, whatever they may be. The teacher is looking for students who want to care about music more than, or in a different way than, they currently do. But, again, she doesn't want them to want this for some extra-musical reason. So it seems that what she wants is for them to respond to musical value exactly to the extent that they're not yet able to.

This is a paradoxical way of stating an ordinary demand for the kind of reason that is my topic. It is possible to have an inkling of a value that you do not fully grasp, to feel the defect in your valuation, and to work toward improvement. The reason for doing that work is provided by the value in question, but the defect in your grasp of that value also shapes the character of the activity it motivates. For consider what kind of thinking motivates a good student to force herself to listen to a symphony when she feels herself dozing off: she reminds herself that her grade and the teacher's opinion of her depend on the essay she will write about this piece; or she promises herself a chocolate treat when she reaches the end; or she's in a glass-walled listening room of the library, conscious of other students' eyes on her; or perhaps she conjures up a romanticized image of her future, musical self, such as that of entering the warm light of a concert hall on a snowy evening. Someone who already valued music wouldn't need to motivate herself in any of these ways. She wouldn't have to try so hard.

The paradox arises from a dilemma concerning two kinds of reasons a potential student of such a class could have for taking it. There is, first, the intra-musical reason, the having of which seems to mark the fact that the class has come to a successful *close*. There is, second, any extra-musical reason, the recourse to which seems to condemn someone to subordinating the value of music to what the teacher would call "an ulterior motive." In the first case, the reason is not the reason of a *student*; in the second case, it's the reason of (what the teacher would call) a *bad* student. I will argue that this dilemma is specious, because there is an agent—the good student—who manages to combine extra- and intra-musical reasoning. Like the

[handwritten margin note: but it seems as if we shouldn't invalidate these attempts]

69

music-lover she will become, she is genuinely oriented toward the intrinsic value of music. For instance, if offered some way of attaining good grades, chocolate treats, etc. without coming to appreciate music, she would reject it. And yet grades and chocolates are integral to the rational explanation of her action of listening to music: she would be asleep without them. "Bad" reasons are how she moves herself forward, all the while seeing them *as* bad, which is to say, as placeholders for the "real" reason.

One characteristic of someone motivated by these complex reasons, by contrast with the simpler reasons of the bad student, on the one hand, and the established music-lover, on the other hand, is some form of embarrassment or dissatisfaction with oneself. She is pained to admit, to herself or others, that she can "get herself" to listen to music only through those various stratagems. She sees her own motivational condition as in some way imperfectly responsive to the reasons that are out there. Nonetheless, her self-acknowledged rational imperfection does not amount to akrasia, wrongdoing, error, or, more generally, any form of irrationality. Something can be imperfect in virtue of being undeveloped or immature, as distinct from wrong or bad or erroneous. (There is something wrong with a lion that cannot run fast, but there is nothing wrong with a baby lion that cannot run fast.) When the good student of music actively tries to listen, she exhibits not irrationality but a distinctive form of rationality.

Her rationality is not, however, of the familiar, clear-eyed kind. Anscombe's *Intention* placed the ability to answer the "why?" question at the heart of philosophical discussions of agency. The agent who can give an account of what is to be gotten out of what she is doing grasps the value of what she will (if successful) achieve through her action. Her answer to the "why?" question might not satisfy every interlocutor, but it is at least satisfying to the agent herself: she takes herself to know why she is doing whatever it is she takes herself to be doing. Of course, not every agent will be able to satisfy herself in this way: some agents are not paying attention to what they are doing, or are being impulsive,[1] or experience a moment of forgetfulness, or have simply failed to think things through sufficiently. In some of these cases, the agent's behavior is arational, since her ignorance is profound enough to disqualify her from acting intentionally; in other cases, her action is intentional, but irrational. The good student of music likewise is unable to articulate, to her own satisfaction, what she expects to get out of her music class. In her case, however, this marks neither the absence of intentionality nor the absence of rationality.

If an agent finds her own answer to the "why?" question satisfying, she must ascribe to herself a certain knowledge of value. Such an agent takes herself to know both that some form of value is on offer and that it is one she herself does or will enjoy, appreciate, or find meaningful. And such a person is often correct—agents often do have such knowledge. How did they acquire it? Since knowledge of value is itself valuable, it stands to reason that one way we acquire such knowledge is the way we acquire many other valuable things: by acting in order to bring about that acquisition. The problem is that unless one is equipped with an ulterior motive,[2] the value of knowledge of some value is not a different value from that value itself. Therefore, those seeking to acquire the knowledge cannot take themselves to know why they are doing so. And yet—I will

---

1. Some, if not all, impulsive agents will take themselves to fail in respect to the "why?" question. "Just because I feel like it" might strike one agent as a perfectly good answer, and another as no answer at all.

2. As in Frankfurt's (1971) example of the doctor who treats drug addicts: he has special reason for wanting to understand the appeal of drug addiction without actually wanting to become addicted.

argue—it is a fact of life that people act not only from, but also, at other times, for the sake of acquiring, knowledge of value.

If those actions are to be rational, then rationality cannot require accurate foreknowledge of the good your rational action will bring you. Thus I will defend the view that you can act rationally even if your antecedent conception of the good for the sake of which you act is not quite on target—and you know that. In these cases, you do not demand that the end result of your agency match a preconceived schema, for you hope, eventually, to get more out of what you are doing than you can yet conceive of. I call this kind of rationality "proleptic." The word "proleptic" refers, usually in a grammatical context, to something taken in advance of its rightful place. I appropriate it for moral psychology on the model of Margaret Little's phrase "proleptic engagement" (2008: 342), by which she refers to an interaction with a child in which we treat her as though she were the adult we want her to become.[3] Proleptic reasons are provisional in a way that reflects the provisionality of the agent's own knowledge and development: her inchoate, anticipatory, and indirect grasp of some good she is trying to know better. Proleptic reasons allow you to be rational even when you know that your reasons aren't exactly the right ones.

A reason for action is a consideration in favor of acting in some way; if the agent in fact acts on the reason, she will be able to offer that reason as an explanation of why she so acted.[4] Sometimes

---

3. Likewise, Bernard Williams (1995) speaks of a "proleptic mechanism" by which he takes at least some instances of blame to function. Williams asserts that a blamer's pronouncement that the blamee "ought to have φ-ed" can serve not as a description of the blamee's current set of reasons, but rather as a way of both anticipating and bringing about the future state of affairs in which the blamee will be in a position to be motivated by the reasons now being ascribed to him.

4. The reason in question is at least a motivating reason, and it may also be a normative one. For a discussion of that distinction, see fn. 13.

we do something for more than one reason: I went to the store in order to get milk and for the exercise. Proleptic reasons are double in a more fundamental way. The good music appreciation student is listening to the symphony assigned for her class because music is intrinsically valuable and because she wants a good grade. If she merely cited the first as her reason, she would be pretending to a greater love of music than she currently has; if she merely cited the second, she would be incorrectly assimilating herself to the bad student. But her motivational condition is also not one in which she has merely added the first reason to the second, because that situation would describe a music-lover who is (strangely) taking a music appreciation class. The fact that music is intrinsically valuable and the fact that she wants a good grade somehow combine into *one* reason that motivates her to listen. The reason on which she acts has two faces: a proximate face that reflects the kinds of things that appeal to the person she is now and a distal one that reflects the character and motivation of the person she is trying to be. Her reason is double because she herself is in transition.

The paradox just described generalizes beyond music education. I will argue that we must acknowledge the reality of proleptic reasons, else we be forced to classify as irrational a large swath of human agency—agency that is purposive, self-conscious, intelligent, and truth-sensitive and that constitutes a kind of building block of or prelude to everything else that we do. I end with a discussion of the currently dominant moral psychological thesis that what practical reasons we have depends on what desires we have. I consider a few variants of such "internalism," as it is called, and argue that none of them can, as they stand, make room for the existence of proleptic reasons.

I. LARGE-SCALE TRANSFORMATIVE PURSUITS

In the preceding chapter, I discussed momentous life changes under the heading of "big choices" or "transformative experiences." I ended by arguing that what Paul and Ullmann-Margalit characterize as decisions or experiences are better understood as temporally extended, agentially directed processes. Let us, therefore, adopt the phrase "large-scale transformative pursuits" to describe such significant life changes as attending college; moving to a foreign country; adopting a child; becoming a painter, a philosopher, or a police officer; achieving distinction in athletics, chess, or music; becoming a sports fan, an opera-lover, or a gourmet; and befriending or marrying or mentoring someone. The features uniting this class of pursuits[5] are that they change what one cares about and that they change it in some substantial way. They typically require years of sustained effort, both in the form of preparation and in the form of the work attending the completed state. They are both transformative and large in scale.

I have labeled the class of pursuits that involve a small-scale change in what one cares about "self-cultivation" (see chapter 1, section III). If I inculcate in myself preferences whose value can be fully cashed out in terms of my current preferences, it is easy to rationalize my action. When a pursuit is large in scale without being transformative, I will describe the agent as ambitious (see chapter 6, section III). Wanting to cure cancer, make a million dollars, or win the Nobel Prize can, if understood in a sufficiently narrow way, count as a large-scale nontransformative

---

5. Though see note ch 1, note 5 for a caveat: this list represents what are, by and large, big changes in anyone's life. I do not deny that there could be people for whom these changes barely register.

pursuit. The key feature of such cases that allows one to clas-sify them as ambitious is the presumption of value-stasis: one needn't oneself undergo a value-change in order to succeed at the project.

Transformative pursuits are recognized as such not only by those who have completed them but also by those who are on their way: one can see in advance that one cannot see in advance all of what is good about parenthood or friendship or scuba div-ing or immigrating to another country. Transformative pursuits aim at values, the appreciation of which is connected to the perfor-mance of the activity (or involvement in the relationship) in ques-tion. Indeed, this is because the pursuits themselves form a kind of value-education, gradually changing the agent into the kind of per-son who can appreciate the value of the activity or relationship or state of affairs that constitutes the end of the pursuit. In the course of becoming a teacher or a friend or a reader of ancient Greek, one learns to appreciate the values that are distinctive of teaching or friendship or reading ancient Greek.

But one does not fully appreciate them until one is at, or close to, the end of the process of transformation. For it is the end state (teaching, parenting, translating) that offers up the actual engage-ment with the value on which any full appreciation of it must be con-ditioned. The joys of teaching are best known to teachers. Everyone goes to college "to become educated," but until I am educated I do not really know what an education is or why it is important. I may say I am studying chemistry in order to understand the "structure of matter," but only a scientist understands what it means for matter to have structure (or, indeed, what matter really is). For the rest of us, that phrase is likely to be backed by little more than an image of a tinker-toy "structure" to which a mental label such as "molecule" is affixed.

The problem posed by large-scale transformative pursuits is this: they require us to act on reasons that reflect a grasp of the value we are working so hard and so long to come into contact with, but we can know that value only once we have come into contact with it. And yet the cost of granting that such ends are pursued for no reason, or bad reasons, would be to restrict the scope of practical rationality very greatly. For most, if not all, of the experiences, forms of knowledge, ethical and intellectual traits, activities, achievements, and relationships that we value are such that the pursuit of them is both large in scale and transformative. It is true that even if we were forced to characterize the choices by which we move ourselves toward all of those ends as irrational, we could still rationalize engagement with the ends once achieved. But if this is all there is to practical rationality, we should be disappointed. For every rational choice to continue in some pursuit will be adventitiously predicated on a series of irrational choices to begin that pursuit. We should expect more from our reasons than maintenance of a mysteriously attained status quo. I propose, therefore, to introduce a species of reasons to meet this expectation.

My music appreciation example built in a demand, on the part of the teacher, that we not separate the rationalization of the pursuit from that of the end. This kind of demand is generally appropriate for large-scale transformative pursuits. We do not want to understand them along the lines of someone who walks to the park for the exercise but stays when she sees they're showing an outdoor movie. For in that case the agent was not, when walking, pursuing the end of seeing a movie. It is possible to rationalize both the walk and the movie watching without rationalizing anything we could call the *pursuit* of the movie. By contrast, large-scale transformational pursuits are characteristically aspirational: when the agent gets where she's going, she sees that she has what she was after all along.

II. ALTERNATIVES TO PROLEPTIC REASONS?

We ought to demand a rational account of how someone can work her way to the valuation characteristic of the various end states to which she aspires. Satisfying this demand, I claim, means postulating a set of reasons—I've called them "proleptic reasons"—tailor-made to rationalize exactly these sorts of pursuits. By way of argument for this claim, let us survey alternate contenders, reviewing the kinds of factors we typically cite in explaining such behavior: a vague grasp of the value in question; a precise grasp of a value in close proximity to the value in question; reliance on the ethical testimony of a mentor or adviser figure; imaginative engagement in a pretense of being as one aspires to be; a desire to have another desire; competitiveness; recourse to self-management techniques of (dis)incentivization. I'll argue, case by case, that vague reasons, reasons of self-management, testimonial reasons, reasons of competition, reasons of pretense, second-order reasons, and approximating reasons rationalize in the right way only insofar as we help ourselves to a dedicated subset of each genus of reasons. It turns out that in order to rationalize aspirational agency, we must invoke not vague reasons but *proleptically vague* reasons, not testimonial reasons but *proleptically testimonial* reasons, etc. In the attempt to avoid proleptic rationality, we find ourselves ushering it in piecemeal, through the backdoor.

(a) Vague Reasons

Someone who has a "vague reason" for φ-ing φ-es with only a vague idea of the value of φ-ing. I have a vague idea of the value of all sorts of pursuits in which I am not currently engaged. For instance, I think there are many valuable careers I did not choose, many valuable hobbies I don't pursue, many valuable books I'm not reading. Such ideas are often not very motivating: I don't plan to read most of those books. Consider a *bad* student of music appreciation, one intent on merely going through the motions necessary for fulfilling a distribution requirement. He might happily grant that music appreciation is a "good and valuable end." He has a vague idea that music appreciation is good. But that's not enough to get him to do the homework, show up to class on time, study for the exam, etc. A vague idea does not entail willingness to put in effort. So let us suppose that the vague idea is not *so* vague—in fact, let us posit that it suffices for motivation. There are many non-aspirational situations in which I have only a vague idea of the value I am motivated to get. I buy tickets to an opera I know I love, not knowing exactly what I will love about this production. Such an activity is not aspirational, because I'm satisfied with my vague idea. I don't now feel the need to work to make up the difference between the vague idea I have now and the sharp one I will have later; I don't experience that difference as a defect in my current state. I need only wait for the world and my interests to line up in such a way as to make it possible for me to do the enjoying or appreciating that I'm already fully capable of.

The aspirant's idea of the goodness of her end is characterized by a distinctive kind of vagueness,[6] one she experiences as defective and in need of remedy. She is not satisfied with her own conception of the end and does not feel that arriving at the correct conception is simply a matter of waiting. She understands her aspirational activity as work she is doing toward grasping this end. So, while vague

---

6. See chapter 5, section VI (b) for a discussion of the difference between the aspirant's vague grasp of a value and the generic or schematic grasp that, according to Richardson (1994), can be filled out only by non-instrumental ("specificationist") practical reasoning.

conceptions of value do help explain how aspiration is possible, it is equally true that the phenomenon of aspiration helps us understand a distinctive form of vagueness—a kind of ever-sharpening vagueness. Large-scale transformation pursuits are done for those vague reasons that are *proleptically* vague.

(b) Self-Management Reasons

My music student plans to reward herself with chocolate for getting through the symphony. I might make plans with a buddy to go running in the morning so that she can hold me to my plan. Reasons of self-management show up whenever I am trying to get myself to do something that I think I should do but may feel insufficiently motivated to do. Some forms of self-management can be very mild, such as simply resolving to (not) do something. In all these cases, I find some way to add motivational backing to a given course of action. Notice, however, that such self-manipulation comes in two forms.

Suppose Sue worries that she'll be tempted to buy expensive holiday presents for her friends,[7] despite her lack of funds. So she adopts one or more of such self-managing tactics as choosing a thrifty friend as a shopping partner, leaving her credit card at home, resolving not to enter a certain expensive store. In the case I'm imagining, Sue does not see her temperamental generosity as problematic. She doesn't have a systemic problem; she just happens to be very short of funds at the moment. Reasons of self-management are, in this kind of case, directed only at *behavior* on a given occasion (or even a series of occasions).

A different kind of holiday shopper might, by contrast, be engaged in a long-term struggle to curb her chronic overspending

---

7. I thank Kate Manne for the example and for helping me to see its importance.

by learning to think less commercially about how to make herself and those around her happy. In that kind of case, self-management is directed primarily at changing how the agent thinks, values, and feels. The music student described earlier would presumably see it as quite problematic if, years hence, she were *still* motivating herself to listen with chocolate. Or consider the case of moving to a new country. I may, at first, have to force myself into social situations. My hope is to thereby come to inhabit the new culture, language, etc. in such a way as to become disposed to eagerly engage in such socializing. I aspire to make this new place my home. This second kind of self-management often goes along with a characteristically aspirational form of *practice*. In some cases, doing something over and over again changes the way I do it. Sometimes I manage myself precisely with the aim of managing myself less and less. And that is just to say: reasons of self-management, too, come in a proleptic variety.

(c) Testimonial Reasons

We often invoke testimony to explain how someone's rationally held beliefs can outstrip the cognitive resources that can strictly be called his own. There is some controversy over whether such testimony is possible in a moral context,[8] but it certainly seems possible to heed the practical advice of your elders and betters—even against your own instincts and inclinations. It is also true that advisers or mentors often, even typically, figure in large-scale transformative pursuits. But the mentor's role in the life of the aspirant is not an unproblematic one. Unlike in other testimonial contexts, the aspirant's goal is nothing other than coming to see the value for herself.

---

8. See Wiland (2014) and McGrath (2011).

The fact that your role model knows so much more than you that you are inclined to defer to her advice means that contact with her is a constant reminder of what you don't have. You don't aspire to do what she does; you aspire to do what she does in just the way she does it—namely, independently.

What would the music appreciation teacher think of a student who takes her class on the advice of his music-loving mentor? I think the teacher would be satisfied with this reason to the extent that she felt the student wasn't. I'm happy to take someone else's word about the truth of many of my historical or scientific beliefs. I'm not, similarly, *happy* with my reliance on my mentor. The species of testimonial reasons that figure in aspiration are special in just the way that the vagueness of an aspirant's conception of her end is special. The testimonial element in aspiration is of a distinctively degenerate kind: the present legitimacy and authority of the mentor's voice are conditioned on, indeed, anticipate, its gradual evanescence. And in characterizing this curious species of testimony we have, once again, helped ourselves to a dedicated, aspirational species of the genus in question.

(d) Reasons of Competition

Many large-scale transformative pursuits are, at some point or other, fueled by a desire to position oneself at the top of some group of people engaged in a similar pursuit. Wanting to be better than others at something is a very powerful motive. The mathematician G. H. Hardy writes that he initially "thought of mathematics in terms of examinations and scholarships: I wanted to beat other boys, and this seemed to be the way in which I could do so most decisively" (1940: 46). We frequently encounter such competitiveness in athletic, musical, intellectual, and artistic pursuits. People even get competitive about their hobbies. But there are—again—two kinds of competitiveness.

In one kind of case, I compete in order to display my excellence or submit it for assessment. So I would like my excellence to be praised and celebrated by others. Or I would like to know how good I am, perhaps to be reassured that I really am as good as people say I am. Competition can be a way of gauging one's excellence, by measuring it against the excellence of others, or flaunting it, by demonstrating its superiority to the excellence of others. Such flaunting can itself spring from a variety of motives—for instance, I might want to flaunt my excellence as a physicist in order to inspire other young women to become physicists. Whatever the ultimate motive, competition of this kind is characterized by a desire to make known to others or to myself a virtue that I *already* have.

In another kind of case, the point of competition is to allow me to strive for excellence in an open-ended way. The thought of being better than the people around me is a powerful motivator for making something of myself when I don't know exactly *what* it is I want to make of myself. Hardy recounts:

> I found at once, when I came to Cambridge, that a Fellowship implied 'original work', but it was a long time before I formed any definite idea of research. I had of course found at school, as every future mathematician does, that I could often do things much better than my teachers; and even at Cambridge, I found, though naturally much less frequently, that I could sometimes do things better than the College lecturers. But I was really quite ignorant, even when I took the Tripos, of the subjects on which I have spent the rest of my life; and I still thought of mathematics as essentially a 'competitive' subject. (47)

If the motivations driving Hardy to become one of the twentieth century's greatest mathematicians were competitive in nature, this competitiveness must have been of a singularly consuming kind. In this kind of case, competitiveness is a way of holding open a door for the person I'm trying to become. I'm competing *in order to become* excellent rather than to show that I already am. When the prize arrives, it turns out to be not what I really wanted; I am already preparing for the next competition. The value for the sake of which I compete is not one on which I have a good grip. I compete for the sake of a future or anticipated value that I, as of now, only incompletely understand. This form of competitiveness is *proleptic* competitiveness.

(e) Reasons of Pretense

David Velleman (2002) has proposed that we emulate ideals by *pretending* to satisfy them. He offers as an example of pretense his own experiences of mock aggression in his martial arts class. He then analyzes a case of quitting smoking as one in which the subject pretends to be a nonsmoker and then gets "carried away" (100 and *passim*) with the pretense. Velleman acknowledges that, on his conception of it, such behavior is somewhat irrational: "When a smoker draws on an ideal for motivation to quit, his behavior is in some respects irrational" (101). He characterizes such agents as "hav[ing] reasons to make themselves temporarily irrational." Velleman seems to think that the irrationality in question is only of a harmless, temporary kind. I find it to be neither harmless nor temporary. The whole idea of such an account is to sever someone's "outer" reasons for adopting the pretense from the reasons as they appear to him once he's inside it. Velleman's thought is that the agent thereby makes a new set of reasons available to himself, which he can leverage into personal change. But once one adopts an account of this kind, one cannot rely on the rationality of the outer reasons to vouchsafe that of the inner ones. Consider that one can have all sorts of reasons for "pretending" to be some way—someone can pay me money, I can do it on a lark, I can be an actor in a play. If I get "carried away" and fail to snap out of it, I seem to exhibit some kind of mental illness. I've become trapped inside my own game. Velleman offers no principled reason why we should not understand the smoker, and emulators in general, as (possibly)[9] luckier victims of the same deep and permanent irrationality.

In aspirational cases, the failure to shed the pretense is salutary rather than pathological. But this is connected to the fact that it is not mere pretense. When I pretend or engage in make-believe, I close my eyes to the world around me, sometimes literally, the better to imagine a world that isn't actually there. It is crucial to my willingness to engage in such activity that I see it as temporary. Large-scale transformative projects—including quitting smoking—are not like this. If I aspire to become a nonsmoker, I am not pretending to already be one. Rather, I want to come to see the world in the way in which a nonsmoker does, because I think that is the right way to see things.[10] I'm not closing my eyes; I'm fighting to open them and to *keep* them open. Velleman's conception of emulating an ideal corresponds to Iris Murdoch's description of humanity in general: "Man is the creature who makes pictures of himself and then comes to resemble the picture" (1996: 252).

---

9. Only possibly luckier, because there are both bad ideals and (morally) good roles for actors.
10. I should note that not every would-be nonsmoker *aspires* to quit. It is possible to have a simpler goal of modifying one's behavior, as in the case of Sue the overspender (see section II (b)). The aspiring nonsmoker is marked by the fact that she wants not only to behave differently, but also to come to see things differently, to cease seeing smoking as, e.g. cool, attractive, fun.

I think the aspirant makes pictures of himself *in order to* resemble the picture.

Pretending is different from trying, but I don't want to deny that trying can involve pretense of a special kind. Imagination does not function only as a momentary escape from reality; I can, perhaps, imagine my way into becoming someone. Here the function of the imagination is not to fashion a substitute world, but to help us move ourselves closer to some reality we already have some grip on. I might, for instance, adopt the mannerisms of the kind of person I'm trying to be. If this were an act of aspiration, it would pain me somewhat to do so, because it is not enough for me to *act* like that person when what I want is to *be* like that person. We cannot analyze aspiration in terms of pretense because the kind of pretense we would need to invoke is an aspirational kind.

(f) Second-Order Reasons

I use the phrase "second-order reason" to describe a reason that is based on a second-order desire.[11] For instance, one might want to be the sort of person who enjoys listening to classical music—one desires to desire music. Could reasons grounded in these second-order desires explain the transformative pursuit of musical education? It seems to me that such second-order desires come in two varieties. The first is the case where I can see precisely what is to be said in favor of desiring music. Having the desire to listen to music

---

11. It seems to me that there can be no such thing as a reason to have a reason that you do not yet have. While second-order desires can exist apart from the corresponding first-order desires, the same does not hold for reasons. For if I had some reason to, e.g., have a reason to listen to music, I would thereby have a reason to listen to music. For the canonical discussion of second-order desires, see Frankfurt (1971).

speaks to some interest or value or preference I already have, such as appearing cultured or getting a good grade in a required class. This kind of second-order desire cannot explain the large-scale transformation into a person for whom music comes to form a core preference. The person who is trying to get an A has no interest in having her desire to listen to music outlast the course. Such a desire to desire music is, as it were, bounded by the first-order desire (for reputation or grades) that fuels it.

In another kind of case, my desire to desire music is not limited by any external advantage—I want to want to listen to music for its own sake, in order to appreciate the intrinsic value of music. This is the kind of reason that can explain major and life-transformative efforts taken on its behalf. But this is also a case where the second-order reason betrays a now familiar instability: I do not know exactly why I want to be the kind of person who desires to listen to music, any more than I know why I want to listen to music in the first place. Second-order reasons of this kind are no less proleptic than their first-order counterparts.[12]

---

12. David Schmidtz's (1994) "maieutic reasons" are close cousins to second-order reasons. A maieutic end is an end achieved by coming to have other ends. Schmidtz offers the example of Kate, who has the end of doing something with her life and pursues this end by going to medical school. Schmidtz claims that she values medicine as an end in itself, but she also values it as a way of fulfilling her maieutic end of doing something with her life. The central claim of Schmidtz's paper is that maieutic ends allow us to choose final ends. But how is the transition between the general (maieutic) end and the particular final end effected? Schmidtz says that "at some point, she concluded that going to medical school and becoming a surgeon would give her the career she wanted" (1994: 228). The question is, as it were, what were the premises from which she concluded this? Was selecting randomly among ends that instantiated her general end? In this case, she did not have a reason to pursue medicine in particular. Or did she have other desires (e.g., wealth) that medicine would speak to? In that case her pursuit of her end would be instrumental, as Schmidtz wants to deny. But there is a third possibility, which is that she settled on her end because she gradually got its value into view—in this case her maieutic reason is itself a proleptic one. Absent proleptic reasoning, maieutic ends cannot explain the rational but non-instrumental development of final ends.

(g) Approximating Reasons

Perhaps the value under which the pursuit is conducted is close, if not identical, to the value of the end. At the end stages of a transformative pursuit I may have access to something close enough to the final value to justify pursuit. For instance, I might appreciate Mozart's light operas, and this gives me reason to listen to his symphonies, and this leads me to Bach. We might try to make up a kind of series of progressively approximating values to lead the music student from music she likes to the music the class is designed to get her to appreciate. Highlights of such a series might look like this: Taylor Swift, the Beatles, Rogers and Hammerstein, Gilbert and Sullivan, Puccini, Mozart, Bach. The question is, does this series represent a subtle shift in value over time, or does it represent one single value getting progressively clarified and approximated to? Does she say, at the end, "Now I see what I was after all along"?

In the first case—subtle shift—we should imagine the value transition as analogous to a move from yellow to blue along the color spectrum by imperceptibly different shades. But this is a variant of the "go for the exercise, stay for the movie" scenario. For the reason grounding the aspirant's activity when she's in the yellow region diverges from the reason in the blue region in such a way as to break up her pursuit into a series of rationally disconnected activities. From the fact that it is impossible to say where one ends and the other begins, it does not follow that there is no difference between the two. If it's a progressive clarification, there's no similar worry: the gradual shift in value would be guided throughout by the agent's sense that some target value is being approximated, like an image gradually coming into focus. But this is just what we mean in speaking of proleptic reasons. For a proleptic reason just is a reason by which an agent grasps, in an incomplete and anticipatory way, the reason that she will act on once her pursuit is successful.

Recourse to other reasons, be they approximating or vague or second-order or testimonial reasons, or reasons of pretense or self-management or competition, does not obviate the need for introducing a distinctive proleptic species of reason. I don't claim that my list exhausts all possible alternatives, but I do think it covers much of the rational territory. Moreover, there is a certain pattern that repeats itself, indicating a general strategy that the champion of proleptic reason should adopt in the face of some additional contender. If someone says that large-scale transformative pursuits can be rationalized by familiar, X-ish reasons, the proleptic reasons theorist will try to demonstrate that only a (proleptic) subspecies of X-ish reasons can hope to rationalize a distinctively aspirational pursuit.

Proleptic reasons are—I conclude—*the* reasons that rationalize large-scale transformative pursuits. A proleptic reason is an acknowledgedly immature variant of a standard reason. A proleptic reasoner is moved to φ by some consideration that, taken by itself, would (in her view) provide an inadequate reason for φ-ing. But she is not moved by that consideration taken by itself; rather, she is moved by that consideration (be it competitive, testimonial, approximating, etc.) as a stand-in for another one. The proleptic reasoner uses the only valuational resources she has at her disposal, namely her current desires, attachments, etc., both to mark the inadequacy of those very resources and to move herself toward a better valuational condition.

The reader may wonder why I invoke a new species of reason rather than speak of a proleptic grasp of a (standard) reason. I do not think that much hangs on whether we attach the property of being proleptic to a reason itself, as opposed to the quality of someone's apprehension of that reason. My interest is in a set of thoughts, actions, desires, choices, and projects that neither exhibit a standard form of rationality nor are to be discounted as irrational. The distinctiveness of proleptic rationality is my topic, whether we spell this out as a distinctive way of grasping reasons or as a grasp of a distinctive kind of reason. But there are considerations that speak in favor of the latter formulation. One context in which we might speak of proleptic reasons is that of explaining why someone did what he did. In this kind of case, a proleptic reason lends intelligibility to some bit of behavior. If we choose to speak of a "proleptic grasp" of a reason, then it will turn out that in proleptic cases, reasons do not explain behavior—rather, grasps do. And it is awkward to speak of actions as being explained by grasps and natural to speak of them as being explained by reasons.

We also invoke reasons when we recommend a course of action. Suppose a mentor tells her student to φ in such a way as to be making a proleptic reasons statement: she can see, on the basis of what she knows about him and of her expertise in φ-ing, that he ought to aspire to φ. She cannot be read as saying that he *has* a proleptic grasp, for her point is to inform him about something he is missing. Nor is she confessing to such a grasp—for presumably, she grasps that same reason non-proleptically. We could describe her as asserting that he ought to have a kind of grasp that he doesn't yet have; but that is a strange way of talking. The more natural thing to say is that she is alerting him to the presence of a special kind of reason.[13]

---

13. The distinction I am making here, between explaining an action that has already been done and recommending one as to be done, should not be confused with the distinction between motivating and normative reasons. All of the practical reasons discussed in the course of this book are (at least) motivating reasons, which is to say, reasons that potentially explain some action. (There are a number of ways of spelling out the distinction in question; here, I follow Smith 1987.) Normative reasons present some requirement on an agent's behavior, from the point of view of, e.g., morality or prudence. Many normative

III. A DILEMMA: FLAILING VERSUS DEEPENING

Let us pause to consider a dilemma for the proleptic reasons theorist:[14] either the aspirant already appreciates, e.g., music to some
degree or she does not. In the first case, she is not aspiring to appreciate music but only to deepen the appreciation she already has. For
if she already has a grasp of the value, then we can explain her taking
the class with reference to this (ordinary, non-proleptic) reason. If,
on the other hand, she does not appreciate music at all, then she
cannot even aspire. She possesses too little of the grasp of the value
to be, in any sense, guided by it. The best such a person could do is

reasons are, of course, motivating reasons. The issue of whether there are normative reasons that are non-motivating is closely related to the question of whether there are external reasons (as discussed later). It is worth noting, however, that all motivating reasons
have some kind of claim to normative force. If I say, "S did ϕ because her neurons fired in
such-and-such a way," I offer a reason in explanation of S's ϕ-ing, but it is not a motivating
reason. The reason is not S's reason for ϕ-ing; it does not rationalize her action. "A reason
rationalizes an action only if it leads us to see something the agent saw, or thought he
saw, in his action" (Davidson (1963) 1980: 3). Motivating reasons explain by rationalizing, and so they must present some justification, however partial, of the action. As Smith
points out, motivating reasons have "the role of justifying from the perspective of the value
that the very reason embodies." However, he insists on assigning to motivating reasons
"the minimal justificatory role possible" and emphasizes the possibility that the justification may only be partial: "A motivating reason, even when it does explain an agent's
behavior, may reveal little of value in what the agent did even from his own point of view"
(38–39). To illustrate this point, he borrows Davidson's example of a man who has always
had a yen to drink a can of paint, and so he does. We have an explanation, though not a
justification, of the man's action. Arguably, this example backfires: for we may not feel that
we have a very good explanation of why the man in question drinks a can of paint. It seems
to me that if an action's justification is only partial, the explanation, too, must be lacking
in completeness. If, for instance, you ϕ-ed because you wanted to ψ, but I cannot see how
anyone could want to ψ, or how anyone could want to ψ under these circumstances, or how
anyone could want to ψ enough to justify the cost of ϕ-ing, then I do not fully understand
why you ϕ-ed. For your action is not as intelligible to me as one without those explanatory
gaps. I suspect, therefore, that motivating and normative reasons may be more difficult to
separate from one another than is standardly supposed.

14. I owe this dilemma to an anonymous referee.

take the class for the wrong reason, and then be surprised to find that she enjoys it.

Let me begin with the second horn of the dilemma. I concede to the objector that without some grip on the value, aspiration threatens to devolve into what we might call flailing. Someone who simply has the idea of becoming better in some vague sense, without a grip on some specific value they will be acquiring, is unlikely to make progress.[15] Consider, as an example, the wonderful chapter in *A Tale of Two Cities* in which Sidney Carton professes his love to Lucie Mannette. Sidney is a self-identified drunken wastrel: Dickens describes "the cloud of caring for nothing, which overshadowed him with such a fatal darkness" (1875: 66). Sidney has no intention of courting Lucie's affections, proclaiming in one of the first exchanges of the scene that "I shall never be better than I am. I shall sink lower, and be worse." He is grateful and relieved that she does not return his feelings:

> "If it had been possible, Miss Manette, that you could have returned the love of the man you see before yourself—flung away, wasted, drunken, poor creature of misuse as you know him to be—he would have been conscious this day and hour, in spite of his happiness, that he would bring you to misery, bring you to sorrow and repentance, blight you, disgrace you, pull you down with him. I know very well that you can have no tenderness for me; I ask for none; I am even thankful that it cannot be." (66)

Nonetheless, Sidney takes joy in telling Lucie what she has meant to him, explaining that she awakens in him the painful glimmer of the possibility of being a better person:

---

15. See note 2, introduction, for a qualification.

"Since I knew you, I have been troubled by a remorse that I thought would never reproach me again, and have heard whispers from old voices impelling me upward, that I thought were silent forever. I have had unformed ideas of striding afresh, beginning anew, shaking off sloth and sensuality, and fighting out the abandoned fight. A dream, all a dream, that ends in nothing, and leaves the sleeper where he lay down, but I wish you to know that you inspired it." (66)

Lucie beseeches Sidney to aspire, telling him, " 'O Mr. Carton, think again! try again!' " Sidney refuses, insisting that it is too late for him. Sidney can't even get started, because he does not know quite what he would be trying to do. His grip on the good is so attenuated, so dreamlike, that what he glimpses is only the bare possibility of being different. He does not actually see what value he would be acquiring or approximating to by becoming different, and so he feels that change is impossible for him. He cannot, as it were, envision himself becoming different with any concreteness. Sidney doesn't aspire, he merely flails. It is worth noting, however, that flailing is not nothing. It means something that Sidney feels a regret he never thought he would feel again, and although this feeling is not enough to get him to make something of his life, it does move him to perform the grand gesture of sacrificing himself for Lucie at the end of the novel. Nonetheless, it doesn't give him the materials for working to become a better person. Aspiration, by contrast, really does call for some sense of the *specific* value one is guiding oneself toward. Does it, then, follow that the aspirant can simply be motivated by an ordinary reason? I do not think it does.

The objector goes wrong in assuming that the project of deepening one's grasp on a value can be explained by non-proleptic reasons.

If your activity of music listening is directed at desiring music more than you currently do, or to the extent that you currently don't,[16] then that activity cannot be explained (non-proleptically!) by the desire you currently have. For the desire you currently have, considered in abstraction from its aspirational (proleptic) component, would only explain pursuit of the satisfaction of that desire. It cannot explain the deepening or intensification of that desire.[17] The way around the dilemma, then, is that while the proleptic reasoner must indeed have some grasp on the good she pursues, her large-scale transformative pursuit of it is directed precisely at the part of it she cannot yet grasp.

IV. INTERNAL REASONS

Proleptic reasons constitute a new challenge to the thesis of *internalism* about practical reasons.[18] Internalism is a thesis about what it takes for someone to have a reason to do something. Internalists hold that an agent's reasons must in some way be relativized to what she desires, where that term is construed broadly to include interests, commitments, attachments, preferences, etc. First espoused by Bernard Williams ([1980] 1981), internalism has since found wide acceptance, though at the same time many of those who

---

16. We must also assume that it is not indirectly aimed at satisfying some other desire that is served by having the desire to listen to music (see the earlier discussion of second-order reasons). Thanks to David Finkelstein for prompting this clarification.

17. Thus the defender of aspiration can agree with Harman (2014) against Paul (2015) that the agents described by Paul have some grip on the end value. The claim that, e.g., pregnancy and childbirth are aspirational phenomena doesn't rest on the assumption that we are bereft of information as to what it will be like.

18. Externalists such as Parfit (2011) go beyond negating internalism when they assert that not only are there external reasons, but *all* reasons are external, i.e., not relativized to motivation.

call themselves internalists are inclined to reject some element of Williams's characterization of the position.

Consider the following internalist theses:

(M) motivation condition: if R is a reason for S to φ, S is such as to be able to be moved by R.

(J) justification condition: if R is a reason for S to φ, R can be derived from S's set of desires by a rational procedure.

Internalists have traditionally held both (M) and (J), and expressed their combination in some formulation such as this:

(MJ) R is a reason for S to φ iff, were S to deliberate in a procedurally rational way from his current set of desires, he would come to be motivated to do so by R.[19]

Internalists have wanted both to deny that someone could be in the condition of being barred from access to his own reasons and to insist that reasons for action justify those actions in the light of the agent's desires. In short, I have whatever reasons would move me if I were fully procedurally rational. Recently, some philosophers have called into question whether internal reasons can do both the job of motivation and the job of justification. (MJ) lends itself to the "conditional fallacy," which amounts to a kind of blind spot for

---

19. By omitting reference to beliefs I elide the difference, here immaterial, between *subjective* and *objective* reasons. A subjective reason would be one arrived at by deliberation from the agent's current set of desires *and current set of beliefs*, whereas objective reasons would presuppose deliberating from a belief-set corrected for falsity and supplemented with any missing (and relevant) true beliefs. See Markovits (2011b) for this way of formulating the distinction.

reasons that depend on one's irrationality.[20] Robert Johnson (1999) describes someone who has a reason to see a therapist because he is deluded into thinking that he is James Bond. "James Bond" cannot arrive at this reason himself: for if he were in a position to reason correctly on this point, he wouldn't (so the story goes) have any need for therapy. Likewise, Michael Smith (1995) describes a sore loser so incensed by his defeat that he is inclined to punch his opponent at the end of the game. Given this inclination, he doesn't have a reason to approach his opponent at the end of the game for a handshake, though that is exactly what his fully rational, and therefore less irascible, counterpart has reason to do.

Johnson has argued that the only way around the conditional fallacy is to give up (MJ) by giving up either (M) or (J); and Julia Markovits (2011a) has recently made the case for the former option. She argues that we have independent reason to give up (M), since there are circumstances in which we shouldn't be motivated to φ by the best reason for φ. For instance, a pilot executing an emergency landing might be well advised not to act for the sake of saving hundreds of lives, because being motivated by this reason might put so much psychological pressure on him as to interfere with his performance of the task. She advocates a weaker version of internalism based only on (J).

I will argue that internalists—even weak internalists—are guilty of selling proleptic rationality short. But first some preliminaries. The weak internalist takes it that the reasons we have *depend rationally* on our desires. Internalists might spell out this rational dependence in a variety of ways: in terms of instrumental rationality

20. Though Markovits (2011a) argues that one can broaden the class of counterexamples to include ones—such as Kavka's toxin puzzle or cases where one has pragmatic reasons to hold a belief—in which the agent's inability to access the relevant reason is due not to her irrationality, but rather to certain strictures that rationality places on us.

(Hume, as understood by Williams [1980] 1981), of the presence of a sound deliberative route, of the absence of rational defects (Korsgaard 1986), of procedural rationality or the reasoning of an ideally rational agent (Markovits 2011a, b); of satisfying norms of consistency and coherence in such a way as to be "systematically justifiable" (Smith 1995: 114). All of these ways of cashing out the dependence indicate some analogue to *formal* validity: the method in question does not add any content to one's ends, but rather takes the content already present in them and shows what reasons follow from it. The idea is: given that "James Bond" has an interest in his mental health and also has some form of mental illness, it follows that he has reason to seek help—even if he, himself, is not in a position to appreciate this reason. Seeking help is the kind of behavior that would be consistent with the aim of mental health, when it is combined with the presence of mental illness. We might also speak of actions that answer or correspond to one's ends. The weak internalist might put his point thus:[21] you have the reasons that an impartial third-party observer would take you to have if he were reasoning about what reasons you have in a procedurally rational way from your desires.

One more quick point of clarification: internalists can—and do—offer us internalist accounts both of *pro tanto* reasons and of *all-things-considered* reasons. Take Williams's ([1980] 1981) example of Owen Wingrave, whose family insists that tradition gives him reason to enlist, in spite of his deep hatred of all things military. When Williams says that Owen has *no reason* to enlist, does he mean that Owen lacks even a *pro tanto* reason to do so? It is hard

---

21. Markovits puts the point in this way in note 13 of her 2011b paper, though the note appears only in the online version of the paper, https://sites.google.com/site/juliamarkovits/research; as she points out there, both Smith (1994: §5.9) and Railton (1986: 174) offer reformulations of internalism in the same vein.

to imagine someone who, in Owen's circumstances, sees literally nothing speaking in favor of enlisting: surely the fact that his family strongly wants him to enlist is at least a (very weak) consideration in favor of doing so? Presumably, even if he allowed that Owen saw some (minimal) reason to enlist, Williams would still want to resist the family's insistence that enlisting is what he has an all-things-considered reason to do. For whatever glancing respect he harbors for tradition, or whatever weak desire he has to please his parents, is dwarfed by his powerful hatred of the military. In what follows, we will set *pro tanto* reasons aside: "S has a reason to φ" means, henceforth, that φ-ing is what S has a reason to do, all things considered.

The problem is that the proleptically rational agent has a reason that not only she, but even a fully rational third-party observer, will have trouble extracting from the content of her antecedent desires. Suppose the good student of music appreciation has a choice between spending an hour of her evening listening to a symphony and devoting that hour to a hobby she thoroughly enjoys. Let us assume that listening to music will not serve any end of hers apart from her (still weak) interest in enjoying music for its own sake. The internalist must direct her to pursue the hobby she already enjoys a great deal over developing her nascent love of music. For that action coheres better with her current set of desires and interests. But if this were always good advice, we would hardly ever have reason to develop new interests, values, relationships, etc. For there is virtually always something else we could be doing that we enjoy more than, and that satisfies our other ends better than, the new form of valuation we have yet to fully acquire.

The problem is not merely that *she* does not, from where she currently stands, have a rational line of sight to the end whose value justifies her activity. For weak internalists are willing to grant that agents have more reasons than they can see their way to acknowledging. The problem is that unlike in Johnson's "James Bond" case or Smith's sore loser case, the impartial rational spectator is no better off than the agent herself. If he could somehow reason from the person's *future* condition, in which (let us suppose) love of music has become the central aesthetic pleasure of her adult life, it would be clear that she ought to listen to the symphony. But the internalist is restricted to *extracting* what the agent should do by applying a procedurally rational method to her antecedent desires, cares, interest, loves, etc. The internalist must counsel us to stick with immediate and available pleasures over embarking on the arduous process of developing a sensibility for new and perhaps higher ones. He seems to be giving us a form of advice that would have irked no one so much as Bernard Williams himself: be philistines!

My claim is that the internalist cannot capture the affective difference between the person I have called the "bad student," who is satisfied with her minimal appreciation of music, and the person who likewise harbors a minimal appreciation but aspires to become a music lover. I want now to consider some responses on the part of the internalist—some desires that he could point to in order to explain why the second has reason to listen while the first might lack it.

First, consider the desires that correspond to what I have called the reason's "proximate face." The aspiring music-lover has promised herself chocolate for making it through the movement and sustains her listening by imagining making a dramatic entrance in a concert hall on a snowy moonlit evening. The bad student lacks these forms of motivation. Will the internalist be able to point to these differences in their ends as accounting for the differences in their reasons? No. In order to successfully motivate oneself through some mechanism such as appetite or fantasy, the subordinate reason's *motivational* force must outstrip that of one's ultimate aims—but its justificatory force cannot do so. So, for instance, if I am trying to motivate myself to lose weight by promising to buy myself a nice dress, but losing weight will in fact frustrate more of my ends than it will satisfy, then my desire for a dress cannot be a source of good reasons. For the very fact that it is irrational for me to be trying to lose weight entails that it is irrational for me to be setting up incentives for myself to facilitate that project.

Alternatively, consider the class of desires that pertain, in a higher-order way, to the distal face, e.g., a desire to desire to listen to music more than one does, a desire to see what all the fuss is about, music-wise, or a desire to become a music-lover. Even if it is true that the good student has these desires and the bad one lacks them, pointing to that difference cannot help the internalist explain the fact that the good student has a reason to listen. For the rational ground of these higher-order desires does not lie in any extraneous benefit that having a stronger desire to listen to music, understanding the source of the fuss, or becoming a music-lover would afford her. At least not in the case I'm imagining: someone who wants to become a music-lover in order to, e.g., please her parents raises no problem for the internalist. For her "additional desire" plugs into independent motivations that can indeed rationalize her choice in a straightforwardly internalist way. But in the case of the good student, the rational ground of her higher-order desires—the reason she has them—is once again simply the intrinsic value of music. And this is a value she is, currently, ill placed to appreciate. So *all* of these desires bottom out in a valuation of music that is quite weak— much weaker than the one she will have at the end of her aspirational trajectory.

But why, the internalist wonders, isn't this weak desire to enjoy music enough to get the aspirant going? Contrast Satisfied Sue with Aspirational Anne. Anne and Sue both enjoy and appreciate music to precisely the same degree—they are, e.g., disinclined to turn off the radio if classical music is playing, but cannot stay awake through a symphony. The difference between them is that Sue is satisfied with the degree to which she desires to listen to music and does not aspire to appreciate it more than she does. Thus it is Anne, and not Sue, who has a reason to take a music appreciation class. Anne's weak desire, being a common ground between her and Sue, cannot be what underwrites this reason. Nor, once again, can we shift the explanatory work onto the second order: Anne is not like metasatisfied Mike, who desires music to the same weak degree that Anne and Sue do, but desires to desire it more than he does because that will appease his wife. Mike's motivational set, unlike Sue's, offers us grounds for distinguishing the second order from the first. Sue's desire to desire music is based on the same weak grasp of the (intrinsic) value of music as her original desire.

Perhaps, instead of claiming that the aspirant's reasons are based in her desires, we should allow that they might be based in her beliefs. There is a kind of internalist[22] who holds that one of the things that can rationally ground a desire (or a desire to have a desire) is a belief in the value of the object that you desire (to desire). Why couldn't an agent's *belief* that music is intrinsically valuable be justified independently of, and therefore underwrite, her project of changing her affective response to music? If this is possible, and I think it is, then there is a version of this agent that is fully analyzable in terms of internal reasons.

The person who believes that music is valuable but doesn't enjoy music, or doesn't enjoy it very much, comes in two varieties. The first takes herself to know *perfectly well* the value of music, despite

---

22. Namely, the kind of internalist who thinks that beliefs can give rise to desires. See Nagel (1970: ch. 5) for the canonical statement of this view.

the fact that she takes less pleasure in listening to music than she thinks she could. She might work on herself to try to get herself to enjoy music more (or at all), simply for the reason that her life could contain more aesthetic pleasure than it does. Her music listening can, indeed, be rationalized by way of internal reasons—but those reasons are not proleptic, because she does not take herself to have anything to learn, value-wise. Manipulating one's affective responses so that they match the way one independently knows they should be is a real phenomenon, but it is not the one I seek to explain here.

If, on the other hand, she takes her own belief in the value of music to be in some way a defective appreciation of its value, since full appreciation would presuppose enjoyment of music, her belief will not suffice to rationally ground her attempts to access it. For she does not take her belief to already afford her (full) rational access to the value she is working to come into (better) contact with. This second case is the proleptic one that I claim internalists cannot accommodate. Such a person is willing to work harder to enjoy music than her belief can, by the logic of internalism, rationally support. Her willingness stems from her sense that there is more value out there than she has yet been able to take account of either cognitively or conatively.

Why can't the internalist simply allow that the good student has, in addition to any of the desires mentioned earlier, an *aspiration* to appreciate music? Internalists are famously open-minded about exactly what forms of motivation or ends or conation might constitute the ground of one's reasons. I have claimed to use the word "desire" broadly—as internalists themselves often do—to cover this whole class. They might suspect that, in this discussion, I have actually used it more narrowly, in such a way as to unfairly exclude the one kind of pro-attitude relevant to differentiating the good student from the bad one. But this is not the case. I do not want to deny the internalist recourse to the concept of being disposed to be motivated in a way that outstrips the reasons derivable from their current motivational set. The problem is that she cannot make room for the fact that any of those motivations are *rational*. For the internalist, letting "aspiration" into one's subjective motivational set simply means letting in a tendency to be motivated in an incoherent and procedurally irrational way. What the internalist cannot do is to derive the good music student's reasons not merely from her aspiration but from her *rational aspiration*. For her theory, as I've been arguing, gives us no way to see how that phrase could be anything but an oxymoron.

At this point, we may feel some nostalgia for old-school internalism. Markovits ascribes reasons to me on the basis of what a third-party, impartial, perfect reasoner would take as answering to my present motivational condition. Williams, by contrast, is interested in what reasons I, with all my imperfections, could arrive at. It is true that Williams must understand what I "could arrive at" in a way that includes the concept of rationality, i.e., as "could *rationally* arrive at"—but he nonetheless has a broader and in a certain way softer construal of what it means to arrive rationally at some conclusion. He doesn't seem interested in specifying a procedure that could be vouchsafed as formally valid and therefore employed in an identical form by *any* rational agent. Rather, he seems to want to claim that an agent must be in a position to somehow or other see her way to any reason we are to count as her own. Hence his famously—to some, aggravatingly—open-minded conception of what such "deliberation" consists in: "Practical reasoning is a heuristic process, and an imaginative one, and there are no fixed boundaries on the continuum from rational thought to inspiration and conversion" ([1980] 1981: 110).

Williams's followers have tended to be much more restrictive than he was in what they are willing to count as rational deliberation. It has seemed to some that without such restrictions it is not clear what the theory means to rule out, and thus what the contrast with externalism is meant to amount to. Others have harbored substantive worries about some of the forms of reasoning that Williams wants to admit. For instance, Smith objects that "the imagination is liable to all sorts of distorting influences, influences that it is the role of systematic reasoning to sort out" (1995: 116).[23] Finally, as I have observed, the conditional fallacy has driven still others (e.g., Markovits) to place at the heart of internalism the idea of what can be deduced by a valid procedure from a given set of desires.

Whatever the disadvantages of Williams's internalism, it might seem to be in a better position to accommodate proleptic reasoning than weak internalism. Indeed, I believe Williams himself may have thought that by emphasizing the role of the imagination in reasoning, he was skirting the worry about philistinism I've been pressing here. When Williams warns against an overly narrow conception of what a "sound deliberative route" may consist in, reminding us that "the imagination can create new possibilities and new desires" ([1980] 1981: 104–105), he may have large-scale transformative pursuits in mind. For it is true that we use our imaginations to grasp the value that a radically new form of life has to offer us. The problem is that we cannot do so well enough to generate an internal reason. The music student uses her imagination to generate a fantasy about a snowy evening, and this imaginative work may well be crucial to her forward progress. But she cannot, in fantasizing in that way, foresee the *real* value that music will bring for her. Imagination

---

23. This for a variety of reasons.

simply doesn't have that power. No matter how loosely we hold the reins, deliberation will not plot a course from the agent's present condition to what I have called the distal face of her proleptic reason. We cannot attribute to the aspiring X-er imaginative or heuristic resources that so far outstrip her current motivational condition that she is able to imagine her way into the intrinsic value of X.

Internalists may respond to this line of reasoning by beginning to doubt whether they *want* to accommodate proleptic rationality. There is no knowing whether an agent's course of action *will* end in φ-ing until the course has, in fact, ended. Are we to ascribe proleptic reasons only retrospectively, on the basis of successful φ-ing? Internalists may raise the same kind of objection to recognizing proleptic rationality that Smith raises to Williams's idea of the imagination as a source of reasons. They may doubt whether there is a fact of the matter as to whether what an agent does in the service of such an indeterminate goal is, or is not, proleptically rational. They may question whether it is even possible to ascertain that someone who takes herself to have a proleptic reason in fact does not, or vice versa.

I grant that the early stages of value-acquisition may indeed be tenuous enough to be immune to rational critique. Aspiration begins as something like wish or hope, and we would tend not to tell someone she "shouldn't" have such-and-such long-term wish or that her cherished hopes for her future self are "irrational." Rational criticism does, however, eventually become appropriate. At some point on the way to her goal, the agent enters a space in which it becomes fitting for someone—though perhaps not just anyone—to say either "Try harder, you can do this" or "Give up, this isn't working for you." These are the kinds of locutions by which we key someone in to the presence or absence of proleptic reasons. We can see the direction someone is heading, assessing her trajectory on the basis of the work she has done so far. We gauge whether she has it in her to make it to the endpoint, whether it is reasonable for her to proceed, or more reasonable for her to try something else. Or, rather, those of us with the relevant expertise and the relevant familiarity with the aspirant do this.

Though proleptic reasons are amenable to rational critique, the character who is in a position to offer this critique is not Markovits's impartial, detached, perfectly rational observer. This observation may further incline the internalist to reject the rationality of proleptic reasons, but I think it should instead lead her to question the un-argued-for assumption that the "perfectly rational agent" is the perfect arbiter of all practical reasons. If it were true that excellence with respect to procedural rationality alone—a kind of analytical prowess—put someone in a position to determine what reasons a person has, philosophers would be much better at offering advice on any sort of practical topic than we in fact are. It is important to keep in mind that the set of examples with which we philosophers discuss practical rationality does not represent a random sample. Philosophers tend, quite reasonably, to gravitate toward examples that provide immediate spectatorial access. The "impartial rational observer" can determine, without wanting anything, doing anything, or having any special expertise, that breaking an egg is a rational means to the end of making an omelet and that leaving the egg intact is not a rational means to the same end. In order to make the relevant determination, all one needs is an understanding of what eggs are and what omelets are. When speaking to an audience—philosophers—without any special practical competence, it is useful to avail oneself of examples that *can* be assessed by any rational observer.

But we should guard against taking such armchair assessability to be a feature of practical rationality itself. For instance, consider the difficulty of determining whether it is an intensive course, years of casual listening, or a season of concert attendance that represents the rational means, for the would-be music-lover, to realize her aspirations. One doesn't know the answer to this question merely by knowing what the relevant items *are*. And not even a master of procedural rationality should, I think, venture to answer this question if she has never had any interest in music.

At least some forms of practical rationality or irrationality may be evident only to those whose sensibilities—desires, emotions, intellects—have been shaped by the practice in question. In addition, such judgments often call for personal acquaintance with the subject whose proleptic rationality is being called into question. And even when an expert is assessing a subject she knows well, she will often be unable to judge whether the aspiration is rational or not until she has some actual extent of practice before her. Thinking about whether or not something will work out is not always a reasonable substitute for trying to work it out. It does not tell against the rationality of aspiration that a judgment as to whether someone has a proleptic reason is likely to be made on the basis of something like a trial period or evidence of similar past attempts, and that it is likely to call for personal acquaintance with and personal affection for both the subject in question and her aspirational target. Judgments of practical (ir)rationality sometimes call for practical experience.

We acquire most, perhaps all, of our practical knowledge by responding to past experience. My interest has been in those cases in which the experience that we respond to is one that we ourselves have sought out; moreover, we sought it out for the (proleptic) reason that it produce this response. In those cases, we have guided ourselves to the new values or desires or commitments that our experience engenders. That process of self-guidance is a kind of practical learning. Because a process of learning some new form of valuation is not the same as a process of articulating or rendering consistent the values one already has, proleptic reasons break every internalist's mold.

MORAL PSYCHOLOGY

Chapter 3

Intrinsic and Extrinsic Conflict

I. INTRODUCTION

(a) Singling Aspiration Out, Fitting Aspiration In

In part I (chapters 1 and 2) of this book, I introduced examples of aspiration and argued that they cannot be analyzed as the straightforward products of decisions to become a new kind of person or by way of standard kinds of reasons. In part II (chapters 3 and 4), I work in the other direction. I begin with standardly recognized phenomena, ones that can be described without reference to aspiration. I then argue that a complete understanding of those phenomena requires us to invoke aspiration. While part I emphasizes the distinctiveness of aspiration, part II shows that aspiration helps us understand phenomena in which we had independent interest. It fits aspiration into a larger whole.

The centerpiece of part II is a form of conflict—I call it "intrinsic conflict"—that has been singled out, by Harry Frankfurt, as calling for a specialized analysis. In chapter 4, I illustrate the breadth of the phenomenon of intrinsic conflict, and its independence from aspiration, by showing that akrasia (weakness of will) is a form of intrinsic conflict. The existence of intrinsic conflict can be identified without reference to aspiration—but, I argue, the same does not hold for the *resolution* of intrinsic conflict. Chapter 3 shows that intrinsic conflicts cannot be resolved, or even addressed, by any procedure of decision-making. For the intrinsically conflicted agent cannot express her conflict in the form of the deliberative question "Should I do A or B?" Instead, I argue, intrinsic conflicts—to the extent that they both persist over time and are resolvable—are resolved by aspiration. The phenomenon of intrinsic conflict thereby illustrates one function of aspiration.

(b) Overview of Chapter 3

In what I will call an "extrinsic" conflict of desire, an agent's desires pull her toward incompatible actions. Such an agent's problem is that, as a matter of contingent fact, nothing she does will get her everything she wants. There is, however, another kind of desire-conflict, in which the agent's desires pull directly against one other. For instance, generously hoping for someone's happiness gets in the way of resentfully wishing to see him suffer. In a loving but spiteful moment, I might be torn between those desires. Harry Frankfurt called our attention to special difficulties attending the resolution of this kind of conflict, arguing that we do so by *identifying with* the one desire and *externalizing* the other. In this chapter, I will show that Frankfurtian identification/externalization cannot resolve such conflicts, which I call "intrinsic." I will go on to propose an alternative: they are resolved by aspiration. I begin with a brief overview of the argument of this chapter.

Frankfurt does not offer an account of what makes a conflict intrinsic. Taking my bearings from his characterization of the examples he offers, I argue that in order to get the conflict properly into view, we must invoke the agent's values. Intrinsically conflicted agents are conflicted at the level of value, and this means that the conflict fractures the agent's evaluative point of view: in order to get the appeal of one of the things she wants fully in view, she must step out of the point of view from which the other appears attractive. I concede that, on this analysis, it becomes difficult to see how intrinsic conflict is even possible. How can an agent simultaneously inhabit incompatible evaluative points of view? I draw on a parallel with cases of split attention: the desires cut against each other, in that she can have the one desire to the degree that she doesn't have the other. One can experience both of two intrinsically conflicting desires, insofar as one experiences each of them in a qualified way.

Though I ultimately deny Frankfurt's positive conclusion that intrinsic conflicts are resolvable by identification, I offer an argument for a related negative conclusion: intrinsic conflicts are *not* resolvable in the way in which we standardly resolve extrinsic conflicts, namely by deliberation. By articulating this argument, I put Frankfurt into conversation with a number of ethical theorists who have aimed to show that there are value-conflicts deliberation cannot resolve. Arguments establishing the limited power of deliberation have been offered in support of Aristotelianism (by John McDowell) and against both Kantianism (by Bernard Williams) and consequentialism (by David Sobel). What is distinctive about Frankfurt's contribution to this series of arguments is that he is committed to the idea that desires whose conflict is deliberatively irresolvable are nonetheless psychologically compossible. Thus it is for Frankfurt, and not for the others, that the question of the *resolution* of deliberatively irresolvable conflict emerges.

I distinguish two ways in which a conflict might not be resolvable by deliberation: it might be, first, that the agent cannot use deliberation to *answer* the question as to which of two options she ought to choose; or alternatively, it might be that she cannot even *ask* this question. Frankfurt's solution to intrinsic conflict—identification—is predicated on the mistaken assumption that intrinsic conflicts are deliberatively irresolvable for the first reason. For he takes it that intrinsic conflict comes to an end when the agent surveys her two desires and *decides* between them. In fact, I argue, an agent who is intrinsically conflicted cannot achieve the reflective distance from her conflict that is necessary in order to even arrive at the state of uncertainty that would have to prefigure such a decision. Can such an agent resolve her conflict at all? I argue that she can do so by aspiring. Aspiration, the temporally extended process by which someone works to become a different and better person, is the solution to intrinsic conflict.

(c) Defining Intrinsic Conflict

Harry Frankfurt (1976: 248; cf. 1988: 170) differentiates what he calls "two sorts of conflict of desire." He illustrates the distinction with a pair of agents roughly along the lines of these:[1]

TORN AESTHETE: A man would enjoy both attending a classical concert and going to the film that is playing at the same time as the concert. Frankfurt says that he "would resolve the problem this conflict presents just by deciding which of the two things in question he prefers to do." If he decides on the film but cannot get a ticket, "it would be quite natural for him to revert to his second choice and go to the concert" (1976: 249).

BITTER WIFE: A woman wants to mail her husband's letter, as a favor to him. But they have a complicated relationship. She loves him, and she knows it will make him a lot happier if the letter is

---

1. I've modified Frankfurt's original example, in which the spiteful act is a speech act, and it is directed against a casual acquaintance. I cite the original example later in section VI.a.

mailed—unmailed letters are one of his pet peeves. But she is also intensely bitter and angry at him for his many small cruelties toward her, his intense irritability (so many pet peeves!), his lack of romantic initiative. Next to the mailbox she sees a garbage can, and it occurs to her to spitefully throw his letter in the garbage instead of mailing it. Suppose that, in the end, love prevails over spite, and she reaches for the handle of the mailbox—but finds it locked. Frankfurt notes, "This would not naturally lead h[er] to see if [s]he could salvage the satisfaction of h[er] other desire . . . the alternative of injuring [her husband] is not second to the person's first choice of [doing him a favor]" (1976: 249).

Let us call the aesthete's conflict "extrinsic," and the wife's "intrinsic." As a first pass at explicating this distinction, we might suppose that the difference lies in whether the intentional contents of the desires are themselves opposed. The wife, in desiring to hurt her husband, desires the opposite of what she desires when she desires to help him. In desiring to hurt him, she desires that he fare badly, whereas in desiring to help him, she desires that he fare well, i.e., *not* badly. The aesthete, on the other hand, doesn't desire *not* to see a movie. He desires two things—to see a movie and to see a concert—whose conflict is only "in the world." It is not wrong to say that intrinsic conflicts feature such internal contradictions, but offering this as the basis of the distinction is too quick. For there is a problem about how to individuate the desires that show up in these conflicts.

It is possible to pick out the intentional content of a given desire anywhere along a continuum of objects that ranges from certain maximally abstractly formulations ("happiness," "acting well"), on the one hand, to a particular action, on the other. We can exploit this fact to create the appearance of contradiction among extrinsically conflicting desires or the appearance of a lack of contradiction among intrinsically conflicting ones. Someone who desires, e.g., both that the table be heavy and that it not be heavy has what are (at least in one sense) contradictory desires. But perhaps he desires it to be heavy because he does not want it to easily tip over, but he desires it to be light because he wants it to be easily moveable when he relocates. His conflict is extrinsic, despite the fact that we can describe him as someone who desires that contradictory propositions be the case. Redescribed, what he wants is something that is both untippable and movable, and there is no contradiction there. Consider the aesthete again. Insofar as he resolves to go to the movie, and he sees that this entails not attending the concert, we may say he desires not to attend the concert. His desire to attend the movie *is* a desire not to attend the concert. In the case of the wife, we could "hide" the intrinsic quality of her conflict by describing it as a desire to mail the letter vs. a desire to throw it in the trash.

In order to get the intrinsic quality of the wife's conflict into view, we must also rule out certain kinds of backstories explaining her desires. Suppose, for instance, that she wants to throw the letter away to teach her husband a lesson about taking her for granted; it is part of a (perhaps ill-conceived) plan to save their marriage. She is hurting him in order to help their relationship. Alternatively, she knows the letter is full of damaging revelations—she is "helping" him in order to destroy his reputation. If she is helping him in order to hurt him, or vice versa, then the options of mailing and trashing are, as for the aesthete, preferentially ordered. Should it turn out that she cannot hurt (help) him by mailing (trashing) the letter, and she can hurt (help) him, to a lesser degree, by trashing (mailing) the letter, it would be quite natural for her, in Frankfurt's phrase, "to revert to her second choice." Likewise if both desires serve some third value, such as promoting her political career: "On the one hand, male voters like him. On the other hand, female voters hate him. And they're the ones I really need to court at the moment. If I work things so that he initiates the divorce, I'll get a sympathy bump as well." It is true that she wants to hurt him (in order to court female voters) and to help him (in order to court male ones), but that is not really the level at which her conflict lies. Here again, it is easy to imagine her falling back on her second-best option: if she cannot succeed with the female voters by trashing the letter, she will court male voters by mailing it.

Specifying intrinsic conflict requires more than pointing out that an agent has a desire to φ and a desire not to φ. We need to add that this level of description picks out the level at which she is really conflicted. In the next section, I propose that we can do this by shifting ground: instead of considering the two desires in isolation, we must situate them in the broader evaluative outlooks of which they are a part. The problem for the wife is that her two desires conflict at the level of value.

II. VALUING: A HYBRID ACCOUNT

Like Niko Kolodny (2003), Samuel Scheffler (2010), and Jay Wallace (2013), I deny that valuing can be simply identified with believing or with desiring. Valuing includes both cognitive and conative elements. Scheffler explains (21) why it is a mistake to think that we value everything we believe valuable: our capacity to believe that things are valuable far outstrips our capacity for personally investing ourselves in those objects we can truly be said to value. In order to value something, we must engage with it in a way that takes time, effort, and practice. Given our finite life spans and limited resources, we cannot devote ourselves to valuing all of the things we see as valuable.

Wallace, drawing on Scheffler, has emphasized the ways such devotion manifests itself in affective connections between the subject and the valued object. He describes the valuer as "subject to a range of characteristic emotional reactions, depending on how things are going with the object of concern" (23). Coming to value something entails opening yourself up to being hurt in relation to that thing: you become vulnerable to forces that threaten the valued object or threaten to separate you from it. But valuing involves more than caring: when we value something, we also *evaluate* it as in some way good or worth caring about. It is possible to be emotionally vulnerable to something one thinks badly of and wishes one did not care about. When I value something, by contrast, I approve of my own affective entanglement with it. Thus valuing seems to include *both* an affective component and a cognitive one. But there is more.

Kolodny (2003: 150) has drawn attention to the connection between valuing and the recognition of practical reasons. When one values something, one is motivationally disposed in relation to that thing: to protect it, preserve it, engage with or in it. Someone who values something is not only affectively responsive to the object but also motivationally engaged with it; the things I value delimit the shape of my practical rationality, in that my values determine what shows up for me as a reasonable thing to do. For instance, if I value philosophy, then I am disposed to respond motivationally to opportunities to engage in it. Likewise, if I value my relationship with my friend, I am disposed to, e.g., respond to her emails, call her, make plans to get together. If I believe philosophy or my friendship to be valuable but am not inclined to engage in philosophy or make any effort to be in contact with my friend, then I do not really value either one. And this is true even if I have an emotional vulnerability that manifests in, e.g., feeling guilty about the fact that I never do any philosophy or call my friend.

Scheffler notes a fourth element to the account of value. In addition to the cognitive, affective, and motivational ways in which we respond to objects of value, Scheffler says that valuing includes an element of self-monitoring (29): when we value something we react to our own responses to the valued object, experiencing the affective, conative, and motivational responses described earlier as merited or appropriate.[2] In order to show that this is indeed an additional condition, not entailed by the first three, let me offer a few examples.

(1) I find myself developing a passion for motorcycle riding at a period in my life when I cannot afford the investment of time or money such an activity demands. In addition, my children are young, and I deem it irresponsible to risk my safety. I genuinely believe that riding a motorcycle is a valuable activity, and I don't think I'm wrong to be thrilled by the prospect of doing so, but I experience my own motivational disposition to engage in the activity as inappropriate: now is not the time.

(2) An older brother finds himself with a growing passion for magic just as his younger brother is displaying talent in magic. The older brother might judge that magic is valuable, be motivated to do it, feel excited at the prospect of pursuing it, and saddened at the thought of giving it up. Nonetheless, he might judge that these reactions are not warranted. He might recognize that while magic really is valuable, his own passion for it is suspect, a manifestation

---

2. In fact, Scheffler makes a somewhat more restricted claim: that we experience the emotional or affective response as appropriate. As my examples show, however, one can extend this condition to cover motivational and cognitive responses as well.

of his reluctance to allow his brother an arena in which to shine.

(3) A photographer, looking at a photograph of a gruesome scene, is struck by its beauty. She takes pleasure in the beauty of the image and is initially inclined to put it up on her wall when she checks herself: "What is wrong with me?! I ought not put this up on the wall, I ought not take pleasure in it, and I ought not even judge it to be beautiful."[3]

In the first case, the agent disapproves only of the motivational response; in the second, of the motivational and affective responses; and in the third, of all three. If it is correct to classify the agents in (1)–(3) as not being (paradigmatic) valuers of the domain in question, then these examples indicate the presence of a self-monitoring component to the activity of valuing: the valuer makes sure that her various responses to the valued object fall in line. The valuer thus experiences her own motivation to pursue, protect, and engage with it as fitting; she will not, as in my third example, feel alienated from her own assessment of the object as valuable. The self-monitoring activity also has a negative side. Insofar as she is disposed to experience the positive responses of pursuing, protecting, enjoying, etc. as appropriate, that same disposition will bring her to reject, disapprove of, and feel alienated from a *contrary* set of attitudes: feelings of disgust, hatred, or indifference toward the object; motivations to destroy, avoid, or disengage from the object; beliefs that the object is worthless, evil, or in some other way not-valuable. And this brings us to the bitter wife.

---

3. This example is inspired by the remarks of the composer Karlheinz Stockhausen about the 9/11 terrorist attacks. For a discussion, see Castle (2011).

Her desire to mail the letter is not a stray impulse, but part and parcel of a larger complex of valuing. She has feelings of warmth and affection for her husband, is motivated to do things that will make him happy, and believes in the value of their relationship. And she experiences all of these reactions as appropriate responses to the value of their relationship. She thus satisfies the conditions on valuing her relationship with her husband.[4] But this does not prevent her from *also* experiencing reactions of spite or hostility toward her husband: she is motivated to do things to damage their relationship, she has feelings of contempt toward him, she believes that she is being exploited and that her husband is undeserving of her love. This set of responses sits ill with her valuation of her relationship: insofar as she values her relationship, she cannot but experience them as inappropriate. We should not, however, infer from this fact the conclusion that she *doesn't* value her husband or their relationship.

An intrinsically conflicted agent experiences a desire (or feeling, or belief) that her values bring her to see as inappropriate. The stray desire throws a wrench in the works of her valuational machinery. We can now compare the wife with some of the non-intrinsically conflicted variants I sketched earlier. If the wife were inclined to throw the letter away in order to teach her husband a lesson, as part of a plan to save her marriage, she would not be intrinsically conflicted because she would not experience that motive as inappropriate to her valuation of their relationship. If she saw both options in terms of her political career, then she would not be intrinsically conflicted because she would not value their relationship in the first place. In this example, she values her political career, and this does

---

4. For the purpose of analyzing this example, I adopt Kolodny's (2003) construal of love as the valuation of a relationship. I should note that nothing in my argument hangs on this particular analysis of love.

not require her to reject either of her two impulses. Finally, the aesthete is not intrinsically conflicted because his valuation of music does not require him to disapprove of his desire to see a movie; nor does his appreciation of cinematic value call for a rejection of his desire to attend the concert. The aesthete's conflict consists in the fact that *pursuing* or realizing one of his values gets in the way of his *pursuing* or realizing his other value. His problem is that he cannot *do* or *achieve* or *bring about* both. The wife's problem is not, in the first instance, that mailing the letter gets in the way of trashing it, or vice versa—though this is, of course, true—but that she has difficulty even *desiring* both of the things she finds herself desiring.

The intrinsic character of the wife's conflict emerges when we situate her desires in the larger framework of her values. If two attitudes constitute an intrinsic conflict, this is because one of them is part of a larger unit of the agent's psychology—a value—where that larger unit, in turn, calls for her to regard the other attitude as inappropriate. The evaluative nexus of love calls for her not to desire to trash the letter. Her hatred, too, seems to represent a form of valuing: she has the relevant evaluative beliefs (her husband is unromantic, thoughtless), affects (resentment, spite), and motivations (to trash the letter); moreover, in her spiteful moments, these strike her as exactly the appropriate reactions to him and their relationship. Her hatred is, thus, an organized evaluative nexus in just the sense that her love is; and from the point of view of that hatred, her desire to mail the letter makes little sense.

Torn between loving attention that manifests her valuation of her relationship and spiteful revenge that inclines her to destroy it, the wife suffers from a kind of double vision. She sees the goodness of mailing with one eye and the goodness of trashing with the other. But she cannot get both of these "goods" into view at once. There is no problem for the aesthete in admitting that cinematic value and musical value are both forms of value. The wife's choice, by contrast, cannot but fracture her evaluative point of view. For her motivation to mail the letter, given the valuational network in which it is integrated, puts a kind of pressure on her *not* to be motivated to trash it. Her conflict seems to be situated at the level of the values themselves, because her conflict is between items she cannot value together. Two desires conflict intrinsically if their conflict divides the agent's evaluative point of view against itself. Experiencing these two desires seems to require that she be two valuers at once.

III. THE POSSIBILITY OF INTRINSIC CONFLICT

The wife cannot, of course, actually be two valuers at once. How, then, is intrinsic conflict possible? The wife is poised between thinking of the prospect of mailing her husband's letter in a loving, forgiving, generous way and thinking about it in a bitter, spiteful, vengeful way. Someone who takes pleasure in her husband's comfort seems to be a different kind of person from someone who takes pleasure in his suffering. Could someone *feel* the generous desire to make a person happy and at the same time equally and fully *feel* the spiteful desire to hurt that person? Having one of these feelings seems to get in the way of having the other. For that is precisely what we mean by saying that her conflict is intrinsic: her valuation of her relationship militates not only against satisfying, but even against feeling, her spiteful desires.

And yet we should not concede the impossibility of synchronic intrinsic conflict; for we will find that we cannot easily redescribe such conflicts in terms of diachronic vacillation. Consider what happens if we try to compose the bitter wife out of alternating periods of loving-wife and spiteful-wife. We will find ourselves imagining someone who wholeheartedly loves and cherishes her husband at one moment, then switches to spitefully plotting his demise, and then flips back to adoring love. That is a person suffering some deep psychological pathology. Spite and love in a mentally healthy person inevitably color each other. The fact that the wife also wants to hurt her husband cannot but have an impact on, i.e. detract from, the quality of her love for him. I do not want to deny that the wife might go back and forth between the mailbox and the trash can, driven at one moment by love, at another by spite. But the vacillation that serves as a familiar marker of intrinsic conflict is not of the Manichean kind to which an eliminative reduction of synchronic intrinsic conflict would have to restrict itself.

Recall what it is like to fight with someone you love. It would not be surprising to hear anger in her voice. It would be shocking to hear anger *unaccompanied by love*. The latter is the experience of being the object of contempt or loathing; and that is not the experience the husband would have were the wife to express her feelings to him as she heads toward the trash can. Likewise, the love that comes to dominate her thinking as she turns back to the mailbox is love of a particular kind: the love of someone who struggles against hate, who loves by trying to love. The wife's conflict, even when it involves vacillation, presents in the form of love marred by spite, or spite inflected by love. We must, then, examine how the value-condition of love can be mixed, synchronically, with that of spite.

Let's start by considering ordinary cases of divided attention. Suppose that I am trying to work through the argument of a paper while my infant child cries loudly in the background. One thing that might happen in this situation is that the presence of the one prevents me from attending to the other altogether. I might be so absorbed in the paper that I don't register my child crying or so distressed by my child's crying that I forget about the paper. But I also might be in a condition between these two, a condition of split attention. I know my partner is handling the baby, so I set out to focus on the paper, but my grasp of the argument is hazier than it would be were the room silent. Or I am holding the baby and attending to her needs, but not as well as I would be were my mind not on the paper. In these cases, the quality of my attention to the one suffers in virtue of my attention to the other. Note that attention does not always suffer from being divided: I might be perfectly capable of cooking a dish I know well while thinking about the paper, but incapable of attending to my child while thinking about the paper. In cases of the second kind, we are moved to introduce "degrees" of attention or awareness. And this, I suggest, is how we should understand the case of the wife.

A purely loving wife thinks about how to make her husband happy; a purely spiteful wife takes undiluted pleasure in the prospect of his pain. The bitter wife's thoughts incline in both directions at once. She cannot fully devote her attention to either value—the value of his happiness or that of his misery—because she is always distracted by a demand to look at the world in an incompatible way. The struggle she experiences in virtue of her mixed condition is manifest in every aspect of her agency: her facial expressions, her idle movements, her inner monologue, her feelings, her speech.

People in situations such as the wife's exhibit some of the behavior we see in cases of split perceptual or cognitive attention.[5]

---

5. I cannot offer a precise account of the relation between the nature of the attention split in desire-conflict cases, on the one hand, and that in dual-task cases. My thought here is only that looking to the latter can shed light on the more general phenomenon of qualified psychological compossibility. It may be that the desire-conflict case shares only some

They aim to "silence" one desire and raise the volume on the other. So the wife might, in a more loving moment, avert her eyes from the trash can or make a mental note to stop associating with recent divorcees. When memories of his behavior that morning begin to ignite the familiar flame of indignation, she takes a deep breath and thinks instead about something nice he did for her. In a spiteful moment, she does the opposite: calling up friends she knows will supportively encourage her to vent her bitterness, replaying the details of their morning fight in her mind. We can imagine parallels with the baby/work example: putting on noise-canceling headphones so that I can attend to the paper or, alternatively, resolving not to bring work home so that I can attend to the baby.

My proposal is that we can make room for having two conflicting value-perspectives at the same time by admitting the possibility of possessing each value in some degree. Noticing a jealous impulse in oneself can't but diminish the quality of one's generous desire to help; acknowledgment that one does still love one's husband cannot but get in the way of fully reveling in spiteful pleasure. If we allow that each value is incompletely or imperfectly present to just the degree that the other is present as well, conflict can be the object of experience. Intrinsic conflict is possible if the conflicting evaluative perspectives are psychologically compossible; and they are, but in a qualified way.

---

structural features of the dual-task cases, but deep differences render the use of the term "attention" for desire-conflict, if not homonymous, then at least metaphorical. Or, alternatively, it may be that there is one genus of attention of which both of these are species. The second point would have to be established in the light of a general analysis of the practical import of attention (on which, see Wu 2011). Since I cannot undertake such an analysis here, all of my references to ethical "attention" should be understood in the first, more cautious way.

IV. DELIBERATIVE IRRESOLVABILITY

Frankfurt argues that intrinsic conflicts are resolved by *identification* with one of the desires and *externalization* of the other(s). He does not specify the point of contrast with the resolution of extrinsic desire, but the natural one to supply is that extrinsic conflicts are resolved by deliberation: I decide which of the two desires should, given relevant contextual considerations, be favored over the other. Frankfurt hints at such an answer when he notes that desires that conflict intrinsically "do not belong to the same ordering," whereas in the extrinsic case it "would be quite natural for him to revert to his second choice." I have articulated a conception of intrinsic conflict on which it is a conflict between two valuational outlooks that cannot constitute a single point of view. I want now to argue that this way of conceiving of intrinsic conflict supports Frankfurt's intuition that intrinsic conflicts call for a non-deliberative mode of resolution. But it is important to say more than this: for there are deliberatively irresolvable conflicts that are not intrinsic. I want to isolate the particular species of deliberative irresolvability specific to intrinsic conflicts.

When we deliberate, we ask which of two (or more) things we ought to do.[6] This is a comparative inquiry, and the comparison in question is one of value. Deliberation asks us to compare the

---

6. I do not want to deny that practical reasoning may, at times, resolve the question of *how* to bring some proposed goal about in a thoroughly non-comparative way. (For an argument that Aristotelian *bouleusis* was primarily non-comparative, see Nielsen 2011.) We need not always, at every turn, insist on doing what we have ascertained to be better than all other available alternatives. I may, for instance, reason as follows: "How will I get to Paris? By taking a plane. Where do I get a ticket? Online." I can, thereby, reason to the action of turning on my computer without, e.g., having considered and rejected the option of consulting a travel agent. Straightforward implementation of a preselected plan is, no doubt, one function of practical rationality. But it is not a function relevant to the topic of intrinsic or extrinsic conflict of desire. For that topic calls for a form of rationality that might guide agents torn between a multiplicity of available options. Hence my focus on *comparative* practical reasoning, for which I reserve the word "deliberation" here.

(anticipated) value of one option with that of another. Such comparisons are not always possible. When the bitter wife thinks about the ways and degrees to which causing her husband pain makes her happy, she is conceiving of her own happiness in a radically different way from the way in which she conceives of it when she thinks about how doing him a favor makes her happy. The point of view from which making her husband happy is an appealing prospect—a sincere, loving, desire for his well-being —is one from which making him miserable seems in no way good. And vice versa. The two options cannot be surveyed because accepting the deliberative relevance of the one entails denying that of the other. She cannot deliberate from both points of view at once. She cannot ask which is "best overall," because there is no single conception of goodness that will accommodate her two sets of values.

Consider, by analogy, the familiar form of speech act that runs like this: "As your friend, I say go ahead, but as your attorney, I advise against it." Suppose that what I mean by this is that I cannot tell you what to do, all things considered. When I look at your situation from the point of view of friendship, the set of values that shows up is different from the set I see when I look at it in my capacity as an attorney. No third perspective is available to me, with reference to which I could impartially assess both sets of values. I can only offer you the guidance of helping you weigh the considerations in each value-space. I can tell you, e.g., how the legal reasons add up. The last step—that of weighing or otherwise adjudicating the two sets of values—I must leave to you.

Being your friend is an advisory role, which is to say that it puts me in a position to be of deliberative assistance to you; being your attorney, likewise, constitutes such an advisory role. In the case I'm imagining, what I'm telling you is that being your friend-and-lawyer is not an advisory role. It does not represent a position from which I might make recommendations to you. In such cases, we often worry that the nonprofessional perspective will "infect" the professional one and make it difficult for the person to give good professional advice. It is sometimes wise to avoid getting medical or legal advice from close family members or friends, exactly for this reason: such situations present the adviser with what we call a "conflict of interest." Conflicts of interest are interpersonal analogues of intrinsic conflicts.

In the case of intrinsic conflict, we could say that the agent experiences a conflict of interest between her role as loving wife and her role as hateful wife. She is in a situation in which the deliberative question "Which of these two thing should I do?" cannot be raised. We ask ourselves whether we should do something only when that thing seems good to do. And in this case, the first option seems like a credible answer to the question of what to do only insofar as one is deliberating from a point of view on which the second doesn't. We can see the distinctiveness of this kind of quandary by comparing it with one in which the deliberative question is difficult or even impossible to *answer*. As Donald Davidson says, "The situation is common; life is crowded with examples: I ought to do it because it will save a life. I ought not because it will be a lie; if I do it, I will break my word to Lavina, if I don't, I will break my word to Lolita; and so on" ([1970] 1980: 34). Let us add to Davidson's list the familiar examples of Sophie's choice between the lives of her two children and of Sartre's student (he can either fulfill his duty to take care of his aging mother *or* his duty to fight for his country).

In these cases—call them "dilemmas"—the agent experiences unhappiness no matter which choice she makes. Furthermore, she may feel she has no nonarbitrary means to decide between her options. And this might be not a contingent but a necessary fact about the values in question—for we might suppose that the

values of mother and motherland (or fulfillment of the two promises, or the lives of the two children, or the movie and the concert)
are incommensurable.[7] In that case, there is no fact of the matter
as to which ought to be preferred by the agent who must choose
between them. An agent placed in a dilemma between incommensurable values is in a difficult situation, no doubt, but her conflict is
not intrinsic. It is no part of loving one child that it is inappropriate
to love another; nor does one's valuation of one's country make it
unacceptable to value one's mother. When one considers what one
should do, both options (e.g., saving mother and saving country, or
saving the younger and saving the older child, or keeping the promise to Lavina and keeping the promise to Lolita) *show up* as valuable
things to do. The problem lies in figuring out which is more valuable. If there is value-incommensurability, this question might be
unanswerable; but that is not the same thing as saying that the question cannot be asked.

The problem of value-incommensurability, if it is one, is a problem for a subset of *extrinsic* conflicts: ones in which the (purportedly) incommensurable values do not stand to one another in any
of the canonical value-relations (see Chang 1997). Neither one is

7. I follow conventional usage in treating "incommensurable" as a synonym for "incomparable,"
where both are to be understood as having the meaning "cannot be compared." This contrasts
with Chang's (1997) usage, since she restricts the term "incommensurable" to describing a
species of incomparability. (Commensuration, in Chang's terminology, concerns the question of whether we can say *how much* more of a given value the one item has than the other.)
Nothing I say here is in substantive conflict with Chang's treatment of either the genus or
the species; my contention that there are deliberatively irresolvable conflicts is not meant
to call into question her denial of (what she calls) incomparability. For Chang argues that
incomparability and comparability are three-place relations , relating one item to another
in terms of a third—which she calls the "covering value." The covering value is the value in
terms of which the two items are to be (or cannot be) compared. If, as in my cases of intrinsic
conflict, no covering value is nominated, then Chang holds that it is improper to speak of the
items as being (in my terms) commensurable or incommensurable. She would say that they
are "noncomparable."

better than, worse than, or equal to the other. Being in this situation, and recognizing that one is in it, may make it impossible to come up with a fully satisfying answer, or any answer at all, to the question "Which of the two should I pursue?" Note that the difficulties in answering this question are not restricted to cases of incommensurable values. Some choices are beyond my individual capacities for commensuration or would take more time than I have available for making the decision. Or I may successfully commensurate the two options as being exactly equal,[8] in which case I still lack an answer to the question of what to do.[9] In none of these cases—including that of incommensurable value—does it follow from the fact that I cannot deliberatively determine an *answer* to the question of what to do that I cannot *ask* the question. For there is such a thing as being in a state of uncertainty as to what to do. Indeed, agents in these dilemmas are often our paradigmatic examples of being stuck in practical uncertainty. And it is natural to capture uncertainty as a condition in which one is asking oneself a question that one finds oneself unable to answer.

Intrinsic conflicts have a perspective-dividing quality: seeing one option as valuable gets in the way of seeing the other as valuable. This is, again, because the self-monitoring activity connected to our valuing of one of the options requires us to reject the inclination to be attracted to the other option. In extrinsic conflicts that take the form of a dilemma, we are all too able to see both options as valuable. The problem is that we don't want to choose between them. We

---

8. Chang adds: on par with, i.e., roughly equal. But both "equal" and "on par" are problematic for the agent trying to make a decision. Sophie might feel that she is in no better position to choose between her children if she decides that their lives are of equal value (or on par), by comparison with the case in which she decides that she cannot determine the value-relation in which they stand.

9. Though in this case I might be in a position to "just pick." See Ullmann-Margalit and Morgenbesser (1977).

really, really want both goods. Thus dilemmas are in a way the opposite of intrinsic conflicts: the latter are characterized by an inability
to see both values at once, the former by an inability to do anything
but see both values at once. The most heart-wrenching dilemma
displays nothing more than the contingent unrealizability of two
desired outcomes. It does not differ, in the relevant respect, from the
aesthete's conflict between the movie and the concert. What I have
called intrinsic conflicts, on the other hand, are conflicts between the
values themselves.

Intrinsic conflicts are not resolvable by deliberation because one
cannot step back far enough from them to even get the deliberative
question in view. They are deliberatively irresolvable by being, in
the first place, deliberatively *unavailable.*

V. INTRINSIC CONFLICT AND
ETHICAL THEORY

In the moral psychological literature, the topic of deliberatively unavailable conflict has not been singled out for special treatment or
analysis, but it has been doing important philosophical work behind
the scenes. The fact that some conflicts are structured so as not to be
amenable to deliberative resolution has formed the basis for arguments for or against Aristotelian, Kantian, and consequentialist
theories.[10] I offer three examples.

10. Richard Holton (2004) also adverts to the phenomenon as part of his case for the distinctive (and perhaps irreducible) normative status of resolutions. He identifies (what is, in my
terminology,) an intrinsic conflict between, on the one hand, the value of holding fast to
what one has resolved to do and, on the other hand, the value represented by the temptations whose influence the resolution was formed to resist. So Homer resolves on Friday
to go jogging on Saturday morning even if he feels tired then. Come Saturday morning,
Homer cannot weigh the value of sticking to his resolution against the value of yielding to

John McDowell has criticized a picture of virtue on which "the virtuous person's judgment is a result of balancing reasons for and against" ([1979] 1998: 55). He offers an Aristotelian alternative: the virtuous person should not be understood as judging that, on balance, the reasons to act well outweigh the reasons to act badly. Rather, the reasons to act badly are simply not practically salient to him: "Some aspect of his situation is seen as constituting a reason for acting in some way; this reason is apprehended, not as outweighing or overriding any reasons for acting in other ways . . . but as silencing them." Whoever experiences as salient the reasons to desert his comrades has already, according to McDowell, put himself out of the running for courage. Such a person cannot (fully) redeem himself by going on to prioritize other, better reasons. The virtuous soldier is one who just doesn't experience reasons to desert as pressing or salient in the first place.

Bernard Williams makes a similar point about the conflict between partial and impartial values. Williams thinks that the natural way for a husband to resolve the question of which of several drowning people to save is simply to see that one of the drowning people is his wife. But Kantianism, according to Williams, requires the person to take into account the claim of each drowning person to be saved. Though the Kantian may allow the husband, in the end, to privilege the claim of his own wife ("in situations of this kind it is

his tiredness. For part of what it is to appreciate the value of being resolute, in this case, is to deem tiredness an irrelevant consideration. Holton takes it that when Homer resolved, on Friday, to go jogging on Saturday despite tiredness, he resolved that he would not, on Saturday, consider tiredness a reason to avoid jogging. Homer cannot, on Saturday, weigh the value of resoluteness against the value of sleep because asking this question entails already having abandoned the resolution. He can, of course, still weigh the considerations on the basis of which he has resolved—e.g., the fact that running promotes health—against the value of satisfying his desire to sleep. But to open up that deliberation is to abandon the prior work that he did in resolving.

permissible to save one's wife"), Williams finds it objectionable that the husband was required to deliberate in this way: "Such things as deep attachments to other persons will express themselves in the world in ways which cannot at the same time embody the impartial view" ([1976] 1981: 18). The point of view on value in which one impartially considers *everyone's* demand to be saved is incompatible with the one from which one person stands out as a special locus of importance. Williams charges that by forcing the husband to ascend to a level of deliberation that can include the value of others, the Kantian forces him to abandon his love for his wife. Williams, then, thinks that love, at least in some cases, conflicts *intrinsically* with Kantian morality.

David Sobel[11] deploys deliberative unavailability as an objection to consequentialism. A consequentialist defines the best choice as the choice of the option with the most value, and she is committed[12] to there being a fact of the matter about which option this is. One way to spell out that fact is to refer to the putative choice made by an "ideally informed agent" familiar with all the options in question. Sobel argues that the "the notion of a fully informed self is a chimera" (1994: 794) because the great variety of possibilities, choices, and lives an agent might lead are not available to a single consciousness. Consider, for instance, the difficulty of combining in one consciousness the point of view of a life characterized by certain forms of ignorance as to other lives (e.g., that of an ascetic hermit) and the

---

11. I've chosen Sobel as representative of those who hold a family of views objecting to consequentialism by objecting to the possibility of full-informedness. See also Rosati (1995), Velleman (1998), and Anderson (1997).

12. Peter Railton distinguishes himself from other, "overly optimistic," consequentialists in disavowing this commitment (1992: 735–736). He suggests that more modest consequentialists might simply concede that there is a certain amount of indeterminacy as to what someone ought to do. Sobel responds that this concession limits the force of the consequentialist injunction to maximize value (n. 4, p.785).

very lives of which such a person must be ignorant.[13] Sobel's argument for the impossibility of such an agent rests, then, on the claim that some of the values or points of view she would have to "reckon up" represent intrinsically conflicting points of view on value.

The intrinsic conflicts to which these authors refer us do not amount to psychologically real events occurring in a person. If the reasons of the coward and the reasons of the brave man belong to, or in, two different people, it is not clear that any single person can be torn between them. Williams's celebrated phrase, "one thought too many," indicts the husband for having as much as a Kantian *thought*. If the suggestion is that in a given situation one *either* inhabits the value-space of Kantian morality *or* one sees the world as a husband does, then there is no being "torn" between these outlooks. Sobel, likewise, describes the cases that interest him as those in which the very access to the value of one life might preclude another life from being "available to one's consciousness" (794). None of these philosophers is committed to the claim that a conflict from which one cannot step back can nonetheless be experienced.

On the other hand, none of them explicitly *denies* the possibility of such a conflict. And we have seen that it is possible, at least in some cases, to reconcile the presence of two incompatible ethical perspectives: we can understand them as placing competing demands on a subject's ethical attention. In this way we've defended a Frankfurtian commitment to the possibility of the *experience* of intrinsic conflict, such as being torn between love and strife. For Frankfurt insists that even after "identifying" with love and "externalizing" spite, such an agent might still *feel* both love and spite.[14]

---

13. Sobel's argument ranges over a wide variety of examples; I've fixated on the example of Ascetic vs. Epicure for the purposes of brevity.

14. "[H]e may continue to experience the rejected desire as occurring in his mental history" (1976: 250). ""[W]hen someone identifies himself with one of his desires, the result is not

The fact that they do not consider the possibility of psychologically real intrinsic conflicts means that McDowell, Sobel, and Williams are not moved to consider how one might resolve such a conflict. For us, as for Frankfurt, this is an important question.

VI. TWO SUGGESTIONS FOR RESOLVING INTRINSIC CONFLICTS

(a) By Identification (Frankfurt)

Intrinsic conflict cannot be resolved by deliberation. How, then, can it be resolved? On Frankfurt's view, an intrinsically conflicted (or "ambivalent") agent "decides" to cut off one of the two desires, "identifies" with the other, and thereby "constitutes himself" as wholehearted (1988: 170). After having made such a decision, "the person no longer holds himself apart from the desire to which he has committed himself. It is no longer unsettled or uncertain whether the object of that desire—that is, what he wants—is what he really wants" (1988: 170). Frankfurt depicts the agent as deciding between conflicting desires by standing back ("hold[ing] oneself apart") from them and somehow plumping for the one over the other ("mak[ing] up one's mind"; 1988: 172). It is at this point that we see the importance of articulating the precise *way* in which intrinsic conflicts are deliberatively irresolvable. For it turns out that the "decision" to which Frankfurt adverts here is appropriate only to resolving those conflicts where the deliberative question can be so much as posed.

> necessarily to eliminate the conflict between those desires, or even to reduce its severity, but to alter its nature . . . Quite possibly, the conflict between the two desires will remain as virulent as before" (1988: 172).

Consider, again, the many ways in which extrinsic conflicts may not be susceptible to deliberative resolution. Sometimes the agent does not have the time to do the requisite deliberating, or lacks crucial information, or finds her options to be of exactly equal value. In any of these cases, the agent can resolve the conflict by simply picking[15] one option instead of the other. This same method is available for the agent faced with incommensurable values: she can just pick. Of course, this is no guarantee that she *will* pick. Perhaps she is stymied by uncertainty long enough that the opportunity for choice simply passes, and she is stuck with one (or neither) of the options she couldn't choose between.

The point is that deciding for the one option over the other is a method of resolving extrinsic, and not intrinsic, conflicts. For the idea of a decision already invokes options being presented, as it were, side by side. Someone can make a decision between two things only if she can, in all seriousness, ask herself which of the two she should do. Recall our three extrinsically conflicted variants of the wife—the one who is teaching her husband a lesson, the one who knows the letter contains damaging revelations, and the one who is running for office. These people can "step back" and decide the conflict in terms of, respectively, love, hate, or political ambition. If the wife who *is* intrinsically conflicted tries to "step back" far enough from loving her husband that the value of causing him misery comes into view, she's stepped out of the attitude of love altogether.

Frankfurt imagines that the intrinsically conflicted agent who has not "resolved" his intrinsic conflict is "uncertain which side he is on, in the conflict between the two desires" (1988: 172) and that

---

15. I call this "simply" picking to contrast it with decisions that are products of deliberation. I do not mean to suggest that such acts of the will (and their attendant methods, e.g., coin flipping) are simple to understand. But it is not my task, here, to account for them. See Ullmann-Margalit and Morgenbesser (1977) for a discussion.

he is looking to resolve this uncertainty. But uncertainty is, in fact, a mark of extrinsic conflict, in particular those extrinsic conflicts that constitute dilemmas. The moviegoer might be so heavily invested both in seeing this movie and in attending this concert that he finds himself wavering between the two options, unable to decide which to do. He might say to himself, "I do not know whether I really want to attend the movie, or whether I instead prefer the concert." He might, then, use deliberation as a way of resolving this uncertainty. Agents who are intrinsically conflicted are, by contrast, not uncertain as to which side of the conflict they are on. If there is no question an agent seeks to answer, she cannot be described as uncertain.

Because the intrinsically conflicted agent cannot step back and get both options in view, her conflict takes an asymmetrical form. Frankfurt describes an intrinsically conflicted agent thus: "Suppose that a person wants to compliment an acquaintance for a recent achievement, but that he also notices within himself a jealously spiteful desire to injure the man" (1976: 249). The desire to compliment constitutes, at this moment, this agent's "main" perspective, one from which the desire to injure represents, at this moment, the irritating (or disturbing) distraction. Such a person does not seriously entertain the possibility that injuring is the right thing to do; he is looking for ways to silence or ignore this impulse. When the desire to injure appears on the scene, a negative judgment has already been entered against it. The way in which such an agent combines love and spite is akin to the way in which we "combine" incompatible demands on our perceptual or cognitive attention: we attend (however briefly) to one of the two, and experience the other as a diminishment or defect in that very attention. We actively try to silence the one demand and accentuate the other. We may flit back and forth over some stretch of time, but at any given moment, we favor either the one side or the other.

In theory, it seems that we should allow for the case in which one feels *exactly as much* love as spite in a given moment, but it is in fact hard to imagine what that is like. When an ethical outlook dominates, then there is something the agent is doing, e.g. pursuing her husband's happiness, and something that is distracting her from doing that, e.g. pursuing his misery. Someone perched on the knife edge of love and hate cannot be described as doing both. Trying to love and hate at the same time is like trying to philosophize and take care of the baby at the same time—under the presupposition that one cannot do both. Such an agent would be frozen, like a deer in the headlights. She would be neither loving nor hating (nor deliberating between loving and hating, since that can't be done). If such a state is a psychological possibility, it does not represent a state of uncertainty or reflection. Rather, it is some form of mental disturbance in which the presence of conflicting desires is so extreme as to be valuationally disabling. Without empirical investigation, it is hard to know what to say about this condition, but I suspect we may end up saying that the attempt to feel too many things at once leads to not feeling anything at all. We should not be fooled by the fact that a "frozen" agent—if she exists—may look, from the outside, like one who is stepping back and reflecting. It is important not to confuse a state of distress with a state of inquiry, though both dispose someone to stand still and not do anything. If "frozenness" is possible, it is not typical; and it does not vindicate the possibility of resolving intrinsic conflict by deliberating (or deciding).

Frozenness aside, intrinsic conflict is characteristically asymmetrical. Its resolution must, therefore, take a distinctive form. What one wants, in seeking to resolve an intrinsic conflict, is to fully inhabit a point of view, to act undistractedly, to stop hearing a "wrong" voice. An intrinsically conflicted agent will not necessarily vacillate between her two outlooks—it might be the case that one of them always dominates—but those who do will also look to resolution as an end to this vacillation. Frankfurt misunderstands the problem of intrinsic conflict as one of uncertainty. His solution—identification—doesn't solve the real problem. Frankfurt acknowledges that "when someone identifies himself with one rather than with another of his own desires, the result is not necessarily to eliminate the conflict between those desires, or even to reduce its severity" (1988: 172). Insofar as identification is compatible with the desire remaining exactly as strong—and thus exactly as distracting—as it always was, it doesn't resolve the agent's feeling of conflictedness. Nor does identification insulate someone against future vacillation. Suppose the wife "identifies with" her love, but in the next moment, experiences such a powerful upsurge of spite that she is now gleefully driven by spiteful hatred. She cannot, on Frankfurt's view, still be said to be identified with her love. For Frankfurt denies that there is any *historical* dimension to identification. But if this is right, then Frankfurt can draw no distinction between the desire I identify with and the desire that holds the psychologically dominant position.[16]

Before turning to my solution, I would like to address a worry as to the coherence of my description of intrinsic conflict. I have argued that the agent cannot get the conflict into view by occupying

---

16. To argue that identification/externalization doesn't resolve intrinsic conflict is not to expose these concepts as empty. For Frankfurt, as has often been observed, uses them to do a variety of jobs. There is a psychological job, where "external" means something akin to phenomenologically alien (in the mode of obsessional thoughts). And then there is a normative job, where "external" means something like "not arrived at by/sanctioned by my reasoning." Schroeder and Arpaly (1999) point out that I needn't, for instance, experience psychological alienation from any desire that moves me akratically. Nor do I need to be identified with one that moves me enkratically. Each of these two senses of "externality" comes apart from the other—Schroeder and Arpaly argue that we should prefer an interpretation of Frankfurt on which we privilege the psychological sense, whereas Moran (2002) argues that it is better to emphasize the normative sense. The debate between them is untouched by the criticism I offer here, since neither sense is dependent on conceiving of identification as the solution to intrinsic conflict.

a third, more reflective perspective encompassing both of her intrinsically conflicting values. This is because the values tend to annihilate one another: the value-nexus of each contains attitudes that undermine the legitimacy of the other. In that case, one might wonder how it is possible for the agent to so much as register the conflict. Intrinsically conflicted agents are aware of their conflict, and experience their condition as a kind of turmoil they would like to resolve. Doesn't this imply that there is at least some sense in which they occupy a third perspective?

On my account, the conflict between the two values is indeed experienced by the agent, because she registers the nondominant perspective in the fact that she cannot completely inhabit the dominant one. So in a loving moment, her spite manifests in an inability to be *completely* loving, in the fact that she must try and struggle to love. Why doesn't her very recognition of this fact constitute a third perspective? It could. This agent could observe herself and note that she is a curious specimen, moved by both love and hate. My point is only that whatever attitude she takes, if it encompasses both of the conflicting values, it cannot be a point of view from which she *deliberates*. She cannot take both the mailing and trashing seriously as options for dealing with the letter in her hand. These options can both occur to her, and they can both motivate her, but she cannot deliberate between them. It is important, in this context, to observe that not everything that motivates us is something that can show up for us in deliberation. For instance, if I am self-deceived about my desire to hurt someone's feelings (I think I am just offering her constructive criticism), then I will not ask myself, "Shall I hurt her feelings now?" I may well be motivated by a desire to hurt her feelings, but I cannot deliberate as to whether I ought to hurt them. For a different reason, the person who is intrinsically conflicted can be motivated to mail or to trash, but she cannot ask herself which of the two forms of motivation is better. She could ask herself whether trashing the letter or burning it and leaving the ashes on his desk is a better way to exact her revenge, or whether dropping it in the mailbox or delivering it herself is a better way to help him out. By contrast, the options of mailing and trashing cannot cohere into a single deliberative question.

(b) By Aspiration

Extrinsic conflicts are typically resolved when the agent makes a choice, either in accordance with a deliberative judgment as to which option is better, or in spite of having formed such a judgment (akratically), or in the face of the impossibility of forming such a judgment (no time to deliberate, incommensurable or equal values, not enough information, etc.). If she delays long enough that the opportunity for choice passes, the conflict ends without her resolving it. Either way, such conflict is short-lived. One doesn't go through one's whole life wondering which of two things one should do. Intrinsic conflicts, by contrast, can be life-long. Some relationships just are "complicated," whether they be with individuals (relatives, friends, bosses), aspects of ourselves (body image, heritage, sexuality), larger entities or groups of people (one's country, the institution at which one is employed, the intelligentsia, the media), or even ideas (feminism, relativism, liberalism). Indeed, some "complexity," some of the time, seems to be the norm for creatures like us. Resolution is rarely completed to a point of McDowellian purity; we are likely to, at the very least, undergo the odd twinge reminding us of the rejected point of view. It is better to think in terms of progress toward resolution. This is, perhaps, all that the wife asks of herself: to become more loving, less spiteful.

Resolution, even of this partial or incomplete kind, is different from other ways in which the conflict might come to a close. To resolve an intrinsic conflict, we exercise our agency in the service of seeing things more harmoniously. Not all forms of conflict diminishment qualify as resolution of the relevant conflict—resolving is a specific way of ending. Death ends all conflicts, and divorce could be one way of ending the wife's conflict without, fundamentally, changing the way she sees things. Outside forces can, likewise, end some extrinsic conflicts by removing the occasion for the exercise or activation of some valuational disposition. We can play the part of such an outside force in relation to another, and even sometimes to ourselves. We do this when we alter our own circumstances so that one side of the conflict rarely has opportunity to arise, acting on ourselves in the mode of Aristotle's self-doctoring doctor. Let me set aside these various forms of self-management and restrict the term "resolution" to what we do in a properly first-personal way to change our valuational outlook. For that is what Frankfurt was after in proposing identification as a mode of conflict resolution. Is there some act of her will—not deliberation, not identification, but some other option—the performing of which would resolve an intrinsic conflict? Yes.

An agent resolves her extrinsic conflicts by deciding, possibly as a result of deliberating. An agent resolves her intrinsic conflicts by aspiring. Aspiration is the diachronic process by which an agent effects change on her own ethical point of view. Aspirants aim to direct their own ethical attention in such a way as to more fully appreciate one value or set of values and to become immune or insensitive to those values that intrinsically conflict with the first set. An aspirant is someone who works to improve her desires, her feelings, her ethical evaluations, and, more generally, her own capacity for responding to reasons.

Just as we can distinguish a kick that is willed from a kick produced by reflex, so too we can distinguish two ways in which someone can become less spiteful. A non-aspiring variant of the wife—perhaps she was raised to think that marriages are by nature "complicated"—might surprise herself by gravitating in the direction of unspiteful love. An aspiring variant of the wife might, by contrast, fail in her project of becoming less spiteful. The aspirant has marked out one attitude as a kind of target toward which she orients herself, and another (or others) as a danger from which she must turn herself away. An agent who "identifies," in Frankfurt's sense, with some desire, constitutes herself as being in some condition at the time at which she so identifies. She fixes her own identity, statically, by deciding. The aspirant stands in a dynamic relation to "her true self"; aspiring does not make it the case that she *is* her true self. Aspiring is the method by which she works to become her true self.

The problem of intrinsic conflict is a problem of divided ethical attention, and so one would expect that the solution would come by way of a redirection of attention. Intrinsically conflicted agents are, as we have noted, in the business of redirecting their own attention. They ignore those facts, people, or mental images, attention to which would bring to light one (distracting) set of reasons, and they focus on those associated with another, incompatible (dominant) set of reasons. Intrinsically conflicted agents interfere in their own thinking; intrinsically conflicted *aspirants* interfere for the sake of effecting long-term change. In the next chapter we will look more closely at this difference by examining a non-aspirational manifestation of intrinsic conflict. For now, we can say: a conflicted wife tries not to look at the trash can, in order to ensure that she acts like her less spiteful counterpart and mails the letter; a conflicted and aspiring wife tries not to look at the trash can, both in order to mail the letter and in order to become her less spiteful counterpart. Her goal is to handle these conflict situations in such a way as to eventually mitigate their occurrence. She directs her attention with the aim of giving it a new shape. Both characters attempt to reason as though they were the straightforwardly loving wife, but the aspiring wife, again, does so aspirationally—in order to become the loving wife.

As in the case of the willed and unwilled kicks, skeptical worries will arise. Someone might doubt whether there really is anything *to* aspiration over and above someone's ending up with a different character. A skeptic might deny that there is a principled difference between ending up less spiteful as a result of *willing* that state and ending up less spiteful through accident or external influence. In chapter 5, I argue that it is, in fact, possible to exercise one's will with the aim of becoming a different—better—person. My interest here has not been in defending the possibility of willfully becoming someone any more than in defending the possibility of willfully kicking. My interest has been to articulate the difference between becoming and kicking. So it is perhaps safer, until we have the argument of chapter 5, to state my conclusion in the form of a conditional: *if* there is any resolution of intrinsic conflict, it will have to take the form of aspiration.

But how fundamental is the difference between aspiration and identification? A supporter of Frankfurt might suggest that we reconstitute identification as deciding to aspire or as making up one's mind as to what to aspire to. This will not work. First, *deciding* to aspire doesn't resolve anything. What resolves conflict is aspiration itself, the temporally extended work of changing ourselves, our values, our desires, our outlook. The problem with Frankfurtian externalization is that there is nowhere for the rejected but still existent desire to go but back into oneself. A desire must be *someone's* desire. Aspirants *externalize* the desire all the way into nonexistence.

Second, aspiration is not always or even typically heralded by a *decision* to begin engaging in it. Not that it can't be: perhaps the wife "decides to aspire" at the revelatory moment when she first sees her husband holding their newborn child. Until that point, she has acquiesced in their "conflicted" relationship, but the sight before her occasions in her a resolution to become a different kind of spouse. But that needn't be how it goes. Quite often we simply find that we have, for a while now, been aspiring to become more loving and less spiteful in some relationship. It doesn't undermine the status of the aspiration as the work of the agent's own will that there was no moment at which she "made a decision" to engage in it. Likewise for the case of ceasing to aspire: it can be a matter of consciously, suddenly, giving up, or one can give up little by little, without realizing it, over a long time. The presence or absence of a decision seems to make no difference to cases like these. And that is because they concern a form of willing that does not happen in a moment, but over long stretches of time.

It is a theme of Frankfurt's work, early and late, to reject genealogical explanations in favor of what he calls "structural" explanations. He wants, for instance, to resist the idea—which he associates with Aristotle—that an agent could be responsible for what she does at one time in virtue of something she did at another, earlier time.[17] What matters, according to Frankfurt, is what the

---

17. "This suggests another respect in which Aristotle's theory is unsatisfactory. He maintains that a person may be responsible for his own character on account of having taken (or having failed to take) measures that affect what his habitual dispositions are. In other words, a person acquires responsibility for his own character, according to Aristotle, by acting in ways that are causally instrumental in bringing it about that he has the particular set of dispositions of which his character is constituted. I think that Aristotle's treatment of this subject is significantly out of focus because of his preoccupation with causal origins and causal responsibility. The fundamental responsibility of an agent with respect to his own character is not a matter of whether it is as the effect of his own actions that the agent has certain dispositions to feel and to behave in various ways. That bears only on the question of

agent wills or identifies with *at the time of* action, and not earlier. And so he endeavors to capture the ethically salient features of personhood in terms of relations in which the agent stands to herself (her desires, motives, commitments) at the time of action. But some of the relations in which an agent stands to herself might be essentially historical. To be an aspirant is to proceed away from some (rejected) past set of desires, commitments, etc. toward a different, anticipated future desire set of desires, commitments, etc. Aspiration is a form of ethical movement, and nothing can move in a moment.

Aristotle had no notion of the will.[18] Those of us who do have some tendency to understand it as something that acts ("decides") instantaneously. But the will, like the agent herself, has a variety of tasks, and some of them take longer than others. Frankfurt was on to something important when he pointed us to a conflict that differs in kind from the familiar concert/movie variety. And he was right that the resolution of this other kind of conflict presents a new and exciting philosophical problem. But he did not fully grasp how new and how exciting this problem is. Intrinsic conflicts reveal the diachronic work of the will, and they do so because they cannot be resolved in a moment.

When we are extrinsically conflicted, we are able to survey the values between which we are torn from a reflective distance. What happens next can take a variety of forms: we may deliberatively

whether the person is responsible for having these characteristics. The question of whether the person is responsible for his own character has to do with whether he has taken responsibility for his characteristics. It concerns whether the dispositions at issue, regardless of whether their existence is due to the person's own initiative and causal agency or not, are characteristics with which he identifies and which he thus by his own will incorporates into himself as constitutive of what he is" (Frankfurt 1988: 171–172).

18. For a discussion see Frede and Long (2012: ch. 2).

resolve the conflict, we may decide without deliberating, or we may find ourselves stymied by indecision. When we are intrinsically conflicted, no such synoptic position is available to us. Instead of stepping back to a neutral point of view, aspirants step forward— little by little—into a state of lessened conflict.

Chapter 4

Akrasia

In the preceding chapter, I argued that there is a kind of conflict, intrinsic conflict, that is not deliberatively resolvable: deliberation doesn't tell a person which of her evaluative perspectives to prefer. Rather, the conflict is structured asymmetrically from the outset. If such an agent deliberates from her current ethical position, she must do so by ignoring or setting aside the reasons of her subordinate evaluative perspective. She deliberates from a purified version of her dominant evaluative perspective, as though she were unafflicted by the reasons she cannot factor in.

In this chapter, we will face up to the fact that deliberating *as though* one didn't have certain feelings, desires, and thoughts doesn't change the fact that one has them. The reasons of the subordinate perspective are, despite their exclusion from such deliberation, nonetheless present to the conflicted agent. The conflicted agent feels them and is, at times, moved by them in spite of her deliberation to the contrary. On these occasions, the truth she is trying to ignore in her reasoning rears its ugly head in her action. I will argue that this phenomenon is the same as the one also known as akrasia, weakness of will, or incontinence. At first glance, this may seem a surprising analysis, since that phenomenon is standardly analyzed by philosophers in quite a different way.

I. DEFINING AKRASIA

The familiar case of akrasia is that of an agent who finds herself, e.g., eating or imbibing or smoking or sleeping more than she thinks she should. She judges that she has most reason to refrain from indulging, and yet she willingly indulges. In order to qualify as akrasia, the action must possess both of these features: the agent must see it as irrational, and she must perform it intentionally. The phenomenon is paradoxical because, on a naive approach to action theory, what makes an action intentional is simply that the agent sees it as rational. If she *willingly* indulged, she must have thought that she had reason to; and if she indulged despite the fact that reason forbade it, she must have done so unwillingly. On one popular interpretation of Plato's *Protagoras*, this was precisely the line of reasoning that led Socrates to deny that akrasia is possible.[1] All purported cases of akrasia are, on this "Socratic" picture, to be redescribed as ones in which a person was unable to resist some desire or failed to believe she ought to have acted otherwise. There is no akrasia; there is only compulsion or ignorance.

Most philosophers find the Socratic move unnecessary, judging that the tension between "irrational" and "intentional" can be resolved by differentiating between acting on *a* reason and acting on one's best reason. This solution derives from Donald Davidson's pioneering paper, "How Is Weakness of the Will Possible?" ([1970] 1980). Davidson faulted his predecessors[2] for forcing akratic conflict into the mold of reason vs. passion, which,

---

1. See Santas (1966: esp. 31) on the dilemma; for a different interpretation see Callard (2014).
2. Plato, Aristotle, Aquinas, Butler, and Mill come in for special criticism, but Davidson also generalizes the point: "I know no clear case of a philosopher who recognizes that incontinence is not essentially a problem in moral philosophy, but a problem in philosophy of action" ([1970] 1980: 30 n. 14).

as he understood it, not only made it hard to see how akrasia is possible, but also placed an unnecessarily moralistic restriction on the cases to be accounted for. The akratic who is moved to sensual indulgence against the dictates of temperance or courage or justice is, he notes, only one kind of akratic. Davidson eschewed any substantive restriction on the kinds of reasons the akratic acts on or against, in favor of a more formal approach in which akrasia is understood as acting on a reason that is worse or weaker than another reason one could have acted on. He points out that akratics can act on (and against) just about any kind of reason, offering as an example someone who akratically rises from bed to brush his teeth against his considered judgment that it would be best to stay in bed and go to sleep. In pressing us to recognize *anyone* who acts against her better judgment as akratic, Davidson was, at the same time, urging us to see that reason is located on both sides of the conflict.

If Davidson is right, what makes akrasia irrational is not the failure to act on a reason, but the inferiority of the reason one does act on. What, then, is the nature of this inferiority? Why do we call the judgment that the akratic acts against her "better judgment"? The judgment cannot be better because of the kind of value it promotes, if we want to allow for the possibility of being akratically prudent or perhaps even akratically moral. Davidson calls the agent's better judgment her "all-things-considered judgment." Having compared her reason to indulge with her reason to refrain, the akratic judges that, all things considered, she should refrain. The strength of such a judgment lies in the fact that one of the things considered in it is the reason to act as the akratic goes on to act. While the one judgment says, "I should eat, because the cookie would be tasty," her all-things-considered judgment says, "I should refrain from eating, even though it would be tasty."

Because Davidson claims that the judgment owes its authority to the fact that it has taken account of the opposing consideration, I call this view "inclusivism." Inclusivism is a way of underwriting Davidson's fundamental insight that the authority of the judgment the akratic acts against is *deliberative*. The akratic's action is wrong not because she (necessarily) violates any moral principle or yields to some base passion. Her sin is irrationality as such, a violation of deliberative procedure.

As Arthur Walker (1989) brings out in a survey article on akrasia, the large literature spawned by Davidson's paper converges on little other than an acceptance of the inclusivist assumption that akratics act on a reason they acknowledge as weaker than another they could have acted on.[3] And this assumption traces directly to the formal theory of akrasia: the inclusiveness of the stronger reason grounds the status of the relevant judgment as *better*. Inclusivists hold that the akratic acts intentionally but irrationally, because she fails to act on the sum total of her reasons. The akratic acts on *a* reason, but she fails to act on what she takes to be her best reason (Davidson [1970] 1980: 42 n. 25). She acts on her weaker reason, the one outweighed in the deliberation of which her better judgment is the upshot. This is a popular and intuitive account of akrasia, but it faces what I call the "double-counting problem."

II. ACTING ON A WEAKER REASON?

In my paper "The Weaker Reason" (Callard 2015), I argue that it is *impossible* to act on one's weaker reason. If one has discounted the rational force of one consideration in favor of another, one cannot

---

3. I update Walker's summary with some additional references in Callard (2015: 82 n. 3).

then take the first consideration as a reason to act. If the reason the akratic acts on has been counted in her deliberations, it cannot be counted again, independently, as a reason to act. I argue that on the standard account of akrasia, the akratic emerges as engaging in an unintelligible form of double counting, instead of an eminently intelligible form of self-indulgence. Without presenting the full argument here, let me try to convey some of its force by introducing an absurd case that fits the description "acting on one's weaker reason."

Offered a choice between $100 and $200, J chooses $100. When asked why she made that choice, she says, "$100 is still good—I had *some* reason to pick $100; I just had a *stronger* reason to pick $200. I acted on my weaker reason."

In these kinds of circumstances, we are not inclined to think we have a case of akrasia on our hands. If we can accept the case as described, we will do so by diagnosing J with some more substantial form of rational breakdown than akrasia. The problem seems to be the fact that she has exactly the same sorts of reasons to choose the $100 as she has to choose the $200. Since they are identical apart from amount, any reason J has to take the $100 *has already been accounted for* in her judgment that it would be better, overall, to take the $200. The $100 still has value, of course, but this value cannot, in this context, serve as J's reason to choose it. For the value has already been tallied in the reasoning that concludes in the judgment that it would be best to choose the $200. Akratic actions make a certain kind of sense to us; J's choice of $100, by contrast, doesn't make any sense at all.[4]

---

4. I am not the first to observe that the theory of akrasia needs to account for the unintelligibility of this sort of example. Peacocke raises it as an unsolved puzzle at the end of his 1985 paper: "We do find akrasia especially puzzling when there are no imaginative or perceptual asymmetries: it is hard to understand the man who with two bottles of the same kind of wine

Akratics typically don't find themselves faced with such homogeneous choices. It is intelligible that someone manages to eat the cookie even after judging that she will be happier, overall, if she sticks to her diet. In that kind of case, we can see how the appeal of the akratic action might survive the judgment that it would be better to do something else. But inclusivists cannot exploit this difference between the two cases so long as they retain their commitment to locating the authority of the akratic's "better judgment" in its inclusiveness. For the heterogeneity in the two values can be relevant to the akratic choice only insofar as it presents deliberative obstacles that impede the formation of an inclusive judgment.

Let me explain. Suppose that someone, having been offered an especially delicious cookie, knows that she will feel immense self-satisfaction if she refrains from eating it. But she also knows that she will really enjoy the taste of the cookie. Until she has reckoned which of these two values outweighs the other, she hasn't formed the kind of judgment that is, according to the inclusivist, akratically violable. If, for instance, she simply cannot say whether self-satisfaction outweighs pleasure, or vice versa, she leaves the issue of "best overall action" undecided. Whether she eats the cookie or refrains, the inclusivist cannot call her action akratic—for she did not form a "better judgment" in (what the inclusivist takes to be) the relevant sense.

in front of him, and with no imaginative differences between the two, chooses the one he believes to be the less good vintage" (72–73). Tappolet (2003) proposes that the solution is that the relevant asymmetries are supplied by the presence of *emotion*. But it does not seem to be true that one must invoke emotions in order to set up a case of akrasia: the standard cookie case does not involve emotion, only appetite. I think the fact that akratics are sometimes moved by emotion is itself to be explained in terms of intrinsic conflict: emotions set up the possibility for akrasia exactly when they mark the presence of intrinsic conflicts. (And they often do.)

Value-heterogeneity might occasion a failure to take into account some feature of what one is about to do. Perhaps she was pressed to make an immediate decision (the cookies were about to be taken away!) and she didn't have time to reckon up the value of eating against that of sticking to her diet. Perhaps she couldn't make a total accounting because (she believed that) the value of the cookie— taste—and the value of the diet—health—are incommensurable. In any of these cases her "better judgment" will not be better in the relevant sense: it won't be inclusive of her weaker reason. The inclusivist faces a dilemma. So long as the agent's judgment leaves out the value of the weaker reason, it is not "better" in the relevant sense: the inclusivist cannot take it as being akratically violable. But if, on the other hand, the distinctive value contained in the "weaker reason" is fully accounted for, heterogeneity in value does not help explain how someone might act on a reason. The inclusivist can- not explain why the fact that our akratic options don't look like J's options is relevant to our understanding of akrasia. This is because the inclusivist takes the job of deliberation to be that of making our option's look like J's.

Here is a case that, in a different way from that of J, should moti- vate us to be disturbed by inclusivism: S eats the cookie although she knows it contains a tasteless lethal poison. It will be strange to say of S, "Though she saw that it would be better overall to refrain from eating the cookie, the fact that the cookie was pleasant none- theless motivated her to eat it." People are not "overcome" by desire for a sweet treat to the extent that they disregard their own lives. Once again, there is a way in which akrasia is intelligible to us, and that form of intelligibility is missing from this case. But if inclusiv- ism is true, this is hard to explain. For if the tastiness of the cookie continues to serve as a reason to eat it once outweighed, this should be as true in the poison case as in the dieting case. Though we can speak of *how much* stronger reason A is than reason B, the relation of outweighing is not one that comes in degrees (i.e., either reason A outweighs reason B, or it doesn't). Given that the weaker reason has already been outweighed, it is not clear how its capacity to motivate could depend on the strength of the countervailing consideration. The situation is that on the inclusivist's picture, even after the stronger reason has done its outweighing, the opposing reason stands.

A good account of akrasia should put us in a position to explain why, if we were faced with an agent such as S, we would be inclined not to characterize her action as akratic but rather as, e.g., in possession of a suicidal wish or of a heroin-like addiction to cookies. The inclusivist cannot explain why we are inclined to reinterpret the case as non-akratic when the stakes are raised in this way.

Let me take stock. The inclusivist says that the akratic's better judgment earns the designation "better" by including (i.e., having accounted for) the "weaker" reason on which she acts. On this picture, the authority of the better judgment comes from the fact that it is the akratic's net judgment, reflecting the balance of reasons in his rational bank account. But I have raised doubts as to whether akratics can be motivated by a reason of this kind, any more than a sane person can akratically choose $100 over $200 or akratically throw away her life over a tasty cookie.

What will the inclusivist say to this argument? I am not sure. Perhaps he will find a way out, some escape hatch that invalidates my double-counting argument. Or perhaps he will decide to join the "Socratic" camp and become an akrasia skeptic. I am not going to pursue this dialectic with the inclusivist any further. I hope I have done enough to show that despite the intuitiveness and popularity of inclusivism, an alternative is worthy of consideration.

III. AKRASIA AND INTRINSIC CONFLICT

If we reject Davidsonian inclusivism, we must offer an alternative explanation as to what makes akrasia irrational. I do not want to retreat to the view that akratics act from passion, against reason. I must, however, grant that without inclusivism, it becomes harder to see how there can be reason on both sides of the conflict. If a reason acknowledged to be weaker cannot be the reason upon which the akratic acts, it is not clear what will underwrite the authority of the akratically violated reason. Why do we say she acts against her *better* judgment if that judgment is neither issued by an intrinsically superior motivational source (prudence/morality), nor inclusive of the judgment she acts on?

My proposal, as I suggested earlier, is that we invoke the framework of intrinsic conflict to analyze akrasia. Akratics are agents whose "better judgment" is simply the judgment issued by their dominant evaluative perspective. For this is the perspective from which they deliberate. Like Davidson, I think that the authority of the akratically violated judgment is deliberative:[5] the reason they act *on* belongs to their subordinate evaluative perspective, the one excluded from deliberation.

5. Why think that deliberation *has* any authority? Jonathan Bennett (1974; see also McIntyre 1993; Arpaly 2003; Jones 2003) has drawn our attention to cases in which someone acts well by acting akratically—so called rational akrasia. Someone's dominant ethical perspective might be inferior, especially when the person has been subject to corrupt educators. This is what seems to happen to Huck Finn, who—at least on Bennett's reading of him—has a head filled with bad moral views but a heart that is (roughly) in the right place. We will take the pervasiveness of akrasia as a problem only insofar as we think that, by and large, the perspective that dominates also ought to dominate. This seems to be a plausible assumption but one whose defense lies outside the scope of this book. Like Davidson, I simply assume that there is such a thing as deliberative authority, and thus that it is, at least by and large, rational to act in accordance with one's dominant, deliberative evaluative perspective. For further discussion of the Huck Finn case see section V.

Notice, first, that if this interpretation of akrasia succeeded, it would avoid the double-counting problem. Suppose that someone akratically φ-es, for reason R. Because the conflict between her reason not to φ and R is deliberatively unavailable, R has not been counted in the deliberations that bring the agent to the conclusion that she should not φ. She isn't double-counting when she subsequently acts on R. For that is the first time she takes it to count in favor of φ-ing.

But does it succeed: is it true that the akratic's conflict is deliberatively unavailable? Before assessing whether we can model akrasia on intrinsic conflict, it will be helpful to refresh our intuitions of what the experience of the latter is like. Consider a literary example. Zafar, the protagonist of Zia Haider Rahman's novel *In the Light of What We Know*, was born in Bangladesh but raised in London from early childhood. As a pre-teen he is sent back to Bangladesh to learn something of his origins. He describes his arrival in Bangladesh:

> Spread along the platform was a mass of bobbing black hair like a long wave of silk. Suddenly I felt the first stirrings of what I would later come to recognize as kinship, a feeling that alarmed me, a sense that I was of a piece with a group of people for the most basic reasons, simple to the senses and irrational. They all looked like me. (2014: 53)

Zafar is "alarmed" by a feeling he cannot name, an "irrational" sense that he belongs in or is a part of the foreign community that surrounds him. His rational judgment says that he is an alien interloper in this place. Though he was born there, he cannot remember it and does not consider it home. Had Zafar articulated this judgment more fully, he might, given his character's intellectual bent and multicultural upbringing, have claimed that where you belong depends not on how you look but how you think. But he responds in a visceral way to the sight of people who look like himself, *as though* belonging were a matter of racial similarity. He evidently takes the fact that people look like him as a reason to consider them "his own." For notice that, although he disavows this impulse as "irrational," he also describes himself as moved by "the most basic reasons." These reasons are, in Rahman's beautiful phrase, "simple to the senses."

Zafar experiences a reason to consider himself "home," but this very reason strikes him, on reflection, as irrelevant to that question. If Zafar is intrinsically conflicted, there is no contradiction here: Zafar's dominant, cosmopolitan evaluative perspective is blind to the rational force of kinship. My suggestion is that akratics are like Zafar, being moved by a reason that, from a certain vantage point, strikes them as being no reason at all.

Let us illustrate with a typical case of akrasia. On the one hand, my commitment to dieting provides me with what I take to be a strong reason to refrain from eating another cookie; on the other hand, the deliciousness of the cookie gives me reason to indulge. Nonetheless, I am not undecided or hesitant as to what I should do. I firmly conclude that I ought to refrain *even though eating the cookie would be so pleasant*. I might even insist that *I see that I will have more pleasure overall if I refrain from eating this cookie*. Doesn't it follow that I have accounted for the value of eating the cookie—pleasure—in my judgment that I ought to refrain? Aren't we forced into an inclusivist analysis of such a case?

No. The pleasure of eating a tasty cookie could give rise to a variety of reasons. For instance, I might know that it will make Sally proud if I enjoy the especially delicious cookies she has put so much effort into baking. Or I may hope that the pleasure from eating the cookie will distract me from my heartache. If the pleasure I feel from eating the cookie is meant to make Sally happy or to dull some pain, the justification of my eating is very different from the one in which I pursue it for its own sake. But even that—pursuing pleasure for its own sake—can be done in more ways than one. If I aim to maximize the amount of pleasure that accrues to me over the course of my life, I count only the size of the pleasures and not their proximity; if my aim is to have pleasure *now*, proximity gains relevance. The akratic's "better judgment" may, then, take the pleasure of the cookie into consideration in one way, namely as one pleasure among the many she may have over the course of her life. But it is not because she thinks of the pleasure in *this* way that the akratic is moved to pursue it.

But is it plausible to say that the akratic is possessed of an evaluative perspective that places paramount value on proximity? Let us suppose that, if asked, she would deny that a pleasure is better because it comes sooner. She might, nonetheless, manifest a commitment to this proposition in what she does. For it is certainly true that there was a time in her life when she manifested such a commitment in virtually everything she did. As young children we pursued only proximate pleasures or pains. Being able to adopt the point of view on which one's future good and, eventually, the good of others emerges as something of value is an ethical achievement; likewise for goods that do not relieve basic bodily needs or provide us with physical pleasure. When we learn to value more than the fulfillment of our immediate bodily needs, we shift away from the ethical perspective of early childhood. But we do not lose access to it entirely, both because growing up is, as they say, a process and because there are situations (dancing, partying, sex, vacation, yoga) where the point of view on which we simply attend to the feelings of the moment becomes, once again, appropriate.

When we are akratic, we do not judge that we are in one of situations. Nonetheless, the temptation to eat the cookie is precisely a temptation to act as though we were. To see the eating of the cookie as a good thing to do, despite the fact that we have judged it to violate our long-term benefit, is to apprehend its goodness with blinkers on: in terms of immediate pleasure, without regard for what pleasures and pains are to come. Akratics would not assent to the proposition "Immediate pleasure is the only thing that matters." For their dominant evaluative perspective—the one from which they issue deliberative judgments—precisely does not operate on this principle. Nonetheless, I contend, that proposition is an accurate description of what it feels like to be tempted. When we want to eat the cookie irrespective of what we will have to pay later on, the thought-content of that feeling is that *only this pleasure matters*. We do not *believe* that only this pleasure matters—the source of our deliberative activity outright rejects that thought, as part and parcel of its rejection of that feeling. This is what a subordinate evaluative perspective looks like: it is not a place from which to deliberate or reason about what to do, but it is nonetheless a place from which reasons for action spring.

Has the akratic taken the tastiness of the cookie into consideration or not? My claim is that the tastiness of the cookie gives rise to two different rational considerations. One of these—the fact that the cookie will contribute just this much pleasure to my life overall—gets taken into account, and outweighed, in the akratic's deliberations. The other—the fact that I want something tasty NOW—has not been reckoned in those deliberations. This is because it shows up as a consideration in favor of eating only from a value-perspective that conflicts intrinsically with the one from which she deliberates. These two reasons can both be expressed with the phrase "The cookie is tasty," but the difference between them will often show up in tone or stress. Consider a familiar form of akratic speech: "I know I'll have more pleasure overall if I don't eat it . . . *but* the cookie is *so tasty.*" The "but" clause is not intended as a corrective to her earlier assessment of what she takes herself to know. It does not continue or reopen her deliberations; rather, it pulls away from the whole project of deliberating. It represents a different thought from the one she had when she originally said to herself, "On the one hand, the cookie is tasty; on the other hand, I'm dieting." The difference in tone or emphasis marks a difference in the way the tastiness is apprehended, and this, in turn, corresponds to a difference in her reasons.

The akratic's intrinsic conflict prevents these two reasons from being in conversation with one another. On the one hand, she deliberates in such a way as not to recognize the force of the fact that she wants pleasure NOW, which is to say, as though she were unproblematically committed to prudence. On the other hand, the point of view she adopts insofar as she experiences herself as having reason to indulge is, in turn, one from which she is immune to the force of the prudential considerations that strike her as having such deliberative significance.

But is such action *free?*[6] Someone might worry that by severing the akratic action from deliberation, I have succumbed to the compulsion horn of the Socratic dilemma. It lies outside the scope of this book to offer an account of intentional action beyond that of acting on a reason. One might, however, wonder whether the reasons of the subordinate evaluative perspective are really the agent's own. I think the subordinate evaluative perspective cannot be assimilated to an outside force acting on the agent, and this precisely for the Davidsonian reason that it presents her with considerations in favor of acting a certain way. It is rational enough to count as internal. I have posited that values are what constitute an agent's

---

6. Thanks to Sarah Paul for pressing this objection.

self; but there is no reason to restrict her identity to the subset of those values that cohere with one another or the subset from which she deliberates. She *is* also the parts of herself she would (at times) rather be without.

How, then, will we distinguish akrasia from compulsion, in which the agent is "acted on" by an outside force—even if the force may be "inside" her body, such as drug addiction? Supposing that the addict takes the drug compulsively, what explains her action is the effect of the drug on her brain. Even if she finds taking the drug pleasant, and so has a reason to take it, she cannot *act on* this reason when she takes it. Her desire to take the drug does not give rise to an intention because, *ex hypothesi*, she is *forced* to act the way she does. What she does is not up to her—more specifically, it is not up to what she views as good or bad. In this kind of case, there is nothing that rationalizes her taking of the drug: the explanation of her taking it is not a rationalizing explanation, but a merely causal account of the interplay between her altered brain chemistry and her visual environment. The distinction between akratics and compulsives, then, is that the former act intentionally because they act on reasons.

IV. AN OBJECTION: MORALIZING AKRASIA

The fact that I have spelled out the intrinsic conflict analysis using an example that fits the traditional reason/passion framework may suggest that I have lost sight of Davidson's insight that "incontinence is not essentially a problem in moral philosophy, but a problem in philosophy of action" ([1970] 1980: 30 n. 14). But this feature of the example is inessential to my analysis. The person who judges her cookie eating to be akratic might, on another occasion, attach that label to the voice that tells her to refrain: she is on vacation, it is the time to indulge, but she just cannot shake the sense that she is consuming too many calories. In this case sensual indulgence represents her dominant evaluative perspective—she does not acknowledge the validity of the hedonic calculus, and experiences her tendency to assess the caloric damage of each treat as a tug or impulse whose rational force is situated outside her current ethical point of view. Now is not the time to be thinking that way—and insofar as she is, she finds herself to be neurotic, uptight, hung-up on dieting. Thus the theorist of intrinsic conflict can easily accommodate the kind of reversal Davidson illustrated with the toothbrusher example. Consider Davidson's statement of the case:

> I propose to divorce that problem [sc. weakness of will] entirely from the moralist's concern that our sense of the conventionally right may be lulled, dulled, or duped by a lively pleasure. I have just relaxed in bed after a hard day when it occurs to me that I have not brushed my teeth. Concern for my health bids me rise and brush; sensual indulgence suggests I forget my teeth for once. I weigh the alternatives in the light of the reasons: on the one hand, my teeth are strong, and at my age decay is slow. It won't matter much if I don't brush them. On the other hand, if I get up, it will spoil my calm and may result in a bad night's sleep. Everything considered I judge I would do better to stay in bed. Yet my feeling that I ought to brush my teeth is too strong for me: wearily I leave my bed and brush my teeth. My act is clearly intentional, although against my better judgment, and so is incontinent. ([1970] 1980: 30)

Notice that, despite the fact that Davidson's example is explicitly constructed to reverse the traditional roles allotted to reason and passion—his agent is akratically motivated to *violate* the dictates of sensual indulgence—the conflict he describes nonetheless takes a familiar form: "*Everything considered I judge* I would do better to stay in bed. Yet *my feeling* that I ought to brush my teeth is too strong for me." (emphasis mine) The akratic characteristically describes herself as judging or deciding or deliberating or seeing or believing that one action is right, and then being moved or overcome by some feeling or urge or impulse or desire or tendency toward another. It is true that, as Davidson notes, the second item needn't direct her toward sensual indulgence—it can, for instance, prompt her to pursue her dental health. We might even imagine agents who akratically violate the dictates of prudence or morality. It is telling, however, that in order to imagine such a case, we have to imagine characterizing prudence or morality or health in terms of urges, impulses, feelings, or needs.

Someone who describes an "urge" to be healthy or moral or prudent is at an odd vantage point in relation to those forms of motivation, namely one from which the fact that some action is conducive to health, prudence, or morality (or perhaps "morality") is not a consideration she is prepared to take seriously in her deliberation. She does not see these forms of motivation as forms of evaluation, which is to say, as sources of reasoned judgment. To the extent that one rejects the evaluative content contained within it, moral or prudential motivation becomes a bare pull or tendency. The opposing motive is then represented *entirely* in terms of its evaluative content, as a belief or judgment about what is best to do. From the point of view of the dominant evaluative perspective from which she deliberates, she has indeed taken "all things" into account—but that is only because she is looking at its opposition from a point of view that strips it of its evaluative content.

What, then, has the toothbrusher's reasoning left out? What is the evaluative perspective from which brushing his teeth looks good to him? One can fill out the case in a number of ways, but there is, I propose, a very natural answer as to what overcomes the toothbrusher when his "feeling that I ought to brush my teeth is too strong for me": the force of habit. Habit—as distinct from any kind of unthinking, potentially pathological tendency toward repetition/patterns of behavior—is the ethical point of view that presents something as "to be done" or as "a good thing to do" because one usually does it. Having habits means being such as to value your normal modus operandi. But the value of behaving habitually is precisely shut out of the evaluative perspective that aims to calculate for this occasion specifically ("suggest I forget my teeth *for once*"). In thinking about whether or not to skip toothbrushing, just this once, due to peculiarities of tonight's bedtime activities—he happens to get settled before brushing his teeth—Davidson's toothbrusher is thinking in an essentially nonhabitual way.

My suggestion, then, is that the asymmetry present in our language for describing the akratic's attitude toward, on the one hand, what he does and, on the other hand, what he thinks he should have done is to be explained by the presence in him of intrinsic conflict. Though he does in fact act on a reason, this reason doesn't fit into his dominant deliberative perspective; it is excluded from the deliberations leading him to conclude in favor of another action. This is why he represents it as an overwhelming feeling or urge: it seems to come from within himself, but so long as he is deliberating, he cannot get its evaluative force into view. On this account, akratic action is intentional action—it is done for a reason—while nonetheless contravening the conclusion of the agent's deliberation. He acts against his "best" or his "all-things-considered" judgment by acting from his subordinate evaluative perspective.

Are there cases of akrasia that do not fit this analysis? The following example has been proposed to me: Joe is hurrying to the bank because it's minutes to closing time, and he stands to lose $500 if he can't deposit a check today. He sees a $1 bill up ahead, being blown by the wind, and is inclined to run after it, but reasons that the $1 reward is not worth the risk of arriving late at the bank. Nonetheless, he finds himself drawn to chase it.[7] One might think, given that the value on both sides is money, that Joe's reason to chase is included in the reason to head straight to the bank. But notice that Joe might have responded differently if, instead of a fluttering dollar bill, he were presented with two envelopes, one of which held $500, the other of which had an 80 percent chance of holding $501 and a 20 percent chance of holding $1. It seems relevant that, in the original description, there are features of the case we can point to in explaining why the value of the second option appears to him in a different guise: the joy of chasing the bill or the frisson of delight from finding money on the street. If we remove these elements of the story, it does start to seem plausible that what is going on is either a case of ignorance—he briefly forgets about closing time—or compulsion—he can't control his impulse to run. It is a telling sign in favor of the intrinsic conflict analysis that when we rule out the possibility of an evaluative perspective divergence, we thereby make a skeptical rewrite of the example, into ignorance or compulsion, more attractive.

Thus I am inclined to think that the intrinsic conflict analysis does cover all real cases of akrasia. However, if the reader is convinced that it can model only some cases, that dispute should not

7. Thanks to Nate Sharadin for this example and the objection.

get in the way of the broader points I want to make about the relation between (at least some cases of) akrasia and aspiration. For this reason, I recommend that such a reader henceforth understand my use of the term "akrasia" as restricted to the cases for which she takes the analysis to work.

V. SPECIES OF INTRINSIC CONFLICT

Akrasia marks the fault lines of our ethical selves: it shows us that we have failed to squeeze all our thoughts about value into one picture. This can happen in three ways. First, it can happen that the thoughts of one's subordinate evaluative perspective represent a bad way of thinking we've mostly shed. So we might consider the reformed racist or homophobe who still, occasionally, finds herself beset with emotional reactions she has come to understand as inappropriate. Or we might consider the victim of abuse who finds herself struggling with forms of guilt cultivated in her long ago by her abuser. She takes this guilt to have no rational basis and deliberates from a point of view that doesn't acknowledge its rational relevance. When she akratically flagellates herself for "crimes" her reflective judgment can recognize she has not committed, she makes manifest the continued presence in her of a corrupt evaluative perspective. If she aspires to eliminate this perspective, she seeks a complete resolution of her intrinsic conflict: to become the person who fully appreciates her own worth. She may not have this aspiration—perhaps she has come to see the elimination of this residual guilt as quixotic. In that case, she deliberates as though she fully appreciated her self-worth, despite the fact that her own appreciation is, in fact, marred by guilt.

In a second kind of case, in which the subordinate perspective is less toxic, complete resolution needn't be its extinction. Consider a chocolate "addict" embarking on a healthy lifestyle. Suppose that at first she imposes on herself the rule *no dessert ever.* She is more likely to be beset by temptation at this time than she is years later, once she has learned to partake moderately of the occasional dessert. At first, her only way of getting the good of healthy living into view is to blind herself—deliberatively speaking—to the value of dessert; eventually, she is able to get both into view at once, and her appreciation for chocolate can rise from its subordinate position. Likewise, a teenager may reject all her "childish" pleasures, but rehabilitate some of these once she feels sufficiently confident of herself as an adult. The opening stages of adopting a new evaluative perspective are often characterized by the rejection of goods that are, as it were, the hallmark of the old one. The completion of the transformation might, at least in the ideal case, be marked by a reintegration. And even if the fault lines do not disappear entirely, they are likely to shrink over time, in the sense that fewer kinds of circumstances expose them.

For it is important to observe that the difficulty of effecting a deliberative unity between, e.g., prudence and pleasure depends greatly on the particular shape that conflict takes on a given occasion. We say that someone has a "weakness" for X precisely when X is the sort of object that, under ordinary circumstances, exposes what intrinsic conflict remains to her. So someone may have a weakness for, e.g., chocolate chip cookies but easily reject oatmeal ones—which she likes but doesn't *love.* And the same person easily rejects the world's tastiest chocolate chip cookie when she knows that it has been laced with a tasteless poison. For those features of her circumstances—whether the cookie is chocolate or oatmeal, whether it has been poisoned—are relevant to the question of whether she can, in coming to the conclusion that she ought not eat the cookie, see her own good in a unified way. When immediate survival is at stake, as in the poisoned cookie case, the evaluative perspective of prudence doesn't leave much else to be desired. The childish demand for immediate pleasure is also less likely to be activated by lesser pleasures—if the cookies are oatmeal, she's likely to be more satisfied that prudence has told her a complete story about what goods are out there at the moment.

Let me end by discussing the third kind of case, in which the dominant evaluative perspective is the one that needs to go. Consider Huck Finn, who feels strongly inclined to protect a runaway slave, but judges that he has a duty to turn him in. Huck understands the slave to be stolen property and resolves to do "the right thing and the clean thing, and go and write to [the slave's] owner and tell where he was." Huck is deliberating from an evaluative perspective informed by the moral corruption of his society, one that presents him with no reasoned argument in favor of Jim's freedom. As Jonathan Bennett observes, "So the action, to us abhorrent, of turning Jim in to the authorities presents itself *clearly* to Huck as the right thing to do" (1974: 125, emphasis in original). Having written—but not sent—the letter to Miss Watson, Huck's mind begins to wander, and he recalls their adventures together:

> [I] got to thinking over our trip down the river; and I see Jim before me all the time: in the day and in the night-time, sometimes moonlight, sometimes storms, and we a-floating along, talking and singing and laughing. But somehow I couldn't seem to strike no places to harden me against him, but only the other kind. I'd see him standing my watch on top of his'n, 'stead of calling me, so I could go on sleeping; and see him how glad he was when I come back out of the fog; and when I come up to him again in the swamp, up there where the feud was; and such-like times; and would always call me honey, and pet me,

and do everything he could think of for me, and how good he always was.

Huck can't fit his thoughts of Jim's kindness into his framework of reasoning about what to do. The racist morality Huck has imbibed from Sunday school ("'people that acts as I'd been acting about that [slave] goes to everlasting fire'") does not make room for the values that strike him when he thinks over their time together. He doesn't know how to *think* about those values, because his mode of thinking is one that doesn't recognize them. He can only, as it were, *feel* them. Bennett again: "On the side of conscience we have principles, arguments, considerations, ways of looking at things . . . On the other side, the side of feeling, we get nothing like that . . . Their effect on him is of a different kind: 'Well, I just felt sick.'" (127, emphasis in original).

In this sort of case, the ideal, eventual resolution of the intrinsic conflict would be to abandon much of one's dominant evaluative perspective in favor of the subordinate evaluative perspective that would, in the process, become rationally articulated. Huck would, then, eventually come to see his decision in terms of facts, such as the fact that Jim is a human being, possessed of moral rights and personhood; the consequent fact that the laws under which he is counted as Miss Watson's property are unjust laws; the fact that Jim is Huck's friend, to whom Huck owes loyalty; the fact that Jim is, in addition, a particularly good person, and thus one worth having as a friend. And so on. As Huck's subordinate deliberative perspective came to dominate, these considerations could take their rightful place in Huck's deliberations.[8]

---

8. Twain does not take this cheerful path. Instead of learning to think for himself, Huck substitutes the authority of Sunday school for that of Tom Sawyer, at whose behest he (effectively) tortures Jim while holding him captive.

In the short term, we cannot but experience our own akrasia as irritating. It is frustrating to see that I, via my recalcitrant vision of the good, stand in the way of my attainment of the good. But if the intrinsic conflict analysis is correct, the fault lines that erupt in akratic action are at the same time the indications of my potential for growth in respect to value-apprehension. Recall Zafar experiencing "the first stirrings of what I would later come to recognize as kinship." He is encountering a reason he does not yet know how to accommodate, the understanding of which will become a lifelong project for him. Because we can be intrinsically conflicted, we are not trapped in the evaluative condition we happen to be in. The fact that we can be akratically insensitive to our dominant evaluative perspective is the flip side of the fact that we can be sensitive to evaluative content that doesn't fit into that perspective. We are not restricted to taking in the reasons we currently have the framework for processing. Just as our students' progress in philosophy depends on their willingness to read difficult, opaque books, human progress in value depends on our openness to *feeling* some goodness before we can make reflective sense to ourselves of that goodness. The possibility of akrasia is thus tethered to the possibility of aspiration. In the next and final section of this chapter, I explain the connection between those two phenomena.

VI. AKRATICS AND ASPIRANTS

Socrates contravenes the akratic's self-ascription of the belief "I ought not to have φ-ed." He thinks that if she had really believed this, she would not have φ-ed.[9] The intrinsic conflict analysis requires no

---

9. This much is common ground between most interpretations of the *Protagoras*. For an argument that it is compatible with acknowledging the phenomenon of akrasia, see Callard (2014).

such radical resistance to the akratic's self-understanding, but it does call for us to acknowledge the inflated rhetoric in the akratic's characteristic expression of regret: "I *knew full well* I shouldn't have . . ." For there is a part of her that doesn't know this at all. On the intrinsic conflict analysis, Davidson's description of the judgment the akratic violates as an "*all-things*-considered" judgment comes off as a bit overstated. Far from considering *everything*, the agent does not even succeed in considering all the reasons relevant to her action. Still, if I am right, we can make good sense of the akratic's feeling that it was perfectly obvious to her, in a fully unqualified way, what she ought to do. Because intrinsic conflict is not subject to deliberative resolution, the akratic's decision-making is, instead, modeled on that of the person to whom it *is* fully obvious that she ought not to indulge in temptation. Call that person "the paragon" with respect to the value in question.

The toothbrusher's less hidebound paragon sees immediately that, given her values, it's not worth rising from bed; likewise, the paragon of moderate consumption judges readily that the pleasures of indulgence are easily outweighed by the pleasures of restraint. It is easy to see what *those* people's value would dictate, and it is this ease that colors the akratic's proclamations as to what *she* ought to do. The akratic's rhetoric is inflated by the fact that she is deliberating as though her subordinate evaluative perspective were not there.

It is important that the modeling the akratic engages in restricts itself to the question of which evaluative framework she inhabits. The paragon of dietary prudence is unmoved by the value of getting something *now*. Likewise, the toothbrusher's paragon does not think along the lines of "toothbrushing before bed is how it must be done." She is immune to feeling the force of habit. The values of the paragon externalize some of the akratic's motivations by casting them as forces that act upon her. By seeing her temptations as temptations, she refuses to inhabit them, to see the world through them. It doesn't follow, however, that the akratic concludes that she ought to do what the paragon would have done; for the paragon would, e.g., not have to forbid herself from entering the room with the cookies.[10] Adopting the paragon's valuational perspective allows the akratic to judge that, e.g., *given* the likelihood of her yielding to temptation upon entering the room, she ought not enter.

But it is also possible that the akratic thinks the paragon *wouldn't* enter the room. The akratic's version of the paragon of, e.g., prudence might differ from the person we call the paragon of prudence—or even the person she *will* be inclined to call prudent once she is closer to grasping that value herself. For instance, the akratic who is very prone to self-indulgence may understand the valuational space of prudence in a hyper-ascetic way. Perhaps *her* paragon hates chocolate and doesn't even see the fact that the cookies contain chocolate as *any kind of reason* to approach them. It is unsurprising if the akratic's partial grasp of her target value should yield some amount of cartoonish exaggeration. She is prone to an unnecessarily extreme and restrictive conception of the value-space in terms of the few elements of it she grasps clearly.

All of this is true not only of the akratic but also of her *enkratic* counterpart. The enkratic faces the same temptation as the akratic, but triumphs where the akratic fails. The enkratic deliberates to the same conclusion as the akratic, but manages to act in accordance with that judgment. The akratic and the enkratic have an important common ground in the experience of intrinsic conflict that precedes their bad (akratic) or good (enkratic) action. Both characters are distinct from the paragon, and thus neither fully inhabits the evaluative

10. See Smith's (1995) example, discussed in . chapter 2 section IV.

perspective from which they deliberate. But—and this is just as important—they do not, qua akratic or enkratic, engage in reasoning that is directed at inhabiting it more perfectly. They see the situation they are in as one that they are in a good position to negotiate.

For it is essential to the very definition of some behavior as akratic or enkratic that the agent in question formed a "better judgment." They took themselves to have an adequate answer to the question "What should I do?" If such a person succeeds, enkratically, in the aim of getting herself to act in accordance with her paragonic perspective, she can explain, to her own satisfaction, the value of her action. Enkratics know why they are doing what they are doing, and akratics know why they should have acted otherwise. They do not, as far as this action is concerned, feel a defect in their grasp of the relevant value. This is not to say that they take themselves to have a full grasp of the value, but only that any defect in their grasp of the full value of the target is, for these practical purposes, irrelevant. They know how important it is to do as their better judgment dictates.

Aspirants try to resolve their intrinsic conflicts; akratics and enkratics try to act in spite of them. Aspirants try to get a better grasp of the target value, so as to approach the paragon; akratics and enkratics make do with whatever grasp they have, by deliberating as though they were the paragon. The proleptic rationality characteristic of aspiration is directed at the reasons that I take myself to be in the process of acquiring, whereas the standard deliberative rationality of the enkratic or akratic is a matter of acting on the reasons I already have. Akratics act *from* a grasp of value, however partial. Aspirants act *toward* a grasp of value. Does this show that akratics cannot be aspirants?

No. Many, if not all, of those subject to intrinsic conflict aspire to become unconflicted; these people are not, in virtue of the fact that they aspire, immune to akrasia. But the explanation of this, given the tension between akrasia or enkrateia, on the one hand, and aspiration, on the other, is that aspirants do not think in an unremittingly aspirational way in relation to the target value. Someone who aspires to value something more than she does needn't always, only, think in terms of what she is missing. For even as she is acquiring the relevant value, she also already has (some of) it—and this grasp will often have to suffice. The learning of a value takes time, and sometimes a decision needs to be made *now*.

This reveals an important feature of aspiration. We cannot hold off from making use of our values until such time as they are securely in our possession; for what happens in the meanwhile is also life. Sometimes we are called to deliberate from the very values that, over a longer swath of time, we could potentially come to acquire more fully. We reason, locally, *from* the very values we may, more globally, also be reasoning *toward*. The practical reasoning we do from these values is, to be sure, hampered by our insecure possession of them. Intrinsic conflict makes straightforward deliberation—deliberation from all our reasons—impossible. Nonetheless, given the impossibility of immediately resolving the conflict, our only option is to act in spite of it. Thus we deliberate as though we were the unconflicted paragons of valuation that we may or may not be trying to be. Either way, the fact that we are *not* those people may slip out. This happens when we are moved by what we experience as an appearance of the good despite the fact that we ourselves, wearing our paragon hat, classified it as a "mere temptation."

PART III

MORAL RESPONSIBILITY

Chapter 5

The Problem of Self-Creation

In part I (chapters 1 and 2), we considered aspiration from the vantage point of decision theory: How could it be rational for someone to pursue a project that is not the optimal way of satisfying her current set of preferences? Our answer was that the rationality of aspiration cannot be captured within the synchronic framework of decision. The aspirant's reason is proleptic, with a proximate face that speaks to the person she is now and a distal face fully visible only to the person she will become. Proleptic rationality is essentially extended in time, being a form of value-learning.

We then turned in part II (chapters 3 and 4) to the moral psychology of aspiration, attempting to give an account of what proleptic rationality feels like. The aspirant is trying to see the world through another person's eyes, namely, through the eyes of the person who has the value she aspires to acquire. Her condition cannot be captured in the Frankfurtian framework: she neither "identifies with" nor is "alienated from" the evaluative perspective she imperfectly inhabits. Rather, she is in a state of intrinsic conflict between the evaluative perspective she seeks to acquire and the one she seeks to depart from.

In this final part of the book (chapters 5 and 6), we will examine the implications of the phenomenon of aspiration for the theory of autonomy. The aspirant does not *end up with* a new value in the way that one might end up with an ulcer or an inheritance. She orchestrates her value-acquisition, driving herself toward a different value-condition from the one she is in. From this vantage point, aspiration emerges as a kind of *work*. The work is visible in her struggles to sustain interest in the hobby or relationship or career or religion or aesthetic experience that will later become second nature; in her repeated attempts to "get it right," attempts that must be performed without the benefit of knowing exactly what rightness consists in; and, most generally, in the fact that she always wants and strives to be farther along than she is. An aspirant's value-transition is her own work, which means that she is a certain kind of cause: a cause of herself.

This is not to deny that the aspirant receives help. Major value-acquisitions reflect the influence of one's environment, especially the people in it. Parents, teachers, and lovers have transformative effects on the people they parent, teach, and love. But they cannot, at least typically, have these effects on someone unless she participates in the process. They assist, rather than substitute for, the activity of the agent herself. My aim in these two chapters is to offer an account of the work an agent does in making herself into a person with new values. I call this work "self-creation."

That label may sound overblown, given that the person must have been around to do the creating. Nonetheless, he didn't then exist *as* the person he becomes. The advantage of "self-creation" over "self-change" or "self-revision," as I might also have called it, is that the former term serves as a reminder that we are not interested in minor or superficial ways in which someone might change himself. Self-creation in the sense I'm interested in is not going to be a matter of a person making physical changes to his body, altering his musculature or the color of his hair. Caring about something new can have physical repercussions, but the change one is effecting on oneself is not, in the first instance, a physical change. Nor is it a psychological one. It will, to be sure, have psychological repercussions: one's new form of valuation lends itself to new emotions, feelings of attachment and vulnerability, curiosity, interest, excitement. But these, too, are consequences of something deeper, which is the *ethical* change occasioned by committing oneself to some form of valuation. Our interest is in self-directed value-acquisition, which is, first and foremost, a change of a person in the ethical dimension. In this chapter, I propose to explain how the aspirant can be an ethical source of himself.

I begin with a discussion of why this question is so difficult to answer. I describe two received models for self-directed agency and argue that neither offers us a framework for understanding self-creation. First, I consider the possibility that one creates oneself by an act of the will in which one endorses some way of being, sanctioning it with an evaluative stamp of approval. I call this the "self-endorsement model," and I argue that because one is in a position to endorse only what one *already* values, self-endorsement cannot represent a way of *acquiring* values. Next, I turn to what I call the "self-cultivation model." Self-cultivation is the process of working to satisfy anterior normative commitments about what kind of person to become. I adapt a paradox described by Galen Strawson (1994) to show that we cannot tell a story of genuine self-creation as a story of self-cultivation. The paradox runs as follows. If, on the one hand, the value I cultivate in myself follows rationally from values I already have, then I do not do any creating. For in this case my "new" self was already contained in my old self. If, on the other hand, the new value is rationally unconnected to my earlier values, then its advent in my life cannot be my own doing. In this case, the self I end up with may be new, but it is not the product of my own agency. Rational value-cultivation is not self-*creation*, and nonrational value-cultivation is not *self*-creation.

I analyze the underlying problem as follows. Call the self that does the creating "S_1," and call the self that is created "S_2." For the theorist of self-endorsement, S_1 is the endorsing self, S_2 the self it endorses; for the theorist of self-cultivation, S_1 is the cultivating self, S_2 is the self it cultivates. Both theorists depict S_1 as normatively prior to S_2 in the following sense: they present S_1 as the agent's authoritative self, the self whose agency (via endorsement or commitment) determines how S_2 ought to be. I argue that if we attempt to derive the norms governing S_2 from the values or commitments already present in S_1, we will never be able to describe self-creation. Instead, one must reverse the priority relation between the two selves. In section IV of this chapter, I show that we can do so by conceiving of the temporally posterior created self as authoritative over the self who creates her. The aspirant does not see herself as fashioning, controlling, sanctioning, making, or shaping the self she creates. Instead, she looks up to that self, tries to understand her, endeavors to find a way to her.

Skeptics of self-creation, Strawson among them, are wont to cite with approval a passage in which Nietzsche scoffs at the philosophical impulse "to pull oneself up into existence by the hair, out of the swamps of nothingness." He describes the very idea of self-creation as a "rape and perversion of logic."[1] Such skeptics may worry that an account such as mine succumbs to the basic error Nietzsche is describing: in positing the normatively prior self as temporally posterior, I am presenting a teleological account of (a species of)

---

1. *Beyond Good and Evil*, sec. 21. Are these skeptics right to see Nietzsche as an ally? He is, after all, apt to wax eloquent on the power of the strong to create themselves. See the passages cited in Owen and Ridley (2003) in response to the more straightforwardly fatalist reading offered in Leiter (2001).

self-directed agency. Is such teleology naturalistically suspect—does it rest on some notion of backward causation or causeless effects?

I argue that the primary task of someone responding to Strawson's dilemma is that of giving an account of how one set of norms—the norms governing S_1—is related to another set of norms—the norms governing S_2. This question about normative grounding needn't be identified with the question as to the *causal* grounding relations between S_1 and S_2. Nothing prevents the theorist of aspiration from offering a traditional (i.e., non-teleological) account of the causal grounding of the genesis of S_2 in the representations, desires, etc. of S_1. But if we want to know whether those very desires and representations succeed or fail, we must assess them with reference to the as yet nonexistent S_2.

In aspiration, it is the created self who, through the creator's imperfect but gradually improving understanding of her, makes intelligible the path the person's life takes. Aspiration is that form of agency in which one acts upon oneself to create a self with substantively new values. One does this by allowing oneself to be guided by the very self one is bringing into being.

[handwritten margin note: ✳ details for how this happens still seem to be missing]

I. SELF-ENDORSEMENT

A number of philosophers have taken an interest in our power to endorse or withdraw approval from some feature of ourselves. Harry Frankfurt distinguishes between two kinds of drug addict: the unwilling addict rejects his own impulse to take a drug, by contrast with the willing addict who approves of his own addiction. Frankfurt (1971) says that the former does not desire as he *desires to desire* and (in Frankfurt 1988) that the latter *identifies* with his desire. Christine Korsgaard (1996) might describe that same addict as endorsing (or failing to endorse) the practical identity of being an addict (ch. 3). Gary Watson covers the same territory by contrasting a person's evaluative and motivational systems: the former issues judgments as to the value of the desires populating the latter. If approval is withdrawn, as in the case of the unwilling addict, the agent is "estranged from his . . . inclinations" (1975: 210).

Abstracting from their differences, we can group these views together as describing self-endorsement, i.e. an activity in which an agent, or some part of her, steps back from, appraises, and attaches a positive or negative evaluation to the aspect of herself she evaluates. I do not doubt that self-endorsement is a real and significant aspect of agency, but I will argue that it cannot serve as a means of self-creation. We do not change who we are by reflectively approving or disapproving of ourselves.

Self-creation, as I understand it, involves the creation of values. But values are also what we use in forming our endorsements or rejections of some feature of ourselves. Can one use one value to generate or eliminate another? Consider some possibilities for how this might go. Suppose that I have exactly three values: V_1, V_2, and V_3. I cannot simply ask myself, "Is V_1 valuable?" for then I will be putting my finger on the scales. I do value V_1 and will end up evaluating V_1 from a point of view that assumes the value of V_1. But I might successfully set that value aside by asking myself a hypothetical question: "Should someone who values only V_2 also value V_1?" or "Should someone who values only V_2 and V_3 also value V_1?" In this way, I can investigate the question of whether to value V_1 without presuming its value. But notice that if I answer no to both of these questions, this has no implications for what I should do or value: I am not someone who values only V_2 or who values only V_2 and V_3. The hypothetical model allows an agent to evaluate one value from the point of view of another, but at the expense of being uninformative of her actual situation. Such hypothetical reasoning does not put the agent in a position to change her value-endorsement.

This observation might lead the theorist of self-endorsement to abandon the project of evaluating a value by way of some value set that does not include it, in favor of evaluating a value by looking at its place in one's value-system as a whole.[2] One can observe, while still valuing X, that one's valuation of X does not cohere well with the rest of what one values. Suppose, then, that someone realizes that one of her values—say, her valuation of her appearance—detracts from her ability to value something else—say, equality or independence—to which she is more fundamentally committed; or that given her feminist values she really ought to value a certain form of political activism to which she is currently indifferent. Do we, in this case, have a form of self-endorsement that amounts to self-creation?[3]

No: the realization in question stops just short of the relevant change. We are to imagine the agent asking herself a question

2. Laura Ekstrom (1993) modifies Frankfurt's account by adding such considerations of coherence to it. She aims thereby to defend Frankfurt against Watson's charge that any higher-order desire must itself be endorsed by a yet higher-order desire, generating a regress. On Ekstrom's picture, my desire is "mine" because I "authorize" it in virtue of its occupying a position of coherence among my desire set: "The coherent elements 'fit with' the other items one accepts and prefers, so that, in acting upon them, one is not conflicted" (609). Ekstrom's defense suffers from a systematic ambiguity as to whether what makes a desire mine is the fact that it coheres with the rest of my desires or the fact that I take it to cohere with them and therefore authorize it: endorsement and coherence compete for centrality in her account. Even if it worked, however, her defense could not go so far as to offer a theory of self-creation. For Ekstrom identifies a person's values with those desires that "fit with" one another ("I propose to define coherence with one's character system . . . as determined by what it is valuable to pursue within that system"; 610), and this means that one cannot so much as articulate the question as to which values, i.e. which (among many) coherent system of desires, one should "authorize."

3. Supposing, for the sake of argument, that it really is rational to become more coherent. For an argument against the existence of demands of this kind, see Kolodny (2005, 2008).

such as "I know I value X, but *ought* I to value it, given my valuation of Y and Z?" or "I know I don't value W, but *ought* I to value it, given my valuation of X, Y, and Z?" If she concludes that she ought to value W, this does not constitute an adoption of that value, but rather a change in her judgment as to what she ought to value. Such an agent comes to see that she is not as she ought to be. The project of assessing oneself for coherence presupposes the possibility of separating the question of what values one has from the question of what values one should have. That separation characterizes the agent who answers the question, for she concludes that she shouldn't (or should) have a certain value *that she continues to have* (or not have).

The judgment that she would be more coherent if she valued X cannot itself constitute a change in what she values. Nor can we say that the formation of the judgment that I ought to value X amounts to the creation of a second-order value. If there is such a thing as valuing a value, this value cannot be what is produced by my coherentist self-policing. Rather it must, like my first-order valuing of X, figure among the objects I police. When I ask myself what I must value in order for my values to be coherent, I step back from my higher-order values as well as my lower-order ones, since I am asking myself not what I *do* value, or what I *do* value valuing, but what I ought to value, or ought to value valuing.[4]

---

4. One may worry that this argument generalizes in a problematic way: Isn't there such a thing as *cognitive* coherentist self-policing, in which one assesses one's beliefs for coherence? If we assume it is possible to generate and destroy beliefs by examining oneself for coherence, that is because we take the cognitive case to have the following peculiarity: judging that one ought to believe that p is or entails believing that p. This rule may or may not hold for believing, but it certainly does not hold for valuing. For valuing, as argued earlier, has not only a cognitive but also a motivational and affective element. The last feature is worth singling out as particularly recalcitrant: judging that one ought to feel something does not even tend to give rise to the relevant feeling.

It might seem, however, that coherentist self-policing is but one small step away from value-change. The realization that it would be rational to gain or lose a value may not itself amount to value-change, but it could constitute an impetus to value-change. In the face of her acknowledgment that she is not the person she ought to be, the agent might be moved to go ahead and change (or commit to changing) herself into that person. In the next section, I will consider whether we can model self-creation using the process of bringing oneself into line with one's judgments about one's values. This process includes, but extends beyond, the moment of self-assessment to encompass the agency that flows from and is governed by whatever assessments one makes.

II. SELF-CULTIVATION

In chapter 1, I described a form of preference change that I called "self-cultivation." The person who cultivates herself engenders preferences in herself whose value she antecedently appreciates. For instance, her interest in living a healthier life moves her to join a gym, in the expectation that she will thereby, over time, engender in herself an inclination to exercise. When we cultivate ourselves, we don't just stand back and assess ourselves; we actually try to change ourselves. Thus self-cultivation might seem to be a more promising model for self-creation than mere self-endorsement. Philosophers such as Jean Hampton, Michael Smith, Michael Bratman, Richard Holton, and Joseph Raz have all articulated what can, broadly speaking, be characterized as theories of self-cultivation. For they all describe a process by which a person can act so as to determine her future self.

Hampton describes a "self-authorship" process: "There are many times in our lives when we choose what we will be. For example, when a young girl has the choice of entering into a harsh regimen of training to become an accomplished figure skater, or else refusing it and enjoying a more normal life with lots of time for play, she is being asked to choose or author whom she will be. When a graduate student decides which field of her discipline she will pursue, or when a person makes a decision about his future religious life, or when someone takes up a hobby—all of these choices are ways of determining one's traits, activities, and skills, and thus ways of shaping one's self—of determining one's self-identity" (1993: 150). Hampton contrasts this "authentic" form of self-determination with one in which a person allows herself to be shaped by social or environmental pressures into becoming what people want her to be. "Self-authorship involves . . . a decision to develop the traits, interests, and projects that are not only consistent with meeting your objective human needs but that are also ones you want, and not ones that others prefer that you want (and perhaps try to persuade you to want)" (155). Thus she grounds the process of self-authorship in the desires of the authoring or creating self.

Smith imagines self-cultivation as a reflective process, akin to the coherentist self-policing described earlier, by which one moves oneself toward a condition of greater consistency among one's desires: "Systematic reasoning creates new underived desires and destroys old. Since each such change seems rationally required, the new desiderative profile will seem not just different from the old, but better; more rational. Indeed, it will seem better and more rational in exactly the same way, and for the same reasons, that our new corresponding evaluative beliefs will seem better and more rational than our old ones" (1995: 116). Bratman (2003) develops Frankfurt's higher-order model in a diachronic direction. He presents the adoption of higher-order self-governing policies as a solution to the problem he calls "underdetermination by value judgment," i.e., the situation in which one is confronted with a choice among what are, from the point of view of one's antecedent desires, a multiplicity of equally valuable pursuits. When there are many good things you could do, committing yourself to one can settle which you subsequently ought to do. Holton defends the possibility of "rational non-reconsideration" (2004: 3), by which a person adheres to earlier resolutions as to what she should now do and does not open the matter for deliberation. Raz (1988), whose view I will describe in more detail later in the chapter, describes the agent at the output of the process of cultivation as doing something akin to keeping promises made by her past self.

In all of these cases, an agent makes and subsequently lives under the normative guidance of some kind of choice as to how she should live.

We certainly do cultivate our physical appearance, friendships, desires, hobbies, traits, skills, traits, activities, and careers. But the difficult case is the cultivation of the state of valuation from which the agent will select *this* physical appearance, *that* friend, rejecting *this* desire in favor of *that* one. Can someone cultivate value in herself? In the course of an attack on the possibility of moral responsibility, Galen Strawson (1994) provides the materials for an argument that value cultivation is subject to the following dilemma.[5]

---

5. Strawson's ultimate target is responsibility for action: he wants to show that because we cannot create our values, we cannot be responsible for anything we do from those values. I discuss the major premise—that action-responsibility derives from character-responsibility— in chapter 6 part V. Since he does not always clearly separate the arguments for these two claims and since I am not discussing moral responsibility, what I offer here is not a direct paraphrase of any passage of his paper. Nonetheless, both the style and the substance of my presentation of the dilemma are heavily indebted to Strawson's way of framing (what he takes to be) an objection to both self-creation and moral responsibility.

The new values, acquisition of which constitutes my act of self-creation, must be either continuous or discontinuous with the ones I already have. If they are continuous, my new values are entailed by my old ones. In this case, I don't really change. If they are discontinuous, the new values contradict or come at a tangent to my old values. In this case, they arise accidentally or through external influence rather than through my agency. I change, but I do not change myself.

Let us see how this dilemma plays out in a schematic case. Suppose that I value E, and I come to value M because I see that M is the means to E (or, more generally, that valuing E rationally requires me to value M). Will this count as self-creation? No: instrumental reasoning works out the consequences of the value condition I already have. It does not discover ends, but only means. But what if, prior to realizing the relationship between E and M, I actively disvalued M? Overcoming my hatred of M might then constitute a substantive change—a change in my ends. But in that case, the mere discovery that valuing E rationally required me to value M is insufficient to explain the change. For why didn't I abandon E instead of embracing M? Perhaps I have *other* values that dictate this decision, or perhaps I simply valued E more than I disvalued M. In either case, we are once again back on the first horn: this isn't a change in value but merely a working out of the consequences of values I already have. If I neither valued E more than disvaluing M nor had other values dictating the overall importance of E, then we have not yet explained my rationale for adopting M. I may have done so randomly or on a whim, but if my new self is the product of such arbitrariness, it is not something I made. Strawson makes this observation when considering a libertarian defense of free will. He asks, "How can the occurrence of partly random or indeterministic events contribute in any way to one's being truly morally responsible either for one's actions or for one's character?" (1994: 18). This point applies equally to cases in which one's efforts of self-change are made for no reason, or arbitrarily. As Strawson points out, someone who succeeds as a result of such an event is "merely lucky." He has ended up with a good self that he did not create.

At each point in the story of E and M, we face the same choice: if the value I engender in myself follows rationally from values I already have, then I do not do any creating. For in this case my "new" self was already contained in my old self. But if the new feature is rationally unconnected to my earlier values, its advent in my life cannot be my own doing. In this case, the self I end up with may be new, but it is not the product of my own agency.

Why does the fact that the t_2 value was derivable from the agent's t_1 values disqualify the case from counting as self-creation? We should allow that the derivation might have required time and effort, so that the agent at t_2 differs substantially from the agent at t_1. Coming to value something that is instrumentally conducive to ends one had all along might occasion observably significant changes in acting, thinking, and feeling. But if we allow that such an agent develops her new self by unraveling the implications of the materials present in her old one, we will find that we have simply pushed the question about self-creation back to an earlier stage: How did she acquire those materials? And so the problem now is not that we must deny that the agent at t_2 is self-created; the problem is that the process seems to have gotten going before t_1. Her valuation of the means is a *new expression* of a value that she acquired at whatever time (before t_1) she came to value that end. We will not have an account of how her ethical self came into being until we have a story of *that* genesis. But if we try to tell one, Strawson's dilemma recurs.

We encounter the same regress if we press, on Bratman's behalf, the question of why a value-choice underdetermined by one's previous commitments cannot constitute self-creation. Suppose Sartre's resistance fighter was not antecedently more committed either to his mother or to his country. Forced to choose, he decides (at t_1) to devote his life to mother over country. Does it really follow from the fact that it would have been equally rational (at t_1) to opt to fight that the filially pious self emerging at t_2 is arbitrary in relation to his self at t_1? Bratman might point out that this would follow only if at t_1 he cared little or nothing for his mother. Suppose, to the contrary, that the soldier at t_1 already cared deeply for both mother and country. In this case the value must already have been created sometime before t_1. The decision made at t_1 is then not value-creation, but one (of at least two) possible developments of his antecedent state of motivation. If we want to know how *that* state got created, we will have to look back further into his past. And then Strawson re-poses his dilemma.

Whenever we tie some new value to an act of self-cultivation, we must admit the arbitrariness of the choice or push the source of the cultivation back a further step. And this regress is a vicious one: as we retreat backwards through a person's selves, we encounter selves that are less and less, and eventually not at all, in a position to do any creating. And shortly thereafter, of course, we run out of self altogether.

Must my later self either come at a tangent to my earlier self or be a rational consequence of it? If the two horns of Strawson's dilemma were exhaustive of the possibilities, self-creation would be—as Strawson thinks it is—a chimera. I will argue that they are not, but I want to note that Strawson's conception of the space of possibilities is widely, though not always explicitly, shared by theorists of the self. Consider, for instance, Robert Noggle's description of "the basic picture of the self" that is "quite common among philosophers" (2005: 108 n. 26). Such a self "evolves according to its own internal logic—its own contents determine whether and how it is to change in response to new information, internal conflicts and changing condition . . . when psychological changes happen in this way, it seems correct to say that the new configuration is an authentic continuation of the previous configuration. On the other hand, a psychological change—especially a change in the core attitudes—that does not occur in this way produces a new configuration that is not an authentic continuation of the previous one . . . If the changes are radical enough, it might be proper to speak of the destruction of one self and its replacement by a new one" (100–101).

As examples of changes in the second category, Noggle offers "sudden organic trauma" and "nefarious brain surgery." He contrasts these with changes that are "internally motivated in such a way that they seem to be *intelligible reflections* of the contents of the core attitudes (100, emphasis in original)." Noggle's division recapitulates Strawson's dilemma: he sees changes in a self as either rational extrapolations of previous conditions ("according to its own inner logic") or traumatic intrusions from without. Noggle's discussion of self-creation showcases how deeply we have been gripped by Strawson's dilemma. The two selves must be rationally connected, or we cannot see the second as the work of the first; but this same continuity prevents novel values from arising.

III. NEURATH'S BOAT

At this point, we may be tempted to conclude that self-creation is, indeed, impossible. Why should we demand that we be able to do more than revise our selves in the light of our current values, becoming more consistent versions of the people we are? We may be inclined to heed Nietzsche's advice to stop trying to pull ourselves "up into existence by the hair, out of the swamps of nothingness." In order to pull ourselves up by the hair we would have to be able to detach ourselves from our bodies. And this may seem to be precisely the logical problem at the heart of the idea of self-creation: we cannot step outside ourselves. It has become a commonplace to describe the developing self using the image of Neurath's boat, which must be rebuilt as it sails.[6] It is impossible to fashion oneself as though one were not already some person with desires and judgments— moreover, with desires and judgments that speak to the question of how one ought to fashion oneself. One can, at most, refashion from within. I want to take a moment to motivate the claim, which may at this point seem questionable, that there is indeed a *phenomenon* of self-creation for which we should try to account. Let me begin by pointing out that Neurath's boat is not Theseus's ship.

The fact that Neurath's boat never docks is indeed an elegant way of expressing the unsheddability of character. One cannot "operate" on one's self from the outside, as a doctor might operate on his own anaesthetized leg. One cannot set aside one's way of looking at the world and somehow examine things from the outside of one's self; as we saw in our discussion of the power of reflection in chapter 3, reflection does not afford a person the opportunity to "step back" from her values. But it does not follow from the fact that reflection has limited power that the self must stay true to its initial form or else be traumatically violated from without. Neurath's boat isn't Theseus's ship, whose job is to stay the same through all its many changes. On Theseus's ship, a rotting plank must be replaced by a plank of a similar shape and size. On Neurath's boat, the only requirement is that it be replaced by sailors on board the boat. Neurath's rowboat might be gradually rebuilt into a trireme

6. See Noggle (2005: 108 n. 26); McDowell (1998: 36–37).

or, for that matter, an airplane without the builder ever setting foot onto dry land. The fact that there is no vantage point one can simply adopt outside one's character doesn't entail that one couldn't *arrive* at the vantage point that is outside one's current character by working toward that condition.

My claim, in effect, is that we are not stuck repairing rowboats; that we regularly build triremes and airplanes out of ourselves. We do this by becoming spectators, taking classes, doing exercises. We find mentors to emulate or fellow travelers with whom to commiserate—and compete. We do the same thing over and over and over again until we get it right, without knowing in advance what "right" is. We do work we don't always enjoy, and we pretend—even to ourselves—that we enjoy it. We leave ourselves open to certain kinds of experiences and closed to others, knowingly risking disappointment and disillusionment down the line. We alert ourselves to and steel ourselves against temptations to abandon course in favor of a more readily available and more immediately intelligible form of value. Candy, television, alcohol, a nap, video games, internet surfing—pick your poison; it's waiting in the wings. We struggle against implicit or explicit messages, from individuals or groups of individuals, to the effect that this kind of value is "not for you." Often these struggles are heightened by the fact that we have internalized the judgments in question. The work that we are engaged in is the work of bringing something into view. But because what we are bringing into view is something practical—a value—the work is a matter of acting and feeling, as well as thinking.

This kind of work involves both moving toward and moving away from a perspective on value. When engaged in it, not only are we gaining something, we are also often losing something. In some cases, the value-perspective that we are losing can be characterized relatively thinly as the non-appreciation of something. But sometimes agents can identify strongly with their pre-aspirational valuation condition. Sometimes people view their own indifference to art or music as connected with being unpretentious and straightforward. Adults who describe themselves as "child-free by choice" view their condition not in terms of the absence of children, but in terms of the presence of the freedom to dedicate themselves to work or friendship or romance or travel. The bitter wife is not merely lacking in love; she actively *hates* her husband. Perhaps she feels, given the way he treats her, that it is only by withholding her affection from him that she can respect herself. Alcibiades sees Socratism as the loss of the only life he knows how to lead, the life of honor. People in these conditions have a strong barrier to changing in respect of the value in terms of which they have identified themselves. They feel, possibly correctly, that there are many good things they would be giving up by acquiring the value in question and that, because the value is one with which they have (at most) only aspirational contact, they would be giving up these known goods for an unknown thing that may or may not be good.

It is, on the one hand, a testament to the flexibility of the human soul that even people who build a sense of identity around not valuing something (music, children, one's husband) can sometimes bring themselves to adopt the opposed value-perspective. People fiercely attached to independence can become wonderful parents. And couples who could not get their future into view without placing children at the center of it can struggle past the sadness of infertility to embrace the freedom of child-free life. It is, on the other hand, a testament to the difficulty of perspectival change that sometimes such people find themselves unable to see things differently, a fact that infuses the rest of their lives with a sense of loss. It seems possible to work to come to see a value one didn't see before, as well as to divest oneself of the value-perspective one currently has: this is the process I have been calling aspiration. Aspirants have a more ambitious goal than self-maintenance. They work to build themselves up into something genuinely new.

On an aspirational account, self-creation is agent-driven learning in the domain of value. The aspirant brings herself to a different view as to what matters in life and comes to appreciate what she once did not. How does this contrast with self-cultivation? Consider an example with which Jean Hampton illustrates her "self-authorship" conception of aspiration:

[I]n the spring of 1991, American newspapers recounted the story of an investment banker who, as a teenager, wanted to be a clown, His parents strongly discouraged it, regarding it as inappropriate for someone of his background and abilities, so he went to MIT and got a job working in Silicon Valley in computers. Still he was dissatisfied and decided things might go better if he had an MBA. With this degree he got a job on Wall Street making a lot of money in a high-powered investment bank. But one day, he claimed, he woke up realizing that if he kept working on Wall Street, he would end up close to death never having gone to clown school. So he quit his job, and did exactly that. This is a nice story of someone who struggled to author himself, while under pressure to be what people in his social group expected of him . . . he faced pressure to submit to a social role, to take on preferences, interests, and projects that he did not really want. He experienced understandable relief when he reclaimed himself. (1993: 154–155)

The striking feature of Hampton's banker/clown, from an aspirational point of view, is how little learning he had to do. His challenge lay in resisting social pressures and exercising autonomy in the service of doing what he really wanted all along. His self was already, as a teenager, developed in the direction of the core value of his life. He did not have to work to discover what he wanted; he had but to claim it, or later to "reclaim," the value that was present in him all along. Such a picture focuses our attention away from the developmental period during which one learns to see something in, e.g., clowning. I do not deny that one important way in which autonomy manifests itself is in the making of choices that align with who you really are, as opposed to who others want you to be. This form of autonomy is not available to everyone, however, since it presupposes the existence of a real or true self. On the aspirational model it can be true that you are at work on yourself, though there is, as yet, no real you; your wants are themselves a work in progress.

One way to see the difference between self-cultivation and aspiration is to look at the role allotted to secondary players. In Hampton's example, other people appear in the form of those who exert "social pressure" to abandon one's true desires. No doubt the man in question also had friends, family members, or associates who encouraged and perhaps facilitated his ultimate career change. One needn't, however, make mention of such people in order to tell this story of "self-authorship." He is in an important respect sufficient unto himself, equipped from the start of the story with the knowledge of what he wants. The aspirant, by contrast, reaches out to others for help in grasping what she wants. Tales of aspirational self-creation will, of course, feature the aspirant in a starring role, but they also lean heavily on a host of supporting players: teachers, mentors, (supportive!) parents, schools, advisers. Everyone relies on the care and love of the people around them, but aspirants rely on the people around them to care about and love the things they themselves are struggling to come to care about and love.

Compare aspirational help with medical help. The patient doesn't know how to cure herself—on this point she lacks knowledge or ability or resources. But there is something she does know: she wants to be cured of the disease. In this kind of case, the agent's practical ignorance or inability is circumscribed by her practical knowledge or ability with respect to her desired end. She knows for certain that she wants a cure. It is not essential for her to acquire the knowledge or ability she lacks: she doesn't need to cure herself. In this sort of case, the person's ignorance/incompetence and her knowledge/competence can be cleanly separated from one another. The aspirant's ignorance, by contrast, runs "all the way down," in the sense that she cannot be sure, until she is no longer an aspirant, that she even wants to acquire the relevant value. And insofar as there is anything about the value she has not yet grasped, she sees it as her job to come to do so. She cannot farm this knowledge out to, e.g., a mentor in the way in which patients can farm medical knowledge out to their doctors. Aware that they have something to learn, aspirants lean on those more securely attached to the value in question, but this leaning is itself aspirational, displaying a pattern of ever-lessening pressure (see chapter 3, section II (c)). Like a child learning to ride a bike, the aspirant gradually replaces her helper's support with her own internal balance. This delicate interplay between one agent and others is one among the features of self-creation that is obscured if we assume the model of self-cultivation. And it is obscured, as I will argue, by the assumption that the created self (the endorsed or cultivated self) depends rationally on the creator self (the endorsing or cultivating self).

But how does the aspirational account of self-creation escape Strawson's dilemma?

IV. ESCAPING STRAWSON'S DILEMMA

(a) *Normative Dependence*

Let me say that there is a *normative dependence relation* between two items when norms apply to the one item in virtue of the fact that, in the first instance, they apply to the other. When two things stand in this relation, the one inherits its normativity from the other. Let me illustrate with an example of a philosophical debate about the source of normativity.

We can assess intentions as good or bad, and we can assess actions as good or bad, and these forms of assessment do not seem to be fully independent of one another. Arguably, Aristotelians and Kantians agree that intentions and actions are subject to normative assessment, and they agree that these assessments stand in a relation of normative dependence, but they disagree as to the direction of dependence. A Kantian (or a Kantian of a certain stripe—it is not important for my point whether she is being true to Kant) says that intentions are the source of the applicability of norms to action. She contends that the fact that the intention has moral worth is what explains the normative status—the worth-having-ness—of the action. On her view, intentions contain a principle on which the agent conceives of himself as acting. The worth of the intention depends on the universalizability of this principle (or "maxim"); this worth then grounds the worth of the action the intention motivates.

Contrast this with a view on which it is actions that are, in the first instance, subject to norms of practical assessment. The Aristotelian opponent of my Kantian holds that actions are the proper objects of judgments of goodness and badness, i.e., praise and blame. The goodness or badness of actions grounds the goodness or badness of character, in that a good character is the character that disposes one to perform good actions; character, in turn, grounds the goodness or badness of an intention, in that a good intention is whatever intention characteristically issues from a good character. Among other differences, these two theorists have a dispute about the location or source of moral worth: the one holds that actions have moral worth because (and insofar as) they are associated with certain kinds of intentions, and the other that intentions have moral worth because (and insofar as) they are associated with certain kinds of actions.

They agree that practical norms apply to both actions and intentions, but they have very different accounts of *how* they apply in each case. They have a dispute about the source of normativity. I am about to engage in just such a dispute with theorists of self-endorsement and self-cultivation.

(b) Priority of Created Self

Just as one can ask whether intention or action is the ultimate locus of moral worth, one can ask whether S_1, the creator self, or S_2, the created self, is the ultimate locus of value. Theorists of self-endorsement and theorists of self-cultivation agree in taking S_1 as the normative ground of S_2. For the theorist of self-endorsement, S_1 and S_2 represent divisions within a person at a given time. S_1 is one's evaluative system, and S_2 is whatever feature (or prospective feature) of oneself one is using that system to evaluate. If S_2 is endorsed, this is *because* S_1 has done the endorsing. For the theorist of self-cultivation, S_1 and S_2 are different time slices of the person. If the person has cultivated a feature in herself, then S_2 should have that feature *because* S_1 did something—made a commitment or a resolution—picking that feature out as the one to be acquired.

The normative priority of S_1 comes through particularly clearly in Joseph Raz's discussion of self-creation. Raz describes S_1 as having done something akin to making a promise, and S_2 as therefore having a new reason for action that is akin to one's reason to keep a promise. Raz says:

> Our life comprises the pursuit of various goals, and that means that it is sensitive to our past. Having embraced certain goals and commitments we create new ways of succeeding and new ways of failing. In embracing goals and commitments, in coming to care about one thing or another, one progressively gives shape to one's life, determines what would count as a successful life and what would be a failure. One creates values, generates, through one's developing commitments and pursuits, reasons which transcend the reasons one had for undertaking one's commitments and pursuits. In that way a person's life is (in part) of his own making. It is a normative creation, a creation of new values and reasons. It is the way our past forms the reasons which apply to us at present. But it is not like the change of reasons which is occasioned by loss of strength through age, or the absence of money due to past extravagances. Rather it is like the change occasioned by promising: a creation, in that case, of a duty one did not have before. For, whatever reasons one had to make the promise, its making transforms one's reasons, creating a new reason not previously there. Similarly, the fact that one embraced goals and pursuits and has come to care about certain relationships and projects is a change not in the physical or mental circumstance in which one finds oneself, but in one's normative situation. It is the creation of one's life through the creation of reasons. (1988: 387)

In Razian self-creation, S_1 holds the reins, creating values and reasons for S_2. Raz responds to the objection that such creation is arbitrary by leaning on the analogy with promising: "It may have been wrong to promise to give my son fireworks, for they are too dangerous. But having made the promise it may now be my duty to give him the fireworks" (388). This analogy plays right into Strawson's hands: *Why* did the father make that promise (i.e., create those values)? Had a yet earlier self promised to make these promises? Or did he promise for no reason, arbitrarily? Raz's vulnerability to Strawson's dilemma is, I propose, a product of his understanding of the normative grounding relation between S_1 and S_2. Promising exemplifies a form of agency in which the earlier self is normatively prior to the later one, and Raz takes this structure to be present in self-development: one's earlier self makes it the case that certain norms govern one's later self.

Let us review the dialectic thus far. We began by considering whether someone could create herself by endorsing or affirming some (prospective) value. We found that if a person stepped back far enough to avoid simply reaffirming what she already values, her endorsements no longer constituted value-generation. The self that is in a position to fairly, impartially evaluate its own values issues not values but, at best, judgments as to rational entailments among values. But could, perhaps, a judgment as to what one's current set of values entails form an initial stage in the process of self-creation? From this question emerges the self-cultivation model, which describes the process of following through on such a judgment by making oneself into the person one judged one ought to be. But self-cultivation is vulnerable to Strawson's dilemma, in response to which we found ourselves in a regress, stepping backwards in an attempt to identify ever-earlier selves from which an act of self-creation might (non-arbitrarily) spring.

The problems seem to emerge from the fact that we press each model backwards, asking, "Who endorses the endorser?" and "Who cultivates the cultivator?" This backward pressure tracks the direction in which normativity is, as it were, flowing. Both models make S_1 the source of S_2's normativity. The regressive line of questioning seeks S_1's normative advantage over S_2, which is to say, the source of S_1's authority to endorse, or make commitments on behalf of, S_2.

It is important to note that Strawson's dilemma does not indicate a problem with the very idea of self-endorsement or self-cultivation. The theorist of self-endorsement can explain why the evaluating self typically has normative authority over the self it evaluates: the former simply *is* the locus of value. It is in the nature of one's values that they are in a position to evaluatively endorse or reject our desires, motives, habits, etc.—but not our values. For those items are *members* of S_1. Only in the case of value-endorsement does the problematic demand to "step back" from our values find application.

Likewise, self-cultivation is an intelligible way to make sense of efforts at self-change. Suppose S_1 concludes, after careful reflection, that he ought to quit smoking. Holton can explain why this resolution not to smoke binds S_2 when the temptation to smoke strikes. S_2 has reason to enact—without reconsidering the issue—the judgment that he made under rationally favorable conditions. We form resolutions (in part) because we anticipate the phenomenon Holton calls "judgment-shift," in which occurrent desire sways our judgment as to what we should do. S_1 was in a better position to adjudicate S_2's decision than S_2 is, so it makes sense that norms should apply to S_2 in virtue of S_1's agency. The problem is that S_1 has no such advantage over S_2 in the case of value-creation.

In the case of value-creation, there is no special feature of S_1 that explains *why* she should be authoritative over S_2. For this reason, the theorist of self-cultivation is left grounding S_1's authority in the act of cultivation itself: S_1's authority lies simply in the fact that she came first. But a vicious regress results from explaining the cultivating self's rule-making authority by appeal to her status as cultivator, for there are other, even earlier selves. Thus S_1 will have to derive her normative license from a yet earlier cultivator, and we will be hurled backwards toward an ever-receding source of ultimate authority. I propose that this regress reflects the fact that, in the case of self-creation, S_1 cannot do the work that self-endorsement or self-cultivation would require of her. She does not have the normativity she is supposed to bestow.

I submit that the theorist of self-creation needs to get the creator self looking forward rather than backward: instead of imagining my future self as beholden to my past self, I suggest we imagine my past self as looking forward, trying to live up to the person she hopes to become. The creator self doesn't *make* a promise; she sees (to take up another facet of the concept of a promise) a *promise* of a better self. When we speak of some prospect as a promising one, we do not use the word "promise" literally since, among other reasons, what doesn't exist yet cannot make promises. But this suggestive locution captures the reversal I propose. Promising presupposes a certain stability and predictability in one's self and one's circumstances. In a case where the values in question are in need of being created, it is only S_2 and not S_1 who would be in a position to take on such commitments. It is not S_1's place to embrace goals on behalf of, form reasons for, or create duties that will bind the created self. By her own reckoning S_1 is not as she evaluatively should be. S_1 is not the lender but the borrower of normative authority.

(c) Strawson's Two Requirements

We can restate Strawson's dilemma in terms of the idea of normative dependence. The one horn—no random changes—calls for a normative dependence relation between the two selves, while the other—no derivable values—demands novelty in the created self. We can represent these demands thus:

The Continuity Requirement says that S_1 and S_2 stand in some normative dependence relation.

The Novelty Requirement says that S_2 must contain a value or values not dependent on the values of S_1.

The continuity requirement and the novelty requirement contradict one another only if we fill out the former by assuming that S_1's values are the source of S_2's. In the next section, I want to flesh out what abandoning this assumption looks like. We will find that when we allow for the possibility that a process of value-acquisition progresses toward its own source of normativity, Strawson's dichotomy gives way to a third option: that the creator self relate to the self she creates aspirationally.

(d) Self-Creation by Aspiration

Consider how people come to appreciate the value of classical music or religious observance or fashionable dress or fine cuisine or political debate. The process might begin because one is suddenly, experientially confronted with a value one's prior valuations did not lead one to anticipate. One might experience such a transformative moment at a performance or in a church or among new friends. Such experiences are "transformative" only in the inchoative sense. They will not bear the weight we will have to put on them, if we try to use them to extrapolate a commitment to the endpoint. The transformed agent will look back, years later, and say of that initial event, "Little did I know, back then, what was really valuable about classical music" (or religious observance or fashion, etc.). She can, at that later point, say, "*This* was what I was after all along," but only because she encountered "this" before knowing exactly what "this" was. The value she comes to endorse is one she knows as a result of working toward a target she could not, at the time, exactly envision.

It is undeniable that many of our values trace their roots to that early-childhood period in which our ethical development was managed by others. Perhaps the Strawsonian will want to say, with respect to these values, that we simply find ourselves with interests and mastery we played no role in generating. And then he will tell us that we can work up additional values by rationally developing the commitments implicit in them. Alternatively, we can once again be passively subject to environmental influence and acquire values that bear no rational relation to those already inculcated in us. But are these the only choices? For all of us have developed passions—for fine food, politics, music, or philosophy—long after leaving our parents' homes. And if we consider the course of such development, we find, I submit, that the Strawsonian picture simply doesn't ring true.

Given the expertise and work involved, it is implausible that anything but the earliest stages of such a transformation can be explained through fully external factors. For instance, the fact that someone found himself, for incidental reasons, in the exceptional gastronomic environment of Osaka, Japan, might be the beginning of the story. Those experiences could ignite a spark of interest, but then something more would be needed to drive someone's systematic development of that initial spark into a full-fledged passion. The "something more" in question is unlikely to be a value to which he was antecedently committed, from which a passionate interest in culinary excellence could be derived.

I don't want to deny that there might be cases in which an accidental and transformative initial experience or an anterior value-commitment suffices to explain someone's value-transition. But in many cases, we embark on these sorts of adventures without think-ing that we know, in advance, exactly what we will get at the end. And that is not to say that we take them up on a whim, or for no reason, or by accident. There is an intermediate possibility that Strawson's dilemma has directed us away from recognizing, namely the possibil-ity that someone has an inkling of a value he does not fully grasp. He doesn't have a fully worked out sense of how this value fits into the rest of his values, because he doesn't have a fully worked out sense of what this value is. How could he, if the value corresponds to the intrinsic pleasures of the fine discriminations he is not yet capable of making? Nor is his pursuit conditioned on the coherence between the new value and the rest of what he currently values. Indeed, his ardent pursuit of it may take him away from much of what he cur-rently cares about.

Most of the profoundly important activities, relationships, and forms of knowledge that human beings pursue are ones a person can fully appreciate, and integrate into her value-system, only once she is well acquainted with them. And our question concerns the proc-ess of becoming acquainted. If you had to acquire values either by accident or by working out the entailments of your prior commit-ments, there would be no such process. You would either already be, in effect, at your value-destination or have no way to get started. But those don't seem to be our only options.

The way in which people stand toward many of the values that they do not fully appreciate is that they partly appreciate them. And with respect to some of these partly appreciated values, they also have the inclination to appreciate them more. They have a sense that their inchoate appreciation is *incomplete*, and act in order to attain a better valuation-condition. The actions they perform are versions of the actions they will be in a position to perform once they have fully acquired the value: i.e., the one who wants to value music acts like the person who already loves music. But she also acts *unlike* the person who already loves music, since that person is not herself acting like anyone else. Such people are, in effect, imitating or trying to live up to someone. They don't pre-approve of the person that they're trying to be; rather, they hope that the person they aspire to be would (and will!) approve of them. They see themselves as the imperfect version of that person who, in turn, serves as the standard by which they are to be assessed.

If you are trying to get better acquainted with some value, then you take your antecedent conception of that value to be inadequate. You act in order to grasp the value better, but your reason for wanting to grasp that value must be the very value you don't yet fully grasp. Life is full of moments in which one contemplates some obscure value from a great distance. We can't comprehend the value of child raising for us, let alone the value of the life of the child we will raise, before starting a family. We go to college for the education college will itself teach us to appreciate; we leave our hometown with the aim of making some foreign place home; we date in order to love, and get married in order to love in a new way; we choose a career because of the as yet unfamiliar joys of expertly doing the work in question. In pursuing these values, our attitude is not merely a hope or wish that we will one day come to appreciate them. We *work* to appreciate them, and this work is rationalized and guided by the values we are coming to know. In these cases, the full justification of what we are doing can come only at the end of the story. It is the end that provides the normative standards for assessing what comes before it.

(e) An Objection: The Value Gambit

Why think of the aspirant as being under the guidance of her future self, as opposed to being under the guidance of the very value to which her future self is (more) responsive?[7] The attraction of this alternative proposal lies in the prospect of avoiding an invocation of teleology. For if the value of, e.g., classical music guides one's aspiration to appreciate it, and if we can suppose that the value pre-exists the agent's arrival at her aspirational goal, then the source of normativity needn't *follow* that of which it is the source. I want to explain why this gambit does not succeed.

The proponent of the value gambit must acknowledge that the aspirant is guided by the intrinsic value of, e.g., classical music in a different way than the person she aspires to become. The latter's response to the value is indicated by, e.g., the joy she takes in the music she listens to, her articulate sensitivity to different renditions of a piece, her regular subscription for season tickets, her disappointment when she must miss a performance, her delight in sharing her love of music with her children. The aspirant, by contrast, is moved by the value of classical music to seek the approval of her music teacher, to commit to meeting a friend at the symphony so that she will not back out and see a movie instead, to pinch herself to stay awake throughout the piece, etc. If we want to characterize the aspirant as guided by the value of classical music, we will have to allow that she is guided in a non-paradigmatic way.

This non-paradigmatic form of value-guidance must be understood with reference to the full-fledged value-guidance into which it aims to develop. Pinching yourself to stay awake isn't a mark of appreciating classical music; it's a mark of *not* appreciating classical music. It is a form of response that comes under the aegis of the value only to the extent that we situate it in a developmental process: pinching in order to eventually attend

7. Thanks to Sam Scheffler and Matt Boyle for pressing this objection.

without pinching. It is only insofar as we bring the aspirant's response into relation with the response of the person she aspires to be that we see the former response as guided by the relevant value. The sense in which it is the value of music that guides her to care about her teacher's approval or to pinch herself is that it is her (ultimate) appreciation of the intrinsic value of music that makes intelligible what she is now doing—including the way in which she is now being guided. The value of classical music makes it right for her to care about her music teacher's approval or to pinch herself to stay awake, but this is because—and only because—she does those things so as to (really, fully) be guided by the value of music.

Aspirationally responding to a value isn't on all fours with non-aspirational response to it, in the way that, e.g., one can respond to musical value both by attending and by discussing. Rather, aspirational response to the value becomes legible as a response to the value only in the light of the proper response into which it develops. And this proper, intelligibility-conferring response is not one the aspirant herself grasps—except, of course, aspirationally. If this is correct, the shift from self to value fails to avoid reference to teleology. If we say that the aspirant is guided by value in a way that is derivative of her later mode of guidance, we adopt a form of explanation no less teleological than the one needed to claim that S2 is the source of normativity. In either case, a later instance of normativity renders intelligible the normativity present earlier.

It might, nonetheless, seem to make a big difference whether what a person is guided by is her self or value. For the first characterization might strike a person as objectionably egoistic. After all, what if someone aspires to be humble or kind—can these aspirations really be understood as forms of concern with *oneself*? I think, first, that we must recall that we are analyzing the self in terms of value.[8] When someone aspires to be the person she will become, she *is* aspiring to a form of value-appreciation; she is looking to fully inhabit a value. Given the theory of the self we are taking for granted, it doesn't matter much whether we adopt the language of self or value. For even if we choose the latter, we will have to allow that the defective way in which the aspirant responds to the value places a distorting emphasis on her own acquisition and ownership of the value. Whether we speak of her as guided by her future self or (aspirationally) by value, we will have to acknowledge that we have depicted the aspirant as more self-oriented than she should be. But this is a feature of the theory, not a bug: aspirants *are* more self-oriented than they should be!

Because an aspirant always has an eye on her own progress—she is engaged with trying to become someone—she cannot be fully, properly responsive to, e.g., music or the feelings of others. The would-be music-lover's attention must be divided: some of it can be directed at the music, but some of it must be set aside for considering the question of how much attention she is paying to the music ("Am I letting myself get distracted?"). When the kindness-aspirant acts unkindly, her ability to appreciate the suffering she has caused is impeded by worries over her own kindness-trajectory ("I've been working so hard on empathy!"). It is no paradox that a kindness-aspirant can't really, fully be kind. She is, after all, *not* fully kind, which is why she is aspiring to be.

V. TELEOLOGY AND AGENCY

(a) Backward Causation?

The aspirational account of self-creation offers us a recognizable story of what it is like to actively acquire values and avoids the

8. See Introduction, part IV.

paradoxes and problems associated with trying to force our under-standing of that transition into the mold of self-endorsement or self-cultivation. It may nonetheless arouse suspicions due to its tel-eological character. We are not, generally, inclined to accept forms of explanation in which that which is later grounds what is earlier.

The opponent of teleology may suspect that I am invoking something like backward causation or time travel: the future can-not cause the past, so how can something that is *in* the future have an effect on what I am doing *now*? Unless the ground of the agent's self-transformation is there at the outset, how is she to move herself to the desired result? In response to this worry, I want, first, to dis-tinguish the claim that S_2 is a normative source of S_1 from the absurd claim that S_2 causes S_1 to come into existence.

When an agent acts on a proleptic reason, she takes steps toward bringing about the normative source of her present condition. She works to make herself grasp the reason (R_2) that is, normatively speaking, the full or complete or nondefective variant of the prolep-tic reason causally driving that work (R_1). Her grasp of R_1 is causally responsible for her grasp of R_2, though R_2 is the source of normativ-ity for R_1 — R_2 is what makes R_1 a *good reason*. My claim, then, is that in the case of aspiration, causal or temporal priority fails to track normative priority. Is this possible? I am inclined to think it must be, since it is actual. The theorist of aspiration gives us what is the only way to account for self-creation in the face of Strawson's dilemma; and self-creation is a fact of life. We ought, therefore, to accept that such a reversal is possible, unless someone can show otherwise. One person who might take herself to be in a position to offer such a demonstration is the theorist of action.

Christine Korsgaard has articulated what we might call a "guidance condition" on rational agency: "A person acts ration-ally . . . only when her action is the expression of her own mental activity" (1996: 33); "A rational agent would be guided by reason in the choice of her actions." The action theorist may argue that in order for some behavior to be assessable as succeeding in a distinctively practically rational way, the norm with reference to which she is supposed to have succeeded must be mentally present to her at the time of action. For only in that way could the norm have guided her action. In order to understand aspiration as the aspirant's own work, we need to be able to understand it as coming *from her*.

I propose to set aside more general worries about teleology and focus attention on the worry specific to the action theorist: Can we represent the aspirant's progress as something she does, given that she lacks a clear or determinate conception of her target until she arrived at it? Does the aspirant satisfy Korsgaard's guidance condition?

(b) Two Conceptions of Agency

If Davidson's causal theory of action, read a certain way, is correct, she will not. Suppose that some behavior counts as an example of agency in virtue of the fact that it was caused by a belief and desire that rationalize it. On this picture, rational guidance is a causal matter. For instance, my trip to the store is caused by the desire to get food and the belief that I can get food at the store. My trip succeeds if I do indeed end up getting food at the store, and it can be assessed in the light of this norm precisely because this norm played a causal role in the genesis of the trip. On at least one way of understanding the desire that functions in such a causal explanation, it must constitute a grasp of what outcome is sought. Some event counts as agency to the extent that its success conditions are inscribed in the attitudes causing it. If practically rational guidance required an agent to know exactly what she wanted out of the outcome, aspiration could not qualify as rationally guided. The aspirant fails to grasp the full normative grounding of her project until it is completed. And if the reason is fully available to the agent only at the conclusion of the aspiration, it cannot (efficiently) cause the behavior that constitutes her aspiration.

A number of philosophers have recently developed a line of thought from Anscombe into a rejection of the causal theory of action. The alternative can be expressed as a response to the well-known problem of "deviant causal chains." The worry is that the Davidsonian has no way of ensuring that it is really the reason, as opposed to something correlated with the presence of the reason, that is doing the relevant causal work.[9] For instance:

> A climber might want to rid himself of the weight and danger of holding another man on a rope, and he might know that by loosening his hold on the rope he could rid himself of the weight and danger. This belief and want might so unnerve him as to cause him to loosen his hold, and yet it might be the case that he never chose to loosen his hold, nor did he do it intentionally. (Davidson [1973] 1980: 79)

Davidson says that he himself "despair[s] of spelling out . . . the way in which attitudes must cause actions if they are to rationalize the action" (79). Some, perhaps ultimately including Davidson himself,[10] have taken the problem as fatal to the causal theory. If we

---

9. This well-known worry can be articulated negatively, as to how one rules out deviant causal chains (Frankfurt 1978: 157–158; Davidson [1973] 1980: 78) or, positively, as to whether the semantic element is doing the causal work (Dretske 1989). For a recent defense of Davidson on this point against a rival neo-Anscombean picture, see Paul (2011).

10. "Several clever philosophers have tried to show how to eliminate the deviant causal chains, but I remain convinced that the concepts of event, cause and intention are inadequate to account for intentional action" (Davidson 2004: 106).

cannot eliminate wrong causal chains, then we may be inclined to give up on the project of basing our answer to the question of whether some event is an action on the way in which that event was caused.

Some of Davidson's critics[11] have sought refuge from this problem in Elizabeth Anscombe's *Intention*. According to the account they find in Anscombe, some behavior counts as an action—and therefore as assessable in the light of some end—not in virtue of the beliefs and desires that constitute its cause, but rather in virtue of the fact that, throughout the course of the action, the agent has a distinctive practical knowledge of what she is doing. So some behavior counts as, e.g., a hand-raising done for the sake of voting, because the agent does it in the practical knowledge that that is precisely what she is doing. This kind of knowledge is distinctive in being non-observational and non-inferential. When *I* try to answer the question as to what she is doing, I must observe her behavior and perceive that her hand is going up. In order to know that she is raising her hand in order to vote on the proposal, I must draw an inference from that (and other) observations. When *she* tries to answer the question as to what she is doing, she needn't observe herself or draw any inference. Thus observational or inferential knowledge of what someone is doing contrasts with the immediate, first-personal knowledge characteristic of the agent acting. Does the Anscombean account of agency offer better resources than the Davidsonian theory to the theorist who is accounting for aspirational agency?

---

11. Here I rely on Paul (2011), which draws together work by Michael Thompson, Sebastian Rödl, Candace Vogler, Richard Moran, Martin Stone, Matthew Boyle, Douglas Lavin, Kieran Setiya, and J. David Velleman. She helpfully abstracts the differences between their views to isolate an Anscombean emphasis on the formal, as opposed to efficient, causal structure of action (cf. Paul 2011: 5 n. 12).

It does not. If the agent's reason is to be the object of her practical knowledge (or even her practical belief), she must fully grasp it in advance of the action's coming to an end. And this is just what the aspirant cannot do. She does not know, or even take herself to know, what she is doing. She is dissatisfied by her own answer to the "why?" question. Whether we make the agent's reason for action the efficient cause of the action or the object of the agent's practical knowledge, we presuppose access to the normative standards governing one's own action. But the aspirant lacks this access, being unable to fully articulate, either before or during her action, exactly what she is doing and why. This is not to say that she has *no* idea what she is doing, but rather that her conception of what she is doing is derivative of a superior conception she will have after she has arrived at her destination.

It will be helpful to contrast aspirational ignorance of the end with the merely general or schematic grasp of an end to which specificationists such as David Wiggins (1975) and Henry Richardson (1994) have called attention.[12] Sometimes an agent's grasp of an end is too abstract to allow her to reason instrumentally in its service; she must, first, figure out in more detail what it is she seeks to do. For instance, if someone would like to have an entertaining evening,[13] he needs to figure out what kind of entertainment (i.e., exciting vs. relaxing, social vs. private) before he can begin to reason about how to arrange it. If a politician would like to create a point-to-point, no-transfer public transportation system for Paris, she needs to make the idea more concrete before she can turn it over to engineers. If you want to do something big for your wife's

---

12. I thank Martha Nussbaum and Elijah Millgram for suggesting that my position be clarified by the contrast with specificationism.
13. This example is from Williams ([1980] 1981: 04); the next one is from Millgram (2008), whose discussion of specificationism informs the presentation of it offered here.

birthday, you must settle whether what form this will take (romantic getaway for the two of you, or party for friends and family, or extravagant gift, or day to herself) before you can begin making the arrangements.

A person who has not yet done the relevant kind of specifying could be said not to know (exactly) what it is for the sake of which she will act and to reason in the service of filling out the end rather than finding a means to it.[14] How does her ignorance differ from the aspirant's ignorance? The distinction between general and particular, on which the specificationist relies, is different from (and cuts across) the distinction between the aspirant's partial or inchoate grasp of value and the full grasp to which she aspires. The former distinction allows one to factor out a known (general) element and an unknown (specific) element, facilitating action that fulfills the end to the extent that it is known. For instance, if I want to have an entertaining evening, I may know that I need to finish my work this afternoon. Without knowing whether my evening will be relaxing or exciting, I know that I won't be able to enjoy it with work hanging over my head. My schematic grasp of my goal may be perfectly adequate to dictate certain means taken in its service. Both my knowledge (that I want to have an entertaining evening) and the action (finishing up my work) that it prompts are shielded from my ignorance (as to what form that entertainment will take). I may not know what I will do, but I know why I am doing what I am doing.[15]

---

14. Though Candace Vogler (2002: 159–169) has argued that specificationist reasoning is a species of instrumental reasoning.

15. When the aspirant buys a bus pass to get to her music class, the purchase inherits her uncertainty about the end: if you press her, you will be able to get her to admit that she doesn't really know why she's buying the bus pass, since she doesn't really know why she's taking the class. What she doesn't know infects every element of the aspirant's action. I thank Anton Ford for helpful discussion of this material.

In these cases, the ignorance of the end doesn't touch action-explanation. Indeed, there is no reason why those who engage in specificationist deliberation need exhibit any ignorance of their end at the time of action. For in many cases nothing prevents them from holding off on acting in the service of their end until they have completed the relevant course of deliberative specification; and in some cases, they will not be able to act until they have done so. (Of course, there may, at that point, still be uncertainties as to the means by which the end will be realized.) It is, by contrast, characteristic of the aspirant that she *must* act in ignorance of what she is doing, since it is by such action that she comes to learn both the value and the nature of her activity. When the specificationist's agent acts, her action is directed at satisfying or realizing her end, as far as she already grasps it, not at learning what that end is. One place to see the difference from aspiration is in each agent's self-understanding as regards the assessment of her action. Aspirants can't confidently and authoritatively assess their own actions. They cannot tell whether they are doing what they are doing well; submit themselves to the assessment of others. Agents with a schematic grasp of their end do not betray a similar reliance on the assessments of others.[16]

The agent who has a schematic grasp of her end acts in a way that can be fully explained by the grasp she already has, however schematic it is. The aspirant acts in a way that can be explained only by the grasp she will have when her agency is complete. The aspirational target cannot be read off the agent's antecedent beliefs and desires unless those beliefs and desires are, in turn, interpreted proleptically, i.e., in relation to what comes after them. The end for the sake of which the agent acts when she aspires is not itself to be assessed in the light of what she currently takes herself to be doing or the desires with which

---

16. I thank Gabriel Lear for this point.

she entered into the pusuit. Rather, the order is reversed: both the intentions with which she acts and the motivations from which those intentions spring are to be assessed in terms of their conduciveness to her aspirational end. Thus we cannot say, of aspirational agency, that the normative assessability of its results derives from the fact that some conception of those results was present to the agent during the course of the agency. In the case of aspiration, the representation in question will have to be assessed in the light of another representation, namely the resultant one. If we want to ground the normativity of aspiration in antecedent representation, we will run in a circle.

We could accommodate aspiration within Davidsonian or Anscombean action theory by breaking it up into its many component actions. We might present each of those actions as caused by, or done with the knowledge of, some reason that rationalized it independently of the value that stands at the end of the process as a whole. On such a piecemeal picture, the many actions add up to a change of value at the endpoint, but that change of value is not a target of her agency. Indeed, the proximate face of someone's proleptic reason will provide us materials for this sort of reduction: we can say that I listened to the opera because I promised myself a chocolate bar when I got to the end. But we have seen, in chapter 2, that such a picture of aspiration will not do: the theorist of aspiration must supply a rationalization of the process of aspiration as a whole. Treating each action in isolation from the ultimate aspirational target produces a distortion of what the agent is doing; on the right way of looking at these moments of agency, they are not self-standing.

(c) Aspirational Agency versus Self-Standing Action

It is, perhaps, no flaw in the Anscombean or Davidsonian account that they do not accommodate aspirational agency. They were, after all, engaged in action theory as opposed to the more general discipline one might call agency theory. And though some actions (e.g., building a cathedral) may take a long time, it does not seem natural to characterize the whole process of becoming a music-lover or a parent as a single action. It is easier to apply that label to smaller projects—such as taking a music class or outfitting the nursery. But if I am right, those actions will, insofar as they form part of aspiration, be of a distinctive kind: they will be actions that cannot be understood except with reference to a larger stretch of agency of which they are a part. Anscombe and Davidson were offering accounts of what we can now characterize as "self-standing actions." The aspirant's agency does not have this quality: her individual actions are not self-standing, and the aspirational whole of which they are a part is not an action. Anscombe and Davidson described a particular kind of agency, namely the self-standing agency of the clear-eyed agent. The theorist of aspiration corrects them only by adding that there is another form of agency, one appropriate to the practical learner.

Let me return to Korsgaard's guidance condition: "A person acts rationally . . . only when her action is the expression of her own mental activity"; "A rational agent would be guided by reason in the choice of her actions." We can now see that statements such as these contain a crucial ambiguity. Suppose we paraphrase the condition at which they gesture as follows. In order for some stretch of agency done at time t to be done for the sake of norm N, it must be true that the agent grasps N at t. What I hope to have illustrated is that there are two ways of grasping a norm (or being guided by reason or having one's action be the expression of one's mental activity). One way is in the manner of the agent of a self-standing action. Such agents' activity is grounded in the bedrock of their current grasp of norms: in Anscombean terms, they act from practical knowledge.

But it is also possible to grasp a norm proleptically. In such a case, the agent's grasp of the norm guides aspirational activity without serving as its normative bedrock, for it is but an attenuated version of the grasp of value she will have once she reaches her aspirational endpoint. *That* grasp constitutes the normative bedrock, the ground on which all of her agency up to that point rests.

The practical reasoners I am describing seek to acquire what Anscombe's agents are fortunate enough to be in a position to exercise. Instead of acting, at each moment in time, *from* practical knowledge, the thread that binds together the various things they do (over the course of months, or even years) is the knowledge *toward* which they act. They are not knowers, but learners. Proleptic rationality illustrates the possibility that we might engage in practical reasoning in order to improve the very conception of the good that drives that reasoning.

Most instances of agency are teleological, in that they are done for the sake of some subsequent end. The agent's behavior is *going somewhere*, and that is because it is guided, from within, by the agent's sense of where she is going. What makes instances of aspirational agency special—puzzling—is that they are cases in which the agent's sense of where she is going is also, in the relevant sense, *going somewhere.*

Chapter 6

Self-Creation and Responsibility

In this chapter, I discuss the implications of the aspiration theory for questions of moral responsibility for one's valuational condition. First, I clarify the aspirational account by distinguishing aspiration both from the "dialectical activity" described by Talbot Brewer and from the phenomenon of ambition. I then argue that the aspirational account of responsibility is asymmetrical, accounting for a person's responsibility for acquiring a good valuational condition in a way that is different from the way in which it accounts for a person's responsibility for acquiring a bad one. I end by using a case study to compare the explanatory power of the aspirational account of responsibility with that of the self-endorsement view, the self-cultivation view, and Susan Wolf's view.

I. ASPIRATION VERSUS DIALECTICAL ACTIVITY

In his book *The Retrieval of Ethics*, Talbot Brewer describes a set of activities he calls "dialectical":

Some such activities have a self-unveiling character, in the sense that each successive engagement yields a further stretch of understanding of the goods internal to the activity, hence of what would count as a proper engagement in it. If the activity's constitutive goods are complex and elusive enough, this dialectical process can be reiterated indefinitely, with each successive engagement yielding a clearer grasp of the activity's proper form and preparing the way for a still more adequate and hence more revealing engagement in it. (2009: 37)

Among such activities, Brewer counts parenting a child, having a conversation, being in love, and appreciating music. What is characteristic of dialectical activity is that its "value cannot be grasped with perfect lucidity from the outset, but must be progressively clarified via engagement in the activity itself" (39). Brewer eventually argues that the set of dialectical activities is (at least roughly) coextensive with the set of intrinsically valuable activities: "[I]t seems doubtful that an activity can count as intrinsically valuable for human beings if it is simple and transparent enough that practitioners can arrive at a full and reflectively stable grasp of its highest possibilities and their value" (40). He holds that in order to be able to account for these activities as unified over time—as opposed to merely broken into disconnected stretches—one needs to abandon a number of foundational assumptions in action theory, namely that desires are propositional attitudes, that they aim to bring about the proposition specified in that content, and that they can be paired with beliefs to produce a rationalizing explanation of action. Brewer calls this set of assumptions "propositionalism," and much of his book is devoted to showing that dialectical activities, and the distinctively "dialectical desires" that motivate one to engage in those activities, call for a non-propositionalist conception of desire.

Brewer's language in describing the agent's grasp of the value and nature of the dialectical activity—that it is partial or unclear or veiled—is similar to the language I have been using throughout this book to describe aspiration. Likewise, his insistence on understanding dialectical activities as extended over time as opposed to broken into disconnected series of actions may remind the reader of one of my arguments in chapter 2, namely the argument that proleptic reasons are needed to capture the unity of the aspirational project. I do not propose to assess the bold theses in Brewer's rich book, but I do want to say why the phenomena he is describing, as he understands them, neither are aspirational nor raise the paradoxes that attend aspirational phenomena; moreover, I do not think that a recognition of the phenomenon of aspiration, taken by itself, requires us to abandon propositionalism. Dialectical activity cannot do the work in my theory that aspiration does, and aspiration could not do the work in his theory that dialectical activity does.

The crucial difference turns on what, precisely, is meant by the idea of a partial or incomplete grasp of value. Let me distinguish two ways in which we might describe some entity as failing to satisfy or instantiate some norm. The first way is by being *imperfect*, and the second is by being *inadequate*. Something is imperfect when there is any respect at all in which it does not instantiate the norm. For any given instantiation of a norm, we can often imagine a better or more complete one. Inadequacy is a much more serious flaw. If something is inadequate, it is not good enough, in the sense of being in need of some kind of remedy. It may not be a problem that a kitchen table is not perfectly clean, but it is a problem if the table is inadequately clean. Brewer doesn't draw this distinction, but a number of features of his view point to the conclusion that when he says the agent does not have a "full" grasp of the value, he must mean that her grasp is *imperfect.* The aspirant, as I understand her, is someone whose grasp both is, and is known by her to be, *inadequate.*

Let me explain why I ascribe the former view to Brewer and why the latter plays such an important role in my own theory. Brewer's characterization of some activity or desire as dialectical is not restricted to agents at an early stage of development: he understands the relevant set of activities, which is to say those that are intrinsically valuable, to be dialectical even for the expert. So even the seasoned practitioner of, e.g., dance, would not find her grasp of the value of dance, and of the activity of dancing, to be, in Brewer's sense, "full." Brewer traces the concept of dialectical desire to the descriptions of the desire for union with God in Gregory of Nyssa, Augustine, and Aquinas (as well as later Christian mystics). Infinitude borne of the impossibility of, e.g., "sating one's appetite for God" (160) is written into the nature of the activity as dialectical. It would not necessarily follow from this picture that the distance from completion marks the state as imperfect as opposed to inadequate—for one could think that all of human life is marked by a deep failure to be in contact with any true value. But this is not Brewer's view. He spends a chapter of his book explaining how these activities are characteristically pleasant, drawing on Aristotle's conception of pleasure as an *energeia* (activity) complete at every moment. Thus he holds that the failure to have a "full" grasp is compatible with having an adequate or good enough grasp of the value. For Brewer is clear that we do engage in these activities for their own sakes and that in so doing we find them rewarding sources of meaning as opposed to painful reminders of our defectiveness.

The aspirant, by contrast, is aware of the defectiveness of her grasp of some value. She is unable to engage in the relevant activity purely for its own sake, precisely because she does not yet value it in the way that she would have to in order to do so. And because she can see that her grasp of the value is inadequate, she is moved to change herself into someone who has a better grasp—thus the music teacher's paradoxical demand that the ideal student of her class, as an aspirant, respond to musical value exactly to the extent he is not yet able to. We cashed out this form of responsiveness as a *proleptic* one, in which the agent is moved by a proximate, but acknowledgedly inadequate representation of value as a stand-in for the real value the agent hopes to thereby attain. Unlike Brewer's dialectical activity, aspirational activity is not done for its own sake. Brewer (121) classifies a dialectical activity as an *energeia* (activity/ actuality), whereas aspiration would have to fall on the side of *kinesis* (motion/change): it fails to be complete at every moment. The activity of the aspirant characteristically aims at self-change: she is taking a music class in order to become a different kind of person, namely one who appreciates music. Unlike aspiration, dialectical activity is not a mode of self-creation; for the same reason, Strawson's paradox does not arise as a challenge for Brewer.[1]

Brewer contends that a dialectical desire cannot be expressed in the form of a proposition describing a state of affairs to be brought about. The aspirant's desire can. Qua aspirant, she desires to bring about the state of affairs in which she is a person who can appreciate, e.g., music. This desire suffices to unify her entire aspirational project, from the moment of its inception until she becomes the person in question. Of course, if Brewer is right, and the activity of (fully) appreciating music must itself be understood as the object of a non-propositional desire, then the same will be true of aspirational

---

1. Brewer does, in one place, make a glancing reference to a "benign paradox of inquiry" attending "any dialectical activity whose constitutive goods have not been fully mastered." The paradox strikes Brewer as benign precisely because the agent engaging in such an activity is, despite the fact that she has not "fully mastered" the good, nonetheless "sufficiently aware of what she would count as good" (47).

desire. For the analysis of aspirational desire is parasitic on the analysis of the desires of the person in the completed condition. My point is only that the aspiration theory, taken by itself, does not give us reason to resist propositionalism. It is also neutral on the question of whether the completed activities have, as Brewer supposes, a component of infinite perfectibility.

II. ASPIRATION VERSUS AMBITION

It has been suggested[2] to me that most of the value-changes we experience stem not from making ourselves into, e.g., a gourmand or an opera-lover, but rather from a simple openness to value. Compare a graduate student who selects her courses with the conscious aim of shaping herself into a successful academic with one who allows interest and passion to determine such choices. This story could play out in a variety of ways, but it is not merely those of a romantic bent who might anticipate the possibility that the second student surpasses the first academically. The first is, perhaps, working on herself with too heavy a hand. A pair such as these might lead one to caution against "too much aspiration," lest the aspirant lead herself down too narrow a path on the basis of a blinkered conception of the value she's pursuing. Are we, sometimes, advised to refrain from aspiring in order to allow ourselves to be open to value as it presents itself? No. I will argue that the right moral to draw from this story is that we are sometimes advised to refrain from being too *ambitious* in order to allow ourselves to aspire. What is the difference between ambition and aspiration?

2. By Rachana Kamtekar and Erin Beeghly, to whom I owe the example of the two graduate students.

Let us, first, review the contrast between aspiration and self-cultivation. Aspirational pursuits combine the property of being large in scale with that of being directed at change in oneself. Self-cultivation overlaps with aspiration on the latter front: when we cultivate ourselves, we engage in a pursuit that is self-directed but small in scale. Because self-cultivation presupposes the priority of the earlier self, it cannot engender major changes, such as reversals in what Ullmann-Margalit calls one's "core values." Thus we found that the self-cultivation model of self-creation underestimated the possibility for radical, rational self-transformation.

We can also contrast aspiration with the kind of pursuit that is large in scale but is not directed at producing a change in the self—these are the pursuits I will call "ambitious." An ambitious agent aims, usually over many years, to achieve something difficult and perhaps important. Nonetheless, the pursuit is not, with respect to value, a learning experience: she is not, as she proceeds, coming to a better and better grasp of why she is doing what she is doing. An ambitious agent's behavior is directed at a form of *success* whose value she is fully capable grasping in advance of achieving it. Hence ambition is often directed at those goods—wealth, power, fame—that can be well appreciated even by those who do not have them.

Ambition is often salutary: the researcher who has the ambition of curing some disease is, if she succeeds, a boon to humankind, as is the politician who aims to ameliorate social ills or the inventor who discovers ways to make life easier for everyone. But because ambition both consumes much of an agent's efforts and does not expand his value horizons, it carries with it the danger of trapping him in what may be an impoverished appreciation of value. This danger is lessened if ambition does not entirely usurp the space for aspiration. For it is important to acknowledge that someone might harbor both ambition and aspiration in the same domain, just as someone might simultaneously aim to both cultivate himself and to aspire. To the extent that she is ambitious, she seeks to realize values already in her grasp; but she might, at the same time, aspire to come into better contact with those same values. Plausibly, the great achievers in human history have been both ambitious and aspirational. Nonetheless, it is possible to criticize someone for approaching some pursuit with too much ambition, too little aspiration. This is, I believe, what the example of the two graduate students illustrates.

The "heavy-handed" student's problem, if she has one, is not that she is aspirational as opposed to open-minded, but that she is ambitious as opposed to aspirational. She is trying to succeed (at getting what she already wants) instead of trying to learn (to want something new). Aspiration is not to be contrasted with openness to value; rather, aspiration *is* openness to value. There is no such thing as generalized openness to value that does not take the form of some concrete pursuit of value. What would such openness consist in, practically speaking? Being open to the value of poetry involves acting differently than one would in order to be open to the value of yoga.[3] If openness is to be a genuinely practical attitude, it must be at least somewhat value-specific. We made this observation with reference to Dickens's Sidney Carton (see chapter 2, section III). Aspirants cannot aspire without some grasp of the value they are trying to acquire. In order for the agent to make any kind of progress—to be aspiring as opposed to flailing—there must be a specific value that she is, so to speak, trying to value. Or trying not to.

For one can aspire not only to acquire, but also to be free from a value. My parents' generation was the first to be faced en masse with the task of revising their sexual norms in the face of encountering

---

3. See my criticism of Paul in chapter 1, section IV.

homosexuality in their own children or in friends of their children. They aspired to rid themselves of the values that would dictate attitudes they found to be incompatible with the love they felt for these children. It is, in part, due to their aspirational work that homosexuality has a very different place in our culture today than it did thirty years ago.[4]

In calling for openness, with respect to sexual morality or anything else, we do not ask for people to instantaneously change who they are or to do so entirely on their own. The call for openness is a call to try to feel the defect in one's valuation, either the failure to value something that is valuable or the mistake of having placed value on something that is not in fact valuable. The call to openness also, characteristically, involves opening oneself to being shaped by others: to listen, to attend, to submit oneself to the judgment of those who have a better grasp than oneself. And this is what the early stages of aspiration look like: having an inkling of interest, being moved to look further, having a sense that one's preconceptions and assumptions may not be right or that one hasn't made adequate room for something, having a sense that there are others who have a better grasp. While the ambitious person may receive assistance from others in achieving his goal, the aspirant needs others to help her with the project of grasping her goal. The ambitious person may, of course, also be ignorant: she may not know how to acquire some particular means to her end or how to jump over some hurdle standing between herself and success. The ambitious person's ignorance is, however, circumscribed by her knowledge: she knows why she wants to get past that hurdle, even if she can't figure out how to clear it. The aspirant's ignorance, by contrast, runs all the way down.

4. Thanks to Kristina Gehrman for this nice observation.

III. RESPONSIBILITY FOR SELF: AN ASYMMETRICAL ACCOUNT

Adults are, to various degrees, responsible for the kind of people they have become. They play some role in shaping their own interests, passions, idiosyncrasies, and moral sensibilities. Genetics, parenting, and many different kinds of environmental factors also contribute, more in some cases than in others. If you become a menace to society after enduring an unusually harsh upbringing, and I do so while having had the benefit of every advantage, I deserve more blame than you do for becoming the kind of person we both are.

These commonsense intuitions point both to the existence of and to the existence of qualifications on someone's responsibility for being whatever kind of person she is. We take ourselves to be responsible not only for what we do (or think or feel), but also for being such as to do (or think or feel) those things. The second kind of responsibility is responsibility for the persisting cognitive, emotional, motivational, and evaluative condition that I've been calling a person's "self" or "who she is."[5] We presuppose responsibility for self when we decry wasted talent and laziness—"You had it in you to succeed!"—as well as when we take privilege or adversity into account when considering otherwise similar applicants—"Describe the challenges you have faced."

---

5. The concept of character has come under attack by "situationalists" such as Doris (2002) and Harman (2003), to whom Kamtekar (2004) responds with a defense. In accounting for responsibility for self, we don't need to address these arguments, for reasons Setiya has given: situationalists deny the existence of character only in the sense of "unified traits that range across much of what we do, their influence apparent in widely varying situations" (2007: 75) Even if we concede the nonexistence of these traits to the situationalist, we can construe the self as composed of dispositions that are more fine-grained and not necessarily widely shared.

The aspirational account supports these various intuitions. On the aspirational account, I am responsible for the values I acquire aspirationally. Since aspiration essentially involves the contribution of one's environment, this responsibility will be a matter of degree. Consider the following (artificially) simple example. Two children both have the ability to play a certain piece of music well, with both technical accuracy and musical sensitivity. The first has natural talent and a piano-teacher mother who guides every moment of his practicing, for which he further has ample leisure; the other is largely self-taught, less naturally gifted, and must squeeze time for practice between chores and schoolwork. We will be more impressed by the achievement of the second student than the first: in comparison with him, the first child seems to have had a lot of the work done for him by his mother, good genes, privilege. Both children deserve credit for having developed the ability to play the piece, but the one deserves more than the other.

In the same vein, I will want to say that I am responsible for my value-achievements to the degree that my aspirational work figures in the explanation of my arriving at the endpoint. I become some way by aspiring when my aspiration to be that way figures significantly in the explanation of my becoming that way. The more it so figures, the more responsible I am. But this is not a complete account; for it describes a merely sufficient condition on your being responsible for your current condition. Or rather, it describes a condition that is both sufficient and necessary for responsibility for being in a *good* condition. I believe we need a different account of responsibility for bad, i.e. blameworthy, conditions. I cannot offer a complete account here of why this is the case or what the account should be. But I find the issue worth addressing in this context, if only in a cursory and promissory way.

It might appear that the account on offer here can easily be extended to bad cases: you are responsible for your good character if you got there by aspiring, and you are responsible for your bad character if you got *there* by aspiring. But there are some reasons to think this may not work. The first problem is presented by the figure of the lazy agent. Jill has, despite ample luck (natural talents, loving parents, etc.), never tried to appreciate any value other than the creature comforts to which her privileged upbringing gave her easy access. Jill's valuationally impoverished condition seems to be her own doing, in the sense that she is responsible for being the (bad) way she is. But she did not *aspire* to be the way she is. In fact, she did not aspire to be any way at all: Jill's problem is complacency.

I suggest that we accommodate Jill's responsibility for her condition by invoking the possibility that someone can culpably fail to aspire. She can be blamed, in effect, for her very self-satisfaction. We can use environmental factors to distinguish (more) culpable failures to aspire from non-culpable (or less culpable) ones in much the way that we do in cases of credit, mutatis mutandis. Having one's route to some positive condition facilitated by privilege, genes, and good luck makes one less responsible for success than the one who had to struggle. In the case of a failure to, e.g., develop one's talents, we can likewise say that an agent is less culpable for his failure to develop himself if major obstacles stood in the way. Jill would be the contrast case, an agent whose failures to aspire are not due to her environment but are directly attributable to her. Thus we can open up, on the side of responsibility for bad character, an avenue of what we might call omissive culpability. This already suggests an asymmetry between the bad case and the good one: on the good side, there is only commissive responsibility, whereas on the bad side, it seems there is both commissive and omissive responsibility. But this is not quite right: the asymmetry runs deeper yet.

For how exactly are we to understand commissive responsibility for being bad? Given that aspiration is an intentional state, no one, except perhaps the devil,[6] aspires to be bad. Suppose we have before us an evil, cruel, heartless gangster. He denies being, or having aspired to be, any of these things. He insists that he both is and aspired to be nothing other than a great leader in his community. Can we hold him responsible for the condition that he ends up in (public scourge), if he ended up being that way as a result of having aspired to be a *different* way (public servant)? To do so would be to introduce an opaque form of self-creation. We will not be able to understand commissive responsibility for being bad on the model of commissive responsibility for being good. It matters, for our conception of the process of aspiration as an agential one, that the goodness one achieves is the same goodness one was (proleptically) after. Otherwise, one is not creating the very self that one becomes.

We cannot say that the dictator is responsible for becoming cruel because he became cruel while aspiring (to be great). For there are cases that fit this formula where we will not want to hold the agent culpable. For instance, suppose it is a result of my successful aspirations to become a great pianist that everyone in my music school comes to hate me for my superiority to them. I become hated by all as a result of aspiring, but I did not aspire to be hated by all. Nor does it seem to be the case that I am responsible for being hated by all. We want to distinguish the evil dictator from someone whose bad condition is a mere side effect of her aspiration. There are reasons, then, to think that someone is to count as having aspired to

---

6. And this case is notoriously hard to understand; cf. Anselm's discussion of the fall of the devil (Casus Diabli), discussed by Tomas Ekenberg (2015).

some condition she is in only if being in that condition figured—however obliquely or opaquely—in the intentional content of her aspirational mental states (desires, beliefs, feelings, etc.).

If this is so, then in virtue of what is someone responsible for becoming an evil person? I want to suggest, in the face of the difficulty of constructing a commissive account of such responsibility, that the error must, like lazy Jill's, be one of omission. The evil person did not aspire to become a good person, though he could have. He had enough contact with the beginnings of goodness through his early childhood that he had the materials from which such an aspiration could spring. I am not, of course, saying that his *actions* constitute omissions. But it is possible to be responsible for being the kind of person who would *commit* those kinds of actions in virtue of having culpably *omitted* to aspire to be a better kind of person.

If this account of responsibility for self is correct, the asymmetry introduced by aspirational accounts of moral responsibility is deep indeed. We are responsible for good ways that we are to the degree that we aspired to be in those ways, and bad ones to the degree that we culpably failed to aspire to be better. The analysis of the bad cases would, on this account, be conceptually derivative of the good ones.[7]

IV. THE ASPIRING GANGSTER?

But is it true that no one aspires to be bad? Consider a gangster in training. It looks as though "gangster" is a description under which someone is blameworthy and, at the same time, a description of a way someone might aspire to be. It is imaginable that someone

7. Thanks to Steve White for showing me the need to revise my views on blameworthiness and for helping me do so.

might try to become a gangster, under that very description. Could someone *aspire* to become a gangster? Recall our two graduate students. Let us exaggerate the differences between them so that the one is maximally ambitious, the other maximally aspirational. The one chooses her courses entirely with the aim of impressing the people whose letters will carry weight; she writes on the most popular topic; she fills her dissertation with the kinds of phrases and points that she imagines will make her sound impressive and right-thinking; etc. The other student chooses advisers because she admires their work and thinks they have something to teach her; she picks a dissertation topic from interest and passion; etc.

These students may be caricatures, but the phenomenon I am caricaturing is very familiar to anyone who has been a teacher. Turning ambition into aspiration is one of the job descriptions of any teacher, but it belongs especially to those of us who, as philosophers, carry the Socratic torch. Socrates may not have had great success with, e.g., Alcibiades, Thrasymachus, and Callicles, but there is no question that he was *trying* to transform their ambitious political strivings into an aspiration to virtue. Aspirants make good learners because, quite simply, they take themselves to have something to learn. We saw that *ambition* was marked precisely by value-stasis. The ambitious person, qua ambitious, is engaged in getting what he wants, as opposed to learning what he wants.

Now return to the gangster in training. This is a popular figure in literature and (especially) movies. All of us have encountered representations of someone working to become a gangster. In order to show that any one of them was an aspiring gangster, we would have to imagine what differences we would introduce into the story in order to retell it as one of mere ambition. And it seems to me we cannot do this. Unlike with the two graduate students, we cannot imagine two young gangsters who are distinguished by the question of whether they aspire or merely have the ambition to become gangsters. We might imagine approving of one such gangster more than another, but this is only because we take him to aspire not to being a gangster, but rather to becoming someone who, e.g., helps his family and gets respect. But aspiring to being that kind of person is aspiring to something *good*.

The young gangster in training may not understand what it is to be a gangster, identifying it with the list of good traits named earlier. He says he wants to be "just like my father," but that is because he doesn't know what his father does. The question is: What does he do when he learns the true meaning of, e.g., "take care of" so-and-so? If he rejects the life with horror, we can say that he *had* aspired to be good and learned that the path he was taking toward that aspiration was mistaken; if he continues to work to be a gangster, his state was never anything but ambition. As an illustration of such a case, consider Henry Hill, the protagonist of the film *Goodfellas*. He describes his initial attraction to mob life:

> As far back as I can remember, I always wanted to be a gangster. To me, being a gangster was better than being President of the United States. Even before I first wandered into the cabstand for an after-school job, I knew I wanted to be a part of them. It was there that I knew that I belonged. To me, it meant being somebody in a neighborhood that was full of nobodies. They weren't like anybody else. I mean, they did whatever they wanted. They double-parked in front of a hydrant and nobody ever gave them a ticket. In the summer when they played cards all night, nobody ever called the cops.

Contrast a speech that might have been given by a reminiscing writer. I'll call him, "Stephen," after Stephen King:

As far back as I can remember, I always wanted to be a writer. To me, being a writer was better than being President of the United States. Even before I first wandered into the newspaper office for an after-school job, I knew I wanted to be a part of them. It was there that I knew that I belonged. To me, it meant being somebody in a neighborhood that was full of nobodies. They weren't like anybody else. I mean, they did whatever they wanted. They didn't own TVs or care what other people thought about them. They read during meals and ignored social conventions; they were rude and they paid no penalty for it.[8]

Both speakers use aspirational language, describing a desire to "be somebody" and to be free from social norms or constraints. They both express admiration for a group they take to be powerful and would like to be part of. Nonetheless, we interpret them quite differently. The writer is plausibly describing an early stage of a learning process, a stage in which he exhibited an inkling of what was to come. The gangster's speech does not point beyond itself. Instead, it indicates to us that he is trapped in a fantasy. There is no analogue for the speech King makes advising young writers: "Writing isn't about making money, getting famous, getting dates, getting laid or making friends" (270). For becoming a gangster *is* simply about those things, and nothing more. Perhaps there are gangsters who would insist, at the end of their lives, that there was something they were

---

8. Inspired by passages from King's *On Writing* (2000), such as "Reading at meals is considered rude in polite society, but if you expect to succeed as a writer, rudeness should be the second to least of your concerns. The least of all should be polite society and what it expects. If you intend to write as truthfully as you can, your days as a member of polite society are numbered, anyway" (142–143). "Life isn't a support system for art. It's the other way around." "If you're just starting out as a writer, you could do worse than strip your television's electric plug-wire, wrap a spike around it, and then stick it back into the wall. See what blows, and how far. Just an idea" (22).

after all along: respect. But we would take a reductive attitude to the phenomenon the gangster calls "respect," denying that it has real value and thereby analyzing it in terms of his associates' attempts to stay on his good side for their own self-interest. The gangster isn't honored; he is simply feared.

When young Henry and young Stephen look at the people they admire, they are both attracted by a kind of power. But Stephen's grasp of that power is aspirational: in pursuing it, he is also at the same time pursuing a value of which it is an intimation. He is reaching beyond himself, proleptically, in the manner of the aspirant. Henry's reason has no distal face. He can't be aspiring, because there is no "there" to aspire to. Suppose there is a gangster otherwise like Henry but who says that "all I'm after, as a gangster, is money, power, and women." He would not be a different kind of person from Henry. The fact that such a person describes himself in cynical terms, whereas Henry employs more romantic language, has no ethical significance. It doesn't *matter* that Henry talks in terms of wanting to be a better person; the defective nature of his target prevents him from counting as the aspirational counterpart to the cynical gangster in training.

If it is true that seeing someone as an aspirant presupposes some appreciation for the value toward which she aspires, then we find in the phenomenon of aspiration a tight connection between our adopting a certain form of explanation for some bit of behavior, on the one hand, and our approval of that behavior, on the other. There is an argument for a view of this kind in the opening discussion of Augustine's *On Free Choice of the Will*. Evodius asks Augustine, "From whom did we learn to sin?" Augustine answers that we cannot "learn" to sin, because learning is the process of acquiring knowledge: "Since learning is good, and the word "learning" (*disciplina*) is correctly applied only when we come to know something (*nisi a discendo non dicta est*), we simply cannot come to know evil things ... It follows that doing evil is nothing but turning away from learning" (1993: 2). One might worry that Augustine's point is a merely semantic observation about the word "learn." Perhaps we do not use the word "learn" to include cases of learning what is evil, but couldn't we? Are we making a principled distinction when we refuse to call the person who *takes herself* to be arriving at an improved cognitive condition "a learner"?

Evodius responds by suggesting that there might be "two sorts of learning: one by means of which we learn to do right, and another by means of which we learn to do evil." Evodius can be heard as asking after the justification for drawing our linguistic (and conceptual) boundaries as we do. Augustine responds by asking him:

AUGUSTINE: Do you at least consider understanding good?

EVODIUS: Certainly. I consider it so good that I cannot see how any human trait could be better. And I would in no way say that understanding can be bad.

AUGUSTINE: When someone is being taught but does not understand, would you say that he has learned?

EVODIUS: Of course not.

AUGUSTINE: Well, then, if all understanding is good, and no one who does not understand learns, then everyone who learns is doing good. (1–3)

Augustine argues that learning entails understanding, and understanding cannot but be good; thus there is no bad form of learning. But why couldn't Evodius insist that there are two kinds of understanding? I want to make a suggestion as to how Augustine leverages Evodius's denial of the title "learner" to one person, namely the one who doesn't understand what he's taught, into a denial of that title to another person, namely the one who "learns" evil. If we were to call the person who "learned" evil things a learner, we would have to do so on the basis that he appeared (to himself) to learn: he took himself to be arriving at an improved cognitive condition. But the person who is being taught appears (to others) to learn. He sits at the foot of the teacher as she expounds truths. And yet that appearance is no basis for calling him a learner. Why not? Because someone who is to learn must *really* be learning and not only appearing to learn. This justification speaks to the work we want our concept "learn" to do—we use it to pick out a certain kind of actual progress toward grasping the way things are. The person who is merely being taught fails to make any such progress—but the same is true of the one "learning" evils.

Augustine's argument aims to expose the internal connection between learning and progress toward enlightenment. I have, in the same vein, described an internal connection between aspiration and genuine value-advance. The two arguments are not, of course, merely analogous. For I have been developing a conception of aspiration as a form of (practical) learning. Insofar as Henry strikes us as having less in common with Stephen than with the cynical gangster, we manifest a concern with aspiration as a form of learning. We could, of course, take a cue from Evodius and carve things up differently. We could speak of appearing to oneself to aspire, a condition shared by Henry and Stephen. Like Augustine, I think it is no accident that we are not antecedently inclined to make use of this category. Aspiration is what excites our interest, because aspiration picks out something of ethical significance. Whether or not someone appears to himself to aspire is not an ethically significant fact about him; by contrast, whether or not someone aspires matters directly to our assessment and treatment of him and to the quality of the life he leads. Aspiration is a useful ethical category in a way that appearing to oneself to aspire is not.

V. RESPONSIBILITY FOR CHARACTER: A TEST CASE

On December 11, 2013, Ryan Loskarn, chief of staff to Tennessee senator Lamar Alexander, was arrested on charges of possessing and distributing extremely graphic and violent child pornography. His arrest was met with shock, dismay, disapproval, and an effort on behalf of his former associates to distance themselves from him as quickly as possible. In an instant, Loskarn went from an up-and-coming political player to being branded with that special kind of evil mark that we reserve for crimes we don't ever want to think about. A month later, Loskarn committed suicide. After his death, a letter was found in which he revealed that he had been sexually abused as a child, at ages five and nine. The letter does not appear to be a suicide note; rather, it seems that he decided to commit suicide sometime after writing it.

Loskarn's letter was met with a wave of empathy, such as we find expressed in Ruth Marcus's *Washington Post* editorial "The Tragedy of Ryan Loskarn." Marcus writes, "Some people do terrible things because they are purely evil, others because they are terribly damaged." Seeing Loskarn as a victim of abuse reframed for us what it meant that he was, as he described himself, an abuser of young children. Details of his troubled past seem to mitigate his responsibility for ending up as he did, since they suggest that, to some degree, something other than Loskarn himself made him into the person he became.

When philosophers discuss examples of agents like Loskarn, they are usually interested in the question of how diminished responsibility for character might detract from someone's responsibility for the actions he performs from that character.[9] That is not the direction of reasoning suggested by Loskarn himself in his letter:[10]

> I understand that some people—maybe most—will view this as a contrived story designed to find some defense for defenseless behavior. That it's an excuse . . . But I'm sharing this with you because it is the truth, not an excuse. And I believe it played a role in my story.

Loskarn ends his letter with an apology "to the children in the images": "I should have known better. I perpetuated your abuse and that will be a burden on my soul for the rest of my life."

Loskarn apologizes to the children because, as he says, he sees himself as responsible for having perpetuated their abuse. He does not seek to be exculpated for responsibility for, as he puts it elsewhere in the letter, "my crime." He offers the details of his abuse because he believes "it played a role in my story." It seems likely that the role such an event would have to play in the self-told story of one convicted for such an offense is exculpatory. Yet Loskarn does not show any signs of seeking exculpation for what he did (or thought or felt). Recall Marcus's description of Loskarn as someone who "did terrible things" but only because he is "terribly damaged." The line plays on the word "terrible," first invoking a sentiment of righteous indignation at the immorality of his (presumably voluntary)

---

9. For a canonical example, see Gary Watson's 1993 discussion of a vicious murderer/victim of brutal child abuse, Robert Alton Harris.

10. Parts of Loskarn's letter are cited in Marcus's article, and it can be found in its entirety at http://www.jesseryanloskarnslastmessage.com/.

evil actions, and then shifts to an empathetic sadness in response to Loskarn's status as a victim with respect to who he *is*. She seems to want to exculpate Loskarn for having become the kind of person that he is, despite holding him responsible for what he actually did. In what follows, I will take for granted both the fact that we can be (to some degree) responsible for our characters and the fact that Loskarn was, and was reasonable in, citing his abuse as grounds for exculpation in respect of responsibility for self as opposed to responsibility for action.[11]

It is unclear where this leaves us with respect to his responsibility for what he did. One might think that, to the extent that Loskarn is not responsible for becoming a pedophile, he is to that extent not responsible for consuming and distributing child pornography. For one might think that any responsibility one has for the actions one performs is derived from one's responsibility for acquiring the character that would dispose one to perform those actions. This is precisely the argument made by Galen Strawson (1994) in the paper[12] in which he offers the dilemma discussed

---

11. Responsibility for self includes responsibility for cognitive, emotional, and practical dispositions, whereas the responsibility for action that I forbear from discussing covers all, and not merely agential, activations of those dispositions. Angela Smith (2012), developing a strand of thought introduced by Robert Adams (1985) and Tim Scanlon (1998: 283–285), argues that my responsibility for what I think or (don't) feel cannot be understood in terms of my having *chosen* the attitude in question. Instead, she thinks that we ought to construe such cases of responsibility in terms of the subject's rational answerability for the thought or (lack of) feeling and that we are responsible when those thoughts and feelings are traceable to our own evaluations. The phrase "responsibility for attitudes" obscures an important distinction between the *disposition* to, e.g., harbor racist beliefs or be jealous of one's sister and the *activation of such a disposition* in the form of thinking a racist thought or feeling a pang of jealousy. Both can plausibly go under the name of an "attitude." Her reasons-account is persuasive as an account of cases where we blame someone for what he said, thought, felt, did, or didn't do on a given occasion, but not as an account of blame for *being such as to* do or feel or think in that way. I do not think this is a flaw in her account, since I do not think she is concerned to discuss moral responsibility for dispositions.
12. As well as in his 1986 book.

earlier, calling into question the possibility of self-creation. He takes responsibility for action to rest on responsibility for character, and he takes the latter to (impossibly) call for self-creation. But we should, at this point, be wary of assuming, simply on the basis of the temporal priority of issues of responsibility for self, that it serves as normative ground for responsibility for action.[13] I do not, therefore, take a mitigation of Loskarn's responsibility for character to entail a corresponding mitigation of his responsibility for what he did. Nor, however, do I assume the contrary. I propose simply to set aside the question of responsibility for action in order to focus on responsibility for self.[14]

Supposing the reader shares my intuition that the revelations in Loskarn's letter mitigate his responsibility for self, let us compare a few ways of accounting for this fact. Let's begin with the self-endorsement model discussed in chapter 5, section I. Recall that on this account, we distinguish those features of an agent for which she is responsible from those for which she is not by looking to her own self-evaluations. We are familiar with the phenomenon of agents such as akratics or addicts who evaluatively reject some part or aspect of their motivational makeup. It might appear that a view on which evaluative self-endorsement is necessary for responsibility is well placed to exculpate Loskarn, given his expressions of self-revulsion. I think that a closer reading of his letter suggests,

---

13. See also the substantial body of work that Strawson's argument has generated (e.g., Fischer 2006: 112–118; Clarke 2003: 170–176, 2005; and Mele 1995: 221–230), much of it addressed to denying or qualifying precisely this premise in Strawson's argument.

14. In drawing this distinction, I do not intend to take a stand on the debate between Shoemaker (2011) and Smith (2012) as to whether moral responsibility comes in multiple species ("answerability, accountability and attributability") or can be analyzed using a single underlying evaluative notion. For even if Smith were right that there is a single underlying notion, it might manifest in different ways depending on the differences in the object—self vs. action—for which the person is to be held responsible.

however, that we cannot explain Loskarn's diminished responsibility by pointing to the negative outcome of a self-reflective procedure:

> I found myself drawn to videos that matched my own childhood abuse. It's painful and humiliating to admit to myself, let alone the whole world, but I pictured myself as a child in the image or video. The more an image mirrored some element of my memories and took me back, the more I felt a connection.
>
> This is my deepest, darkest secret. . . .
>
> In my mind I instigated and enjoyed the abuse—even as a five and nine year old—no matter the age difference . . . By my late teens I reached a sort of mental equilibrium on the matter. I couldn't stop the images from appearing altogether, but I generally controlled when they appeared . . . As an adult I thought I was a tougher man because of the experience; that I was mentally stronger and less emotional than most. I told myself that I was superior to other people because I had dealt with this thing on my own. Those I worked with on the Hill would likely describe me as a controlled, independent, and rational person who could analyze a situation with little or no emotion. That's how I viewed myself. In retrospect, the qualities that helped me succeed on Capitol Hill were probably developed partly as a result of the abuse and how it shaped me.

In many ways, Loskarn identifies both with his abuse ("In my mind I instigated and enjoyed" it) and with the person his abuse made him: "controlled, independent, and rational." He writes, speaking in the present tense, that "in my heart I still struggle to see my five-year-old self as a victim." Loskarn says he "felt a connection" to child pornography, and he does not present himself as safely alienated from this connection. He does not describe his desire as a compulsion that he can evaluatively condemn as in any sense "external." He is unlike Frankfurt's unwilling addict, whose will retreats to the safety of second-order rectitude. Loskarn cannot seem to make a clean break from the negative features of himself—and this is because those negative aspects run very deep. The self-endorsement theory cannot exculpate Loskarn, because he does not succeed in performing the relevant self-alienating task.

The self-cultivation theory does not fare better. Loskarn describes his present self as a product of the "self-control" he learned to exercise to cope with his abuse. In retrospect, he can see that he was "shaped" by his abuse, but at the time he understood himself as cultivating virtues of independence, rationality, and control. When he describes "the mental equilibrium I *had created* to deal with my past," he understands his pedophilia as something he *did* to himself as a way of confining the problematic parts of himself. It looks as though there is some basis for saying that Loskarn *did* cultivate the condition he ended up in.

At this point, we might wonder whether *any* attempt to ground responsibility for self in a kind of self-directed agency will be able to exculpate Loskarn. This is just the point made by Susan Wolf, who assimilates what I have called the self-endorsement view and the self-cultivation view under the label "the deep self-view," according to which

> our wills are not just psychological states *in* us, but expressions of characters that come *from* us, or that at any rate are acknowledged and affirmed *by* us. For Frankfurt, this means that our wills must be ruled by our second-order desires; for Watson, that our wills must be governable by our system of values; for Taylor,

that our wills must issue from selves that are subject to self-assessment and redefinition in terms of a vocabulary of worth. (1987: 49)

[T]he deep-self view . . . allows us to distinguish cases in which desires are determined by forces foreign to oneself from desires which are determined *by* one's self—by one's "real," or second-order desiring, or valuing, or deep-self, that is. (51)

My "deep self" is in charge of governing or determining what forms of motivation will count as true expressions of my agency. When some desire can be traced—either as endorsed or as cultivated—to this deep self, then it represents a desire that is truly "mine." Wolf suspects that all such views will inevitably crumble under regress. "No matter how many levels of self we posit, there will still, in any individual case, be a last level—a deepest self about whom the question, 'What governs it?' will arise, as problematic as ever" (52). She worries that the regress can be ended only with some implausible picture of a "prime mover unmoved, whose deepest self is itself neither randomly nor externally determined, but is rather determined *by* itself—which is, in order words, self-created" (52). She takes the metaphysical difficulties attending the deep-self view to expose the paradoxical quality of the very idea of self-creation. I have argued that the regress that Wolf takes to threaten the very idea of self-creation in fact threatens only one account of self-creation: the account in which the creator self rules over, determines, controls, or governs the self it creates. Self-creation needn't be cashed out in terms of the normative priority of the creator self over the created self. But I want to set aside Wolf's metaphysical scruples with the very idea of self-creation and discuss an objection she raises to the idea that, even if we *could* make sense of such self-creation, it would not suffice for moral responsibility.

She describes a case in which a sadistic dictator, Jo, has indoctrinated his son, JoJo, into his evil values so well that JoJo is fully on board with Jo's inhumane political agenda:

> Jojo is given a special education and is allowed to accompany his father and observe his daily routine. In light of this treatment, it is not surprising that little JoJo takes his father as a role model and develops values very much like Dad's. As an adult, he does many of the same sorts of things his father did, including sending people to prison or death or to torture chambers on the basis of whim. He is not *coerced* to do these things, he acts according to his own desires. Moreover, these are desires he wholly *wants* to have. When he steps back and asks, "Do I really want to be this sort of person?" his answer is resoundingly, "Yes," for this way of life expresses a crazy sort of power that forms part of his deepest ideal. (53–54)

Wolf introduces JoJo to show how even someone who acts from his "deep self"—motivated by values that he endorses, as opposed to ones from which he is alienated—can lack (full) moral responsibility. Comparison between JoJo and Loskarn serves to support Wolf's general intuition that there is a condition on moral responsibility for one's motivational condition that is tangential to questions of whether one endorses or has cultivated it. JoJo enthusiastically avows the values from which his actions spring; plausibly, he has also done work to mold himself in the image of his father, cultivating the character he now has. Loskarn, in quite a different way, identifies with his abuse, internalizes evaluative attitudes that are products of it, and cultivates the character he ends up with. Since she takes the case of JoJo to show that exercises of agency over oneself fail to serve as grounds for responsibility, Wolf grounds our mitigation of JoJo's responsibility in a substantive fact about his ethical point of view: his desire for power, and his ethical ideal more generally, is "crazy." Wolf's analysis of the case is that JoJo is not responsible for his character, because his ethical point of view is insane.

To say that JoJo is insane is, according to Wolf, to say that he lacks "the minimally sufficient ability cognitively and normatively to recognize and appreciate the world for what it is" (56). JoJo's ethical point of view is divorced from reality, and he has no prospect of correcting it. I think there is something right about Wolf's approach, in that it suggests that if we want to understand what is wrong with JoJo and Loskarn, we cannot avoid making mention of the substantive fact that what they value is not valuable. They are mistaken or incorrect in their valuational approach. The aspiration approach likewise rules out the possibility that Loskarn's disposition to watch child pornography was his own creation, precisely on the grounds that watching child pornography is bad. There is no value that one's cultivation of such a disposition would be getting at. But I think the invocation of such a substantive condition is not incompatible with claiming that the condition in question is a fact about that person's self-directed agency. My defense of this claim begins with a critique of Wolf's sanity account.

First, it is not clear to me that Loskarn's values are rightly described as insane in Wolf's sense. Given his inclination to keep his viewing of pornography secret, it seems that Loskarn was not *completely* "unable to understand and appreciate that an action fell outside acceptable bounds" (Wolf 1987: 61). Even if there is some sense in which he did not understand the depth of the evil he was committing, it seems wrong to say he was constitutionally unable to understand this. For by the time he writes the note, he has come face to face with the horror of what he has done. I am not even sure that JoJo qualifies as insane in Wolf's sense. Was JoJo *unable* to appreciate the moral law? Is there *no* set of circumstances we can imagine on which he comes to acknowledge the error of his ways? Since JoJo is fictional, we could simply postulate that there is literally not a single possible world in which some kind of moral awakening occurs during his adult life. But then the JoJo example will be less than useful in our attempt to analyze the ordinary human phenomenon of responsibility. We will want to know how actual people, for whom change tends to be (in a broad sense) possible, if unlikely, can be exculpated for characters for which they are not responsible.

The second problem with Wolf's analysis is that it does not draw sufficiently on the historical conditions under which JoJo acquired his ethical perspective. It is not the fact that his views are bad or insane, but the manner in which those views were developed, that seems to have exculpatory bearing. As it stands, Wolf's account cannot distinguish between JoJo and Jo, whose values are just as insane as his son's. Wolf never directs us to mitigate Jo's responsibility; indeed, she herself seems to tie her exculpation of JoJo to his upbringing: "It is unclear whether anyone with a childhood such as his could have developed into anything but the twisted and perverse sort of person that he has become" (54). We should not conflate the claim that JoJo couldn't, given his upbringing, have become anyone else with the claim that he couldn't, having become that person, come to later appreciate morality. Even the former claim seems too strong—perhaps someone with a less accommodating temperament than JoJo would have more seriously rebelled against his father. It certainly does not seem right to insist that, given his childhood trauma, Loskarn *had* to develop a child pornography habit. But we seem to be on the right track if we are thinking about the process by which JoJo and Loskarn, by contrast with Jo, came to be the way they are.[15]

---

15. Wolf might deny that Jo and JoJo are equally insane. For she could claim that Jo, unlike JoJo, has the *ability* to normatively recognize and appreciate the world, though he does not

On the aspiration account, we must refer to this path and to the nature of the agency contained with it in order to understand whether the person is responsible for making himself who he became. The aspirational account is asymmetrical in that responsibility for good character will be a matter of having made oneself into the person who has that character, whereas responsibility for bad character cannot be understood in a parallel way. The person who ends up with bad values never aspired his way there. We must, then, distinguish culpable from non-culpable (or less culpable) failure to aspire. On what grounds do we judge that a person is less than fully responsible for having failed to aspire to correct his bad values or acquire good ones?

In our discussion of proleptic reasons, we saw that they characteristically manifest in a social form. Aware that they cannot fully get their target into view, aspirants draw on the help of teachers, mentors, parents, coaches, therapists, friends, and fellow aspirants. They interact with, are guided by, and also imitate and pretend to be like the people around them who have a more developed (or, in some cases, just differently developed) form of the value. They rely on their environment not only to supply them with the minimal grasp of value with which they begin, but throughout the process of growing that initial seed into a complete, established form of valuing. Because the defects in her form of valuing do not escape her notice, the aspirant is motivated to subject herself to the assessment of others. Unlike either self-endorsement or self-cultivation, aspiration is not a theory of solitary self-creation. And this allows the

exercise it (62). But she could do this only by insisting on a systematic connection between, on the one hand, the process by which one arrives at (or has inculcated in one) a normative outlook and, on the other, the manner in which one holds the outlook thus arrived at. The aspirational theory of self-creation offers up the philosophical materials with which to underwrite such a connection.

aspirational theorist to cite the fact that someone was cut off from the relevant kind of help in her explanation as to why such a person should not be blamed for her failure to achieve the relevant goal. The aspirational theory places great emphasis on the following common ground between Loskarn and JoJo: they are both relatively isolated from the system of value we would have them learn. In JoJo's case this is a product of the fact that he has been brainwashed by a powerful tyrant. In Loskarn's case, the cause is much more mundane:

> As a child I didn't understand what had happened at the time of the abuse. I did know that I must not tell anyone, ever. . . .
>
> I always worried someone might look at me and know, so I paid close attention to others for any sign they might have figured it out. No one ever did.

Loskarn did not seek out help, because he could not bear anyone to know what had happened to him. He kept himself apart from others. He tried to keep the abuse even from himself, rewriting his memories ("I instigated and enjoyed the abuse") even as he could see that he was falsifying them. He says, "To those who choose to sever all ties with me, I don't blame you. No one wants to think or talk about this subject matter. All I can say is: I understand and I'm sorry." He understands why people would want to be dissociated from him, because he wants to be dissociated from himself, describing himself as "disgusting and horrible." He expects no sympathy, no empathy, no help, nothing but rejection from his community.

Aspirants do the work of becoming new people, but they cannot typically do this work alone. Loskarn eventually does come to want to change his own ways of thinking and dealing with the abuse, but only as a result of a chance occasion to share his past:

In my life, I had only ever mentioned the abuse to three friends, and then fleetingly so. I never spoke to a mental health professional about this or any other matter until I was in the D.C. jail. I talked with a counselor there about my crime and the horrible hurt I had caused so many people. I didn't talk to him about my past. I didn't think it mattered because I intended to kill myself as soon as possible.

The session ended and I left to be taken to a cell. Before I'd gone far, the counselor called me back. He said there was something he couldn't put his finger on and he wanted to talk some more. And then he just stopped and looked at me, not saying a word. He was the first person in my life who I think had figured it out. And he was the first person I ever spoke to in any detail about those memories.

It is only *after* speaking to this counselor that Loskarn is moved to write the letter in which he speaks of having endeavored to "begin the process of trying to sort this out and fix myself." Until that point, his approach was that of making do with the self he had, rather than acquire a new one. He had recourse only to self-management, controlling, limiting, and repressing, but never *changing* the "broken" parts of himself.

Loskarn's experience of abuse is certainly sad, but what is really tragic is his subsequent imprisonment, by shame and secrecy, in his own valuational error. Because Loskarn was a real person, it is easy to have an emotional reaction to reading his letter; and I think the pang of sadness that we feel when we imagine his loneliness contains some intelligence. We wish we could reach out to the child Loskarn, the adolescent Loskarn, the young adult Loskarn and draw him out from his very private suffering into the light of our shared space. He is not responsible for failing to aspire out of his condition because his feeling of shame cut him off from any of the resources such aspiration would have had to draw on.

The aspirational theory is well placed to explain why those who have suffered from unusually harsh conditions in their upbringing are less responsible for failing to create themselves as good people and as valuers of the good. We needn't imagine that an upbringing such as JoJo's or a traumatic experience such as Loskarn's is incompatible with aspirational success. All we need for exculpation is that such a success, though imaginable, calls for an aspirational task at which most of us would have failed. This is, I think, one payoff of the aspirational account of self-creation in the domain of moral responsibility: because it shows us how the claim that people create themselves is consistent with the admission that they need help to do so, it offers us the correct interpretation of cases such as Loskarn's and JoJo's.

Conclusion

I. DEFENDING ASPIRATION

The reader has probably noticed that the posture of this book is a defensive one. It is true that I set out to explain both what aspiration is and how it relates to questions about rational decision, psychological conflict, and moral responsibility. But I do all of that by way of making the case that there is, really, such a thing as aspiration. Did this argument need to be made? At first glance, it might seem as though the phenomenon is too commonplace to require the support of philosophical argument: everyone acknowledges that people do in fact become mothers, lovers of classical music, and gourmands. Isn't it just a fact of life that people become fluent in what was once a foreign culture? Does any philosopher deny the existence of the phenomenon that this book champions?

Yes, I believe many do, without having drawn their own, or their readers', attention to that fact. For they are moved to describe the relevant set of cases in distorting ways, under the pressure of a theory that has implicitly foreclosed the possibility of the distinctively practical form of learning—value-learning—that constitutes the agency of the aspirant. They are inclined to read cases of aspiration either as examples of self-cultivation or as examples of having been shaped by others. In the first case, they can simply describe the cases as standard intentional actions; in the second, the change the person undergoes is not an expression of her own agency. To see no space between self-cultivation and being changed just is to deny the phenomenon of aspiration.

And, as I have noted, the refusal to see this space is not without argumentative backing. When they want to gloss (what I would call) a case of aspiration as simply a case of self-standing intentional action, philosophers will note that intentional action is compatible with a great deal of ignorance as to exactly what one will do, how one is going to do it, and what success will consist in. It is certainly true that unless our action is extraordinarily simple, we act before we have figured out all the details. If we assimilate the aspirant's ignorance to this sort of incompleteness, we will be glossing over the importance of the fact that the aspirant does not know *why* she is doing what she is doing. Her ignorance is one of value. In response, we are likely to hear that if the person under description *doesn't* know why she is doing what she is doing, she is not "doing" the thing in question. If she *does not* grasp the value in advance, then her progress is really the work of others.

In this dialectic our interlocutor seeks to commit us to the position that the aspirant either (fully) grasps or (fully) lacks the value that lies at her target. Such an interlocutor is, in effect, putting the squeeze on the distinctive form of ignorance characteristic of the one who is coming to know. When we say that the aspirant's grasp of the end is "proleptic," what we mean is that her grasp of the value for the sake of which she acts is a dimension in which she improves herself over the course of her aspirational agency. At the end of the process, she will be able to say, truthfully, "Now I see what I was after all along!" Did she grasp this end all along? Yes and no: she grasped it enough to be "after" it, but not enough to see it for what it really is. The pressure to say she either (fully) has it at the time of aspiration, in which case her agency is of the ordinary variety, or fully lacks it, in which case she is not acting, is the pressure to deny the phenomenon. We cannot allow the class of aspirants to be split into those non-aspirants who cultivate themselves and those non-aspirants who are cultivated by others.

Consider a similar "divide and conquer" strategy employed by would-be deniers of weakness of will.[1] The person who is skeptical that there is such a thing as akrasia will not put herself forward as denying some *phenomenon*—for, of course, she does not think that there is any such phenomenon. Instead, she will redescribe the cases that the rest of us took to be instances of acting against one's deliberative conclusions as cases in which people *either* did not draw those conclusions (because, e.g., they had deceived themselves as to which conclusions they drew or revised their thinking at the last minute) *or* could not control themselves and so did not really *act* against the judgment in question. The examples that the theorist of weakness of will adduced to illustrate the phenomenon will be classified by the skeptic into one of these two kinds of non–weakness of will. The skeptic denies that there is unity to the class of phenomena originally presented for theorizing.

Unlike the problem of weakness of will, the problem of aspiration is not a recognized topos in philosophy. This makes it much easier for people to engage in reductive analyses without exciting attention to the fact they are doing so. If one is not *redescribing* cases someone has already classified as aspirational, the division of the relevant phenomena into self-cultivation or being-shaped may not strike one as needing any special defense. At the very least, this book should serve to generate the relevant kind of philosophical

---

1. Santas (1966) offers this presentation of Socrates' position in Plato's *Protagoras*.

pressure: the skeptic of aspiration will have to acknowledge herself as such and explain why it is a mistake to see an underlying unity in the set of cases described in this book.

But I hope, of course, that it can do more than that. I granted from the outset that this book is in important ways introductory—it cannot pretend to have altogether dispelled the aura of paradox surrounding the phenomenon of value-learning. This is because, while I have suggested ways of modifying the existing conceptual framework in the three areas of ethics in which the theory of aspiration is rooted, I have not taken the further step of showing, in each area, what a complete theory inclusive of my accommodation amounts to. Here are a few examples of the lacunae that result from my approach. In relation to part I, I have not offered an account of how we balance aspirational thinking against more standard deliberative demands about how to expend our temporal, financial, and emotional resources; nor have I explained the fact that people seem antecedently drawn in different aspirational directions and limited in their abilities to "muscle" themselves into valuing. In relation to part II, I have not explained how we arrive at an orientation in our intrinsic conflict; nor have I described the special connection that seems to exist between aspiration and the emotion of interpersonal love. In relation to part III, I have not explained how aspirational responsibility for one's values is related to responsibility for action; nor have I offered an account of how the fact that we can identify aspiration only in domains where we acknowledge the relevant value is compatible with tolerance and value-pluralism. I have made room for aspiration by undermining certain settled dichotomies and assumptions but I have not, so to speak, put Humpty Dumpty together again. Why not?

The problem I have faced is not merely one of carving off an appropriate, book-sized project. The incompleteness of the account presented in this book is due, in large part, to a defect of its author: she is not so distant from the philosophical culture she describes to have escaped the very preconceptions obscuring the phenomenon. Like everyone else, I have trouble getting aspiration into view. Like everyone else, my "intuitions" about cases are shaped by a reflexive assumption that takes decision as the paradigmatic moment of rational agency. Rational agents present themselves to my imagination as wholehearted, value-laden subjects; I am not inclined to ask how they *got* all their commitments, projects, relationships, and concerns. I find it natural to conceive of rational agents as reasoning from value rather than toward it. In writing this book, I embarked on a project that entailed fighting against these tendencies in myself; the completion of the project is something that will, I believe, call for fellow soldiers.

My hope, then, is that this book will generate energy and optimism and good faith toward the construction of ethical theories (of decision, psychological conflict, and responsibility) that comfortably accommodate the phenomenon of aspiration. Those armed with such a theory will naturally apprehend coming-to-value as one of the vicissitudes of practical rationality. They will have a theory of value on which it is intuitive to take value as something that can be learned. Their understanding of agency will be such that they will readily see coming-to-appreciate as a manifestation of it. This book is aspirational, not because it is about aspiration, but because it is written by and for those who are just being introduced to the phenomenon. The best I can hope for, then, is that reading this book will allow one to cling more tenaciously to the goal of recognizing the agency of becoming, even in the absence of full theoretical resources for doing so. To that end, I will close with a test case meant to bring out the stakes of acknowledging the reality of aspiration, by showing the work that the concept can do in application.

II. MOTHERHOOD AND INFERTILITY

By "application," I refer not only to the idea that, as philosophers, we apply the concept of aspiration to particular cases of aspiration, but also to the idea that, as human beings, we interact with aspirants and need to treat them as such. Aspirants are characteristically needy people, since (they see that) their own conceptions of value are insufficient. Their group of supporters includes, but is not limited to, people who may have a better grip than they on the particular values and reasons of the person they want to become. They also rely more generally on the kindness or empathy or material assistance of those who love them, since they tend to make mistakes, to need help, to not know exactly what they are doing.

Aspirants represent a distinctive ethical category of agents whose vulnerability renders our correct treatment of them a matter of especially deep ethical significance. This, I take it, is part of what explains our profound shock and anger in the face of cases of child abuse. I believe that we have an especially stringent set of ethical intuitions that govern the ways in which it is appropriate to behave toward aspirants. We sense a special responsibility when we interact with our children, our students, our advisees, those who look up to us, and in some cases siblings and friends. Our feeling that carefulness, sensitivity, tact, and empathy are called for in these interactions betrays an awareness that these people need our help to become the people they seek to be. If we do not do enough, they may never get there; and if we do too much, we get in their way.

The embeddedness of the aspirant in the social world was a theme of the preceding chapter. If one can, contra Nietzsche, "pull oneself up into existence by the hair, out of the swamps of nothingness," it is only because one is not alone in the swamp. The possibility of self-creation does not eliminate the need for parents, teachers, coaches, and, more generally, helpers. Becoming good is something that you do, even if the assistance you get from your fellow citizens is crucial to the success of your project.

I want now to show how the modifications I have suggested to the theory of practical rationality, moral psychology, and moral responsibility support the ethical intuitions that we make use of in our interactions with the kind of aspirant who figured so largely at the opening of this book: the aspiring parent. I hope thereby to reveal how much it matters, even at the level of our day-to-day treatment of those we love, that we be in a position to acknowledge aspiration and the aspirant's distinctive (proleptic) rationality. Applying the concept "aspirant" to the people around us can make an ethical difference to how we treat them.

In the first chapter, we considered a pair of suggestions as to how a decision theorist might explain the making of a life-changing decision, such as the choice to have children. Ullmann-Margalit considered such choices from the third-person vantage point. She determined that there was no rational way of adjudicating the debate between "Old Person," with his current set of preferences to avoid boring family life, and "New Person," who, having had his preferences deeply changed by the advent of children, embraces the conventionalism spurned by Old Person. Ullmann-Margalit argues that one cannot "choose" which of these points of view is better; one can only "pick," as between type-identical boxes of cereal. Paul considered the same choice from the first person. She concluded that one ought to make the transformative choice if one wants to have new preferences, and otherwise one ought to refrain. I want to return to the question of the rationality of the childbearing decision, considered now from the point of view we have neglected: the distinctively ethical second-person point of view. How should we respond or react—as we all must, at some point or another—to friends and family members traveling any distance down the road of childbearing? I have argued that the aspirational approach to large-scale transformative pursuits offers us better answers to both the first- and the third-person deliberative questions than those offered by Paul and Ullmann-Margalit, respectively. But our discussion of self-creation and the case of Loskarn has given us reason to think that it might be in the second-person domain that the approach for which I have been arguing will really shine.

I want to begin by considering how Paul or Ullmann-Margalit might approach the second-personal question. In her article "What You Can't Expect When You're Expecting," Paul develops the consequences of her account of what she calls transformative choice in the area of parenthood specifically. She argues that because having a child is a transformative experience, someone who is infertile cannot know what he or she is missing. She concludes that such a person has no reason to grieve his or her infertility as a loss. She holds that it is rational to be upset over not having X only if you can anticipate the value of X for you, which is to say, if, knowing what you would get out of it, you know why you want it. For Paul, this is a matter of being able to imaginatively project for yourself the future of which you take yourself to be deprived. Since prospective parents cannot do this, it is not rational for them to be unhappy to discover that they cannot have children:

> My argument also has consequences for those who want to be able to physically conceive, carry and give birth to a child, but are unable to do so. If you want to have a child because you think having a child will maximize the values of your personal phenomenological preferences, and as a result of your inability to have a child (and thus your inability to satisfy these preferences)

you experience deep sadness, depression, or other negative emotions, my argument implies that your response is not rational. This is disturbing and some might find it offensive, but it is true. Such a response is not rational. That does not mean your response is wrong, or blameworthy, or subjectively unreasonable. (2015: 21)

Some readers might pause over Paul's description of the parent's rationale for wanting children as "think[ing that] having a child will maximize the values of your personal phenomenological preferences." Recall that for Paul, it is a general truth about decision that "[t]o choose rationally . . . you choose the act that brings about the outcome with the highest estimated expected value. In the case where you have a child, the relevant outcomes are phenomenal outcomes concerning what it is like for you to have your child" (5). Thus when Paul adverts to those who choose to have children in order to maximize their preferences, she intends to rule out those who may want to have children for some external reason, such as in order to have more hands to bring in the harvest. *Those* people can rationally choose to have children. But when she refers to people who have children in order to "maximize . . . personal phenomenological preferences," she is describing what is, in a relatively affluent society, the standard reason for wanting to have children: for its own sake.

We can set aside the question of how exactly to characterize this standard case and whether it is right to gloss wanting children for its own sake as seeking to maximize preference satisfaction. Paul's point is that if a person who is motivated to have children in the ordinary way is unable to have children, any "negative emotions" he or she might experience at this prospect are irrational. Though Paul softens her conclusion by denying that such grief is "wrong, or blameworthy, or subjectively unreasonable," she presumably does mean to contrast this kind of case with one in which people *do* have a real reason to be upset. She is thus claiming that grieving infertile people are confused, by contrast with those who are upset at the loss of—to demonstrate the range of cases—a large sum of money, the use of a limb, or an actual, living child. The irrationality is that of being upset over a state of affairs that they cannot see as bad for them. We might compare them to a child who is upset at being denied her favorite plate to eat on. The child does not have any real reason to be upset, though we might find her response—given that it is her favorite plate—to be subjectively reasonable, and we might refrain—given that she is a child—from calling her response blameworthy or wrong.

There is a parallel line of argument on the side of those who don't want children. Paul is equally bound to charge as irrational the person who *doesn't* want children because she[2] wants to go to college. Such a person is wrong to think that she knows what it will be like either to have a child or to go to college; and she should not be trying to make her decision on the basis of any such projection. She cannot anticipate what it will be like to experience either the love she will feel for her child or the intellectual excitement she will feel in college. And if, for instance, she *must* have the child, because abortion is in one way or another unavailable to her, it is, by Paul's argument, *irrational* of her to grieve the loss of her opportunity for an education.

---

2. From this point on I will speak, as Paul does, about motherhood specifically. Much of what I have to say will hold true to some degree for men, but the points I make here are starker when considered with reference to women. For both the burdens of child raising and the grief of childlessness characteristically fall harder on women than they do on men. It has been, and continues to be, a social and cultural fact that such issues touch women and men unequally. See May, who notes, for instance, that "[c]hildlessness is measured in terms of women. I found no data on childlessness among men" (1995: 11).

Paul anticipates that readers will resist her conclusion, as I do myself. I believe that if we conceive of the grief of our friends or loved ones in this way, we will treat them badly. And we will do so because we will be mistakenly blind to their predicament, which is to say, to the reasons governing their sadness. The aspiring parent does have reason—proleptic reason—to mourn her lack of access to the value in question, as the aspiring college student has reason—proleptic reason—to bemoan her lack of access to an abortion. The fact that the person doesn't have full access to the value of what she has lost doesn't remove the sting of loss. Rather, the person's pain has a distinctive, aspirational character, in that what one mourns is never getting the chance to learn how valuable that child, or that education, would have been. One bemoans the life one never got to know.

Now let us turn to Ullmann-Margalit, who analyzes such decisions as cases of "picking." Her account of the (ir)rational structure of what she calls "big" decisions is also an unsatisfactory basis for a sensitive response to the grief of the unhappily pregnant or the unhappily childless. It does not make sense to grieve the absence of a freedom to pick; if one is reduced to picking between options, then the ability to make the selection is not one that a person can reasonably prize. One is not disempowered in virtue of the fact that the supermarket shelf contains only one token of the type of cereal one prefers. The same is true of a weightier case, such as the college student who would have picked (and not chosen) college A over college B. They are both good schools, and she sees that neither has more to offer her than the other. She might rationally grieve the rejection from B on the grounds that it reflects poorly on her academic worth (if she had reason to believe that), but she cannot mourn her rejection on the grounds that she would have attended B. Since she would merely have *picked* B over A, her rejection from

B does not deprive her of anything. She doesn't have a real reason to be upset about where she's going to college. Things would be different if she were not able to attend any college—this is a transformative experience whose loss would be a real loss to her. And this is so even if—indeed, it is true in part *because*—she cannot quite see what she would be missing.

We want to be able to distinguish cases in which one is deprived of a picking experience from ones in which one is deprived of an aspirational experience. Assimilating aspirants to pickers trivializes the losses experienced by the former when they are cut off from progressing in their aspirations. It is true that both aspirants and pickers are in a situation where they do not know what they are missing. The difference between them is that aspirants were in the process of trying to learn what they were missing. The fact that the erstwhile aspirant (knows that she) will never know what she is missing is a legitimate source of grief for her.

Being cut off from one's aspiration gives one reason to lament because the aspirant's valuational condition was predicated on the value she now knows she won't acquire. Proleptic reasoners act for the sake of a future apprehension of value. They are counting on arriving at a valuational condition, exclusion from which may threaten their grip on value altogether. When such a person feels lost, empty, and adrift, her feeling is a truthful reflection of what has happened to her. There is a distinctive kind of sadness appropriate to losing something you were only starting to try to get to know. This sadness is a rational response to the experience of infertility—as well as to the experience of having to abandon one's educational aspirations for motherhood. The aspiring college student who must give up those dreams to raise a child is liable to feel that she was *counting* on the college experience to make her life meaningful. She doesn't know who she is if she must depart from her educational trajectory.

The historian Elaine May reports on the prevalence of a parallel sentiment among the infertile. In the course of writing her book on infertility in postwar America, she placed an "author's query" in a variety of newspapers and magazines in which she asked childless people to write to her of their experiences. In the book, *Barren in the Promised Land,* she presents representative samples of the more than five hundred letters she received. "Marsha" (names have been changed) writes to her:

> The grief—the loss . . . I spent six years of my life trying to be a mom, and it was beyond my control. For a while I couldn't look ahead. I thought, how do I define myself if I don't do this? What am I if not a parent?

It does not help to tell Marsha that *she never was* a parent and that she is exactly the person she was before embarking on her six-year fertility journey. For she is not the same person, having put her other values on hold in preparing herself for motherhood. And yet when she laments the six years she spent trying to have a child, she is not complaining about the opportunity cost. Her point is not that she wishes she would have made advances in her career or hobbies over that time. She no longer cares about the other things she could have spent that time doing, because the emotional investment in the values of motherhood has sapped her interest in anything else. This sentiment is reflected in the trajectory of another respondent. "Amanda" had initially been ambivalent about parenthood and occupied by a demanding job as a legal secretary. Nonetheless, over the course of treatment she loses interest in her job, and when the process fails she describes her condition:

> I find myself wandering [*sic*] every day about what I will do with my life and how I will fill this void in my soul . . . I want to find

fulfillment in something else one day, but for now I realize that I must first heal and grieve.

Amanda's typological mistake—"wandering" for "wondering"—is evocative of a Freudian slip. For she describes herself as lacking anything of value, meaning, or interest by which she might orient her passage through life. She has quit her job, has given up on motherhood, and feels that there is nothing but "void" in her soul. She has the sense that there will be some valuational future for her, but at the moment she cannot anticipate it. She may well be right that in order to move forward, she must first reconcile herself to what she has lost ("I must first heal and grieve").

If we were Amanda's friend, it would not merely be cold or ineffective to tell her that her grief is irrational. It would be false, since she does have a reason to be upset. She is mourning the loss of her own self. Amanda's feeling of being bereft of value is of a piece with Marsha's feeling that she lacks an identity. One's deepest values, interests, and desires—which, for these women, have all become focused on the project of motherhood—form the core of one's own sense of the person one is. In acknowledging her reason to be upset, we acknowledge that she has lost the person she was trying to become, and thereby the person she now is.

Aspirants open themselves up to a distinctive experience of losing everything without seeming to have lost anything at all. Because the aspirant's value-condition is, by her own lights, derivative of the one she aspires to have, she is vulnerable to the experience of having the valuational rug pulled out from under her. Aspirants have, to various degrees[3] and in various ways, put down roots in a possible world.

3. Thus we could also use the aspirational framework to understand the grief of women whose pregnancies do not lead to motherhood. Even those who believe that life begins at birth

For the sake of simplicity, I have until this point assimilated the inability to have one's own biological children and the inability to adopt into a single condition of inability to have children (in any way whatsoever). Paul's argument is not restricted to counting as irrational those who grieve the lack of biological children while being able to adopt.[4] The difference between the two forms of inability is immaterial to her charge of irrationality. But it is an important distinction for understanding the varieties of aspirational vulnerability and for seeing the ways in which our own responses to aspirants may become deficient in fellow feeling.[5] I recall with shame my first conversation with a close friend who was reeling from the shock of her newly discovered infertility. I found myself driven to raise the possibility of adoption at a point where I should have recognized that topic as premature. Indeed, I believe I did recognize that the words coming out of my mouth were wrong, even cruel. What drove me to imply, as I could see I was doing, that it is self-indulgent to be attached to the idea of having one's own biological children? Why

rather than conception experience stillbirth or late-term miscarriage as something akin to the death of a child (Aloi 2009). Regardless of when one thinks life begins, emotional preparations for it tend to begin well in advance of that. Likewise, women who relinquish their babies for adoption often experience the event as a lifelong wound. The long-lasting grief of birth mothers is well documented in the psychological literature, as is the fact that such grief is what Doka (1989) calls "disenfranchised": "As the child did not die, the birthmother is not expected to mourn. The perception that since the baby was put up for adoption and, therefore, a degree of comfort exists with the decision, further negates the need for grieving . . . There is no public announcement of the pregnancy, the birth or the loss. The relinquishment is not even seen as a loss" (Aloi 2009: 28). A philosophical framework that allows us to see the grief of child relinquishment, pregnancy loss, and infertility as responsive to real—if proleptic—reasons will also expose our reason to provide these women with personal as well as institutional assistance in expressing and working through such grief.

4. Or, for that matter, the reverse: those who are unhappy over being unable to adopt and who could but are unwilling to have biological children.

5. May reports that the following sentiment, expressed by one of the infertile women who responded to her request for experiences, was echoed by many others: " 'The most difficult part of being childless and infertile was the things that friends, family and strangers said to us' " (1995: 13).

did I insinuate that it is a mark of wanting children for the "right reasons"—whatever those are—that one is happy to come by them whichever way? The heartlessness and ignorance of such a response are heightened when it comes from a person such as myself at the time of my friend's discovery, who has had the privilege of easily conceiving and bearing her own biological children. Those willing to adopt, but wishing to adopt infants as opposed to older children, can come in for the same sort of criticism. Why do we find it so natural to task infertile people with curing overpopulation or the plight of foster children?[6]

I think a certain form of callousness is engendered by the difficulty of theorizing or rationalizing proleptic reasons. One form this takes is an unwillingness to recognize aspirational loss as real—we treat aspirants as though they had *no* access to the value in question. For instance, May quotes a women named Deirdre Kearny as "one among many who provided a list of frequently heard offensive remarks":

> I really would like to write a book entitled *What NOT to Say to Infertile Couples!* "Just forget it and go on." "I don't think it would have bothered me if I couldn't have children." (May 1995: 13)

The person who made that last comment, who I'll call 'Bill,' would presumably experience, e.g., losing custody of his children as a profound loss. Now that Bill has children, he values being their parent. But he denies that he had access to this value in advance. He thereby denies that the inability to be a parent is a loss for those who have never been parents.

---

6. I am setting aside the fact that such advice often wildly underestimates the difficulty and expense of adoption.

The form of callousness I exhibited toward my friend took the opposite form: instead of treating her as though she had no access to reasons of motherhood, I was ignoring the proleptic character of her reason. I should have understood that my friend would long to feel her unborn baby kick, to give birth to him or her. I should have anticipated that she would be thrown by the possibility of being deprived of the experiences of pregnancy and childbirth. These desires should not be confused with those of someone (if there could be such a person) who viewed those experiences as the only point of motherhood. The grieving infertile person is not selfishly hyper-attuned to her own experiences. She wants to have these experiences because images of herself being pregnant and giving birth have been the (proleptic) form that her desire to be a mother has taken for her. She knows that being a mother is not the same thing as being pregnant, but for her, for now, her limited grasp of the value does not allow her to separate those two conditions. Being pregnant or nursing a newborn may be as far ahead as she can see into the motherhood project. It is by looking forward to these experiences that she has an antecedent grasp on the good of parenthood. (I doubt many prospective parents fantasize about parenting teenagers.)

Bill's response to Deirdre and my response to my friend share a blindness to the way in which the infertile person is antecedently invested in motherhood. If having a child were like riding a rollercoaster or tasting a new flavor—something you did for the sake of having a new experience—Paul would be right that deprivation makes no mark on the deprived subject. Someone cannot really be "robbed" of such an experience, because he cannot feel the loss. If you have never tasted chocolate, then a chocolate-lover such as myself might jokingly say, "I feel sorry for you." But it is I, and not you, who have reason to be distraught over the prospect of the end of the world's chocolate supply. The same holds for profound life changes one had no interest in: someone who was fully and strictly indifferent to the project of becoming a mother, appreciating opera, traveling to Egypt, or becoming an astronaut would have no reason to be upset if the path toward any of these pursuits were foreclosed to her.[7]

Alternatively, suppose having a child were a midsized decision such as buying a car. S is looking to buy a car in order to get to and from work more easily. It would be perfectly intelligible to raise the possibility of his moving closer to work in order to be in a position to rely on public transportation. It won't usually be[8] out of place to point out incidental benefits of this alternative option, such as mitigating environmental damage, living closer to the action of the city, getting more exercise on the way to the office. S might be happy to combine a solution to his transportation problem with other problems, such as the social life problem, the environmental problem, the healthy lifestyle problem. If having a child were like buying a new car, it would be appropriate to point out to someone who has just learned that she will have difficulty having children without extreme, expensive medical intervention that she can contribute to solving the foster child problem; that having a newborn will interfere with sleep, and therefore with her ability to succeed at her job; that pregnancy is awful for one's teeth and for one's general health; etc.

---

7. Though it is a well-recognized phenomenon that people will discover the limits of their indifference in such a scenario, coming to long for the very option that is now foreclosed. Sometimes this represents a "grass is greener" form of irrationality; at other times, I suspect, one simply learns that one really did want something one took oneself not to want.

8. Though it also might be. You might know full well that he was looking forward to buying this car for years as his first big, independent purchase; it might have an important psychological place in his move toward adulthood. It might still be right to advise him not to buy it, but one might need to put the point with more sensitivity than the conversation described suggests.

But this deliberative presentation of the varieties of parenthood will typically be the wrong way to talk to someone first facing the prospect of infertility. The problem is not that the infertile person is being asked to weigh something important—her future child—against things too trivial to matter in the face of that value. Her health, her job, her finances, and the plight of unwanted children might be deeply important to her, both pre- and post-parenthood. Most parents will at some point have to carefully weigh some dimension of their child's well-being against the importance of helping the less fortunate or their own health and career. The problem is not that the value of the nonexistent child somehow dwarfs all value. The problem is that the prospective parent doesn't yet know how to weigh all these things against one another. Her grasp on the value of parenthood is not like S's grasp on the value of transportation. She does, of course, currently care about the plight of the less fortunate, her own health, job, finances, etc. But her concern for those things has developed over her years as a non-parent. She knows how someone who doesn't have children values her job, her health, her finances, and her moral obligations to the less fortunate. She doesn't have available to her the new way of thinking about these values when they are combined with the valuation of one's child. And she won't, not until she actually is a parent. And that's a merely necessary condition: if she is like me, she may not feel at home in motherhood until sometime after she is taken by the world at large to be one. The transition into motherhood does not involve losing hold of all the things one used to value, but it may shake one's antecedent grip on those values. I became unsure *how* to value the things I used to value—how to value money, health, and morality "as a mother." Reconstructing one's values takes time; large-scale transformative pursuits often involve a kind of rebirth even with respect to those values that straddle the transformative event.

When we point out to the person who has just learned she is infertile the external selling points of adoption, we are bulldozing over the multiple evaluative perspectives that divide her deliberative faculty. We are treating her as though she had a unity she doesn't yet have; and the reason she doesn't have it is precisely that she is trying so hard to become a parent. We are ignoring how hard she has to work to even see the value—that of parenthood—that we are taking her to have reflexive access to. We are ignoring how vulnerable her valuational position, which is to say her own sense of her identity, currently is.

A proleptic reason poses a distinctive expository difficulty that we exploit in our insensitive responses to aspirants. Reasons are answers to "why?" questions—either "Why do you intend to φ?" or "Why did you φ?" An aspirant is not in an ideal position to answer such a question—for her reason always has a proximate face, citation of which represents her activity as lesser than it is, and a distal face, citation of which ennobles her current activity beyond its rightful status. The music student cannot say that she's taking the class for the grade, nor can she say she's taking it because music is intrinsically valuable. The infertile person can't say she wants, for purely selfish reasons, to have the phenomenal experience of pregnancy; nor can she say, as she will be able to, that she's acting out of parental love. A proleptic reasoner will have trouble explaining exactly why she is doing what she is doing, though once she gets to her destination she will say, "This was why." Her current rational understanding of herself is predicated on the better understanding she looks forward to having one day. If we want the best justification for her actions, we have to turn to her future self.

All of this is, at least in the case of parenthood, quite salutary. It would be terrible if we wanted children for (what we could antecedently appreciate as) good reasons. For what we look forward to in looking forward to becoming parents is the activity of loving some specific child for the child's own sake. But, whether adopting or not, no one can know in advance which person she will get. We must be open to loving any child, but that does not mean that we must love every child. We aren't required to harbor a love for babies or children in general, as might be a job requirement for a nursery-school teacher. We must be open to loving someone or a few, specific people. The content of the attitude by which we move ourselves toward parenthood must be capable of molding itself to the personality that is, itself, coming to take a determinate shape. It is good that we enter parenthood for the most inchoate of reasons; the proleptic character of our reasons puts our children in a position to fill out what parenthood means for us.

BIBLIOGRAPHY

Adams, R. 1985. "Involuntary Sins." *The Philosophical Review*, vol. 94, pp. 3–31.

Aloi, J. A. 2009. "Nursing the Disenfranchised: Women Who Have Relinquished an Infant for Adoption." *Journal of Psychiatric and Mental Health Nursing*, vol. 16, pp. 27–31.

Anscombe, G. E. M. 1963. *Intention*, 2nd ed. Oxford: Basil Blackwell.

Anderson, E. 1997. "Practical Reason and Incommensurable Goods." In Ruth Chang, ed., *Incommensurability, Incomparability and Practical Reason*. Cambridge, MA: Harvard University Press, pp. 90–109.

Arpaly, N. 2003. *Unprincipled Virtue: An Inquiry into Moral Agency*. New York: Oxford University Press.

Augustine, 1993. *On Free Choice of the Will*. Translated by Thomas Williams. Indianapolis: Hackett.

Bennett, J. 1974. "The Conscience of Huckleberry Finn." *Philosophy*, vol. 49, pp. 123–134.

Bratman, M. 2003. "Autonomy and Hierarchy." *Social Philosophy and Policy*, vol. 20, pp. 156–176.

Brewer, T. 2009. *The Retrieval of Ethics*. Oxford: Oxford University Press.

Callard, A. 2014. "Ignorance and Akrasia Denial in the *Protagoras*." *Oxford Studies in Ancient Philosophy*, vol. 47, pp. 31–80.

_____. 2015. "The Weaker Reason." *Harvard Review of Philosophy*, vol. 22, pp. 68–83.

_____. Forthcoming. "Liberal Education and the Possibility of Valuational Progress." *Social Philosophy and Policy*, vol. 34.

Castle, T. 2011. "Stockhausen, Karlheinz: The Unsettling Question of the Sublime." *New York Magazine*, August 27.

Chang, R. 1997. "Introduction" to Ruth Chang, ed., *Incommensurability, Incomparability and Practical Reason*. Cambridge, MA: Harvard University Press, pp. 1–34.

Clarke, R. 2003. *Libertarian Accounts of Free Will*. Oxford: Oxford University Press.

———. 2005. "On an Argument for the Impossibility of Moral Responsibility." *Midwest Studies in Philosophy*, vol. 29, pp. 13–24.

Cooper, J. ed., 1997. *Plato, Complete Works*. Indianapolis: Hackett.

Davidson, D. (1963) 1980. "Actions, Reasons and Causes." In his *Actions and Events*. Oxford: Clarendon Press, pp. 3–20.

———. (1970) 1980. "How Is Weakness of the Will Possible?" In his *Actions and Events*. Oxford: Clarendon Press, pp. 21–42.

———. (1973) 1980. "Freedom to Act." In his *Actions and Events*. Oxford: Clarendon Press, pp. 63–82.

———. 2004. "Problems in the Explanation of Action." In his *Problems of Rationality*. Oxford: Clarendon Press, pp. 101–116.

Dickens, C. 1875. *A Tale of Two Cities*. New York: Harper & Bros.

Doka K. J., ed. 1989. *Disenfranchised Grief: Recognizing Hidden Sorrow*. New York: Lexington Books.

Doris, J. 2002. *Lack of Character*. New York: Cambridge University Press.

Dretske, F. 1989. "Reasons and Causes." *Philosophical Perspectives*, vol. 3, pp. 1–15.

Ekenberg, T. 2015. "Voluntary Action and Rational Sin in Anselm of Canterbury." *British Journal for the History of Philosophy*, vol. 24, pp. 215–230.

Ekstrom, L. 1993. "A Coherence Theory of Autonomy." *Philosophy and Phenomenological Research*, vol. 53, pp. 599–616.

Elster, J. 1982. "Sour Grapes: Utilitarianism and the Genesis of Wants." In Amartya Sen and Bernard Williams, eds., *Utilitarianism and Beyond*. Cambridge: Cambridge University Press, pp. 219–238.

Fischer, J. 2006. "The Cards That Are Dealt You." *Ethics*, vol. 10, pp. 107–129.

Frankfurt, H. 1971. "Freedom of the Will and the Concept of a Person." *Journal of Philosophy*, vol. 68, pp. 5–20.

———. 1976. "Identification and Externality." In Amelie Rorty, ed., *The Identities of Persons*. Berkeley: University of California Press, pp. 239–252.

———. 1978. "The Problem of Action." *American Philosophical Quarterly*, vol. 15, pp. 157–162.

———. 1988. "Identification and Wholeheartedness." In his *The Importance of What We Care About*. Cambridge: Cambridge University Press, pp. 159–176.

Frede, M. and Long, A., 2012. *A Free Will: Origins of the Notion in Ancient Thought*. Berkeley: University of California Press.

Goodfellas, 1990. Directed by Martin Scorsese. Warner Brothers Films.

Hampton, J. 1993. "Selflessness and the Loss of Self." *Social Philosophy & Policy*, vol. 10, pp. 135–165.

Hardy, G. 1940. *A Mathematician's Apology*. University of Alberta Mathematical Sciences Society, http://www.math.ualberta.ca/mss/.

Harman, E. 2015. "Transformative Experiences and Reliance on Moral Testimony." *Res Philosophica*, vol. 92, pp. 323–339.

Harman, G. 2000. "Desired Desires." In his *Explaining Value and Other Essays in Moral Philosophy* Oxford: Clarendon Press, pp. 117–136.

_____. 2003. "No Character or Personality." *Business Ethics Quarterly*, vol. 13, pp. 87–94.

Holton, R. 2004. "Rational Resolve." *Philosophical Review*, vol. 113, pp. 507–535.

Johnson, R. 1999. "Internal Reasons and the Conditional Fallacy." *The Philosophical Quarterly*, vol. 49, pp. 53–71.

Jones, Karen. 2003. "Emotion, Weakness of Will and the Normative Conception of Agency." In Anthony Hatzimoysis, ed., *Philosophy and the Emotions*. Cambridge: Cambridge University Press, pp. 181–200.

Kamtekar, R. 2004. "Situationism and Virtue Ethics on the Content of Our Character." *Ethics*, vol. 114, pp. 458–491.

King, S. 2000.*On Writing*. New York: Simon & Schuster.

Kolodny, N. 2003. "Love as Valuing a Relationship." *Philosophical Review*, vol. 112, pp. 135–189.

_____. 2005. "Why Be Rational?" *Mind*, vol. 114, pp. 509–563.

_____. 2008. "Why Be Disposed to Be Coherent?" *Ethics*, vol. 118, pp. 437–463.

Korsgaard, C. 1986. "Skepticism about Practical Reason." *Journal of Philosophy*, vol. 83, pp. 5–25.

_____. 1996. *The Sources of Normativity*. Cambridge: Cambridge University Press.

Leiter, B. 2011. "The Paradox of Fatalism and Self-Creation in Nietzsche." In John Richardson and Brian Leiter, eds., *Nietzsche*. Oxford: Oxford University Press, pp. 281–321.

Lewis, D. 1989. "Dispositional Theories of Value." *Proceedings of the Aristotelian Society*, supplementary volume 63, pp. 113–137.

Little, M. 2008. "Abortion and the Margins of Personhood." *Rutgers Law Journal*, vol.3 9, pp. 331–348.

Marcus, R. 2014. "The Tragedy of Ryan Loskarn." *Washington Post*, February 16.

Markovits, J. 2010. "Acting for the Right Reasons." *Philosophical Review*, vol. 119, pp. 201–242.

_____. 2011a. "Why Be an Internalist about Reasons?" In Russ Schafer-Landau, ed., *Oxford Studies in Metaethics*. Oxford: Oxford University Press, vol. 6, pp. 255–279.

_____. 2011b. "Internal Reasons and the Motivating Intuition." In Michael Brady, ed., *New Waves in Metaethics* London: Palgrave Macmillan, pp. 141–165.

May, E. 1995. *Barren in the Promised Land*. New York: Basic Books.

McDowell, J. (1979) 1998. "Virtue and Reason." In his *Mind, Value and Reality*. Cambridge, MA: Harvard University Press, pp. 50–76.

_____. 1998. "Some Issues in Aristotle's Moral Psychology." In his *Mind Value and Reality*. Cambridge, MA: Harvard University Press, pp. 23–49.

McGrath, S. 2011. "Skepticism about Moral Expertise as a Puzzle for Moral Realism." *Journal of Philosophy*, vol. 108, pp. 111–137.

McIntyre, A. 1993. "Is Akratic Action Always Irrational?" In Owen Flanagan and Amelie Rorty, eds., *Identity, Character and Morality*. Cambridge, MA: MIT Press, pp. 379–400.

Mele, A. 1995. *Autonomous Agents*. New York: Oxford University Press.

Millgram, E. 2008. "Specificationism." In Jonathan Adler and Lance Rips, eds., *Reasoning: Studies of Human Inference and Its Foundations*. Cambridge: Cambridge University Press, pp. 731–747.

Moran, R. 2002. "Frankfurt on Identification." In Sarah Buss, ed., *Contours of Agency: Essays on Themes from Harry Frankfurt*. Cambridge, MA: MIT Press, pp. 189–217.

Murdoch, I. 1996. "Metaphysics and Ethics." In Maria Antonaccio and William Schweiker, eds., *Iris Murdoch and the Search for Human Goodness*. Chicago: University of Chicago Press, pp. 236–252.

Nielsen, K. 2011. "Deliberation as Inquiry: Aristotle's Alternative to the Presumption of Open Alternatives." *Philosophical Review*, vol. 120, pp. 383–421.

Nietzsche, F. 1966. *Beyond Good and Evil*. Translated by Walter Kaufmann. New York: Random House.

Noggle, R. 2005. "Autonomy and the Paradox of Self-Creation." In James Taylor, ed., *Personal Autonomy*. Cambridge: Cambridge University Press, pp. 87–108.

Owen, D. and Ridley, A. 2003. "On Fate." *International Studies in Philosophy*, vol. 35, pp. 63–78.

Oz, A. 2005. *A Tale of Love and Darkness*. Translated by Nicholas de Lange. Orlando, FL: Harvest Books.

Parfit, D. 2011. *On What Matters*, vol. 1. Oxford: Oxford University Press.

Paul, L. A. 2014. *Transformative Experience*. Oxford: Oxford University Press.

———. 2015. "What You Can't Expect When You're Expecting." *Res Philosophica* vol. 92, pp. 1–23.

Paul, S. 2011. "Deviant Formal Causation." *Journal of Ethics and Social Philosophy*, vol. 5, pp. 1–23.

Peacocke, C. 1985. "Intention and Akrasia." In Merrill Provence Hintikka and Bruce Vermazen, eds., *Essays on Davidson: Actions and Events*. Oxford: Clarendon Press, pp. 51–73.

Pettigrew, R. 2015. "Transformative Experience and Decision Theory." *Philosophy and Phenomenological Research*, vol. 91, pp. 766–774.

Rahman, Z. 2014. *In the Light of What We Know*. New York: Farrar, Straus and Giroux.

Railton, P. 1992. "Pluralism, Determinacy, and Dilemma." *Ethics*, vol. 102, pp. 720–742.

Raz, J. 1988. *The Morality of Freedom*. Oxford: Oxford University Press.

Richardson, H., 1994. *Practical Reasoning about Final Ends*. Cambridge: Cambridge University Press.

Rosati, C. 1995. "Persons, Perspectives and Full Information Accounts of the Good,. *Ethics*, vol. 105, pp. 296–325.

Santas, G. 1966. "Plato's Protagoras and Explanations of Weakness." *Philosophical Review*, vol. 73, pp. 3–33.

Scanlon, T. M. 1998. *What We Owe to Each Other*. Cambridge, MA: Harvard University Press.

Scheffler, S. 2010. "Valuing." In his *Equality and Tradition*. Oxford: Oxford University Press, pp. 15–40.

Schillebeeckx, E. 1969. *God and Man*. Translated by Edward Fitzgerald and Peter Tomlinson. New York: Sheed and Ward.

Schmidtz, D. 1994. "Choosing Ends." *Ethics*, vol. 104, pp. 226–251.

Schroeder, T. and Arpaly, N. 1999. "Alienation and Externality." *Canadian Journal of Philosophy*, vol. 29, pp. 371–387.

Setiya, K. 2007. *Reasons Without Rationalism*. Princeton, NJ: Princeton University Press.

Shoemaker, D. 2011. "Attributability, Answerability, and Accountability: Toward A Wider Theory of Moral Responsibility." *Ethics*, vol. 121, pp. 602–632.

Smith, A. 2012. "Attributability, Answerability, and Accountability: In Defense of a Unified Account." *Ethics*, vol. 122, pp. 575–589.

Smith, M. 1987. "The Humean Theory of Motivation." *Mind*, vol. 96, pp. 36–61.

_____. 1992. "Valuing: Desiring or Believing?" In David Charles and Kathleen Lennon, eds., *Reduction, Explanation, and Realism*. Oxford: Oxford University Press, pp. 323–359.

_____. 1994. *The Moral Problem*. Oxford: Blackwell.

_____. 1995. "Internal Reasons." *Philosophy and Phenomenological Research*, vol. 55, pp.109–131

Smith, W. 1872. *A Smaller History of Greece, from the Earliest Times to the Roman Conquest*. New York: Harper & Bros.

Sobel, D. 1994. "Full Information Accounts of Well-Being." *Ethics*, vol. 104, pp. 784–810.

Strawson, G. 1986. *Freedom and Belief*. Oxford: Oxford University Press.

_____. 1994. "The Impossibility of Moral Responsibility." *Philosophical Studies*, vol. 75, pp. 5–24.

Tappolet, C. 2003. "Emotions and the Intelligibility of Akratic Action." In Sarah Stroud and Christine Tappolet, eds., *Weakness of Will and Varieties of Practical Irrationality*. Oxford: Oxford University Press, pp. 97–120.

Ullmann-Margalit, Edna. 2006. "Big Decisions: Opting, Converting, Drifting." In Anthony O'Hear, ed., *Political Philosophy*, vol. 58 of *Royal Institute of Philosophy Supplements*, pp. 157–172.

Ullmann-Margalit, Edna and Morgenbesser, S. 1977. "Picking and Choosing." *Social Research*, vol. 44, pp. 757–785.

Velleman, D. 1998. "Brandt's Definition of Good." *Philosophical Review*, vol. 97, pp. 353–371.

_____. 2002. "Motivation by Ideal." *Philosophical Explorations*, vol. 5, pp. 90–104.

Vogler, C., 2002. *Reasonably Vicious*. Cambridge, MA: Harvard University Press.

Walker, A. 1989. "The Problem of Weakness of Will." *Nous*, vol. 23, pp. 653–676.

Wallace, J. 2013. *The View from Here: On Affirmation, Attachment, and the Limits of Regret*. New York: Oxford University Press.

Watson, G. 1975. "Free Agency." *Journal of Philosophy*, vol. 72, pp. 205–220.

_____. 1993. "Responsibility and the Limits of Evil: Variations on a Strawsonian Theme." In John Martin Fischer, ed., *Perspectives on Moral Responsibility*. Ithaca, NY: Cornell University Press, pp. 119–148.

Wiggins, D. 1975. "Deliberation and Practical Reason." *Proceedings of the Aristotelian Society*, vol. 76, pp. 29–51.

Wiland, E. 2014. "Rossian Deontology and the Possibility of Moral Expertise." In *Oxford Studies in Normative Ethics*. Oxford: Oxford University Press, pp. 159–178.

Williams, B. (1976) 1981. "Persons, Character and Morality." In his *Moral Luck*. Cambridge: Cambridge University Press, pp. 1–19.

_____. (1980) 1981. "Internal and External Reasons." In his *Moral Luck*. Cambridge: Cambridge University Press, pp. 101–111.

_____. 1995. "Internal Reasons and the Obscurity of Blame." In his *Making Sense of Humanity*. Cambridge: Cambridge University Press, pp. 35–45.

Wolf, S. 1987. "Sanity and the Metaphysics of Responsibility." In Ferdinand Schoeman, ed., *Responsibility, Character, and the Emotions*. Cambridge: Cambridge University Press, pp. 46–62.

Wu, W. 2011. "Attention as Selection for Action." In Christopher Mole, Declan Smithies, and Wayne Wu, eds., *Attention: Philosophical and Psychological Essays*. New York: Oxford University Press, pp. 97–116.

INDEX

CPSIA information can be obtained
at www.ICGtesting.com
Printed in the USA
BVHW081924190320
575490BV00001B/6